Gender and Subject in Higher Education

Kim Thomas

The Society for Research into Higher Education
& Open University Press

Gender and Subject
in Higher Education

Published by SRHE and
Open University Press
Celtic Court
22 Ballmoor
Buckingham MK18 1XW

and
1900 Frost Road, Suite 101
Bristol, PA 19007, USA

First Published 1990

Copyright © Kim Thomas 1990

British Library Cataloguing in Publication Data
Thomas, Kim
    Gender and subject in higher education.
    1. Great Britain. Higher education institutions.
    Sexism
    I. Title
    378

    ISBN 0 335 09272 1
         0 335 09271 3 (paperback)

Library of Congress Catalog Number Available

Typeset by Rowland Phototypesetting Ltd
Bury St Edmunds, Suffolk
Printed in Great Britain by St Edmundsbury Press Ltd
Bury St Edmunds, Suffolk

This book is dedicated to my father,
Ken Thomas,
and to the memory of my mother,
Myra Thomas

Contents

Acknowledgements

This book came about as the result of the efforts of a group of women staff at Aston University. The group, who had been campaigning to improve opportunities and conditions for female staff and students at Aston, successfully persuaded the university to fund, for three years, a Ph.D on 'Women in Higher Education'. I was taken on as a postgraduate student in 1983 and completed the thesis four years later. *Gender and Subject in Higher Education* is a revised and shortened version of that thesis. I have never before had the opportunity to thank all the members of the women's group for their part in securing the funding for the Ph.D, and should like, therefore, to do so now.

Thanks are also due to the following, without whom this book could not have been written:

Jan Webb and Henry Miller, my two excellent research supervisors, for their help and advice;
Ian Bates, my husband, for his support in general and for his proof-reading in particular;
All the students and lecturers who gave their time to be interviewed for the research;
Aston University, for funding the project.

1

The Question of Gender

Introduction

The research on which this book is based is concerned both with examining the concrete experiences of male and female students, and with the meanings students attach to those experiences. I suggest that these meanings arise from everyday discourse, which habitually makes use of oppositions such as masculinity/femininity, science/arts – oppositions which make sense only in relation to each other. Within these oppositions, one is rated more highly than the other: in this case, masculinity and science. Masculinity is defined by *what it is not*; the term 'masculinity' does not make sense without a knowledge of the term 'femininity'.

This book looks at these two divisions – masculinity/femininity and arts/ science – and examines the interaction between them in higher education; it regards the terms as social constructions, not as givens. It examines students' understanding of these divisions and how this understanding relates to the role of education in society. The next sections of this chapter will draw attention to the issues discussed in the book and outline the content of the later chapters.

The issue of gender

Gender is a social construction; it concerns the differing qualities culturally attributed to women and men (Oakley 1972). Sociologists, Acker (1981) has argued, have often failed to recognize that sex differences are the result of cultural and social influences:

> Writing of men, sociologists show an acute awareness of the social constraints upon their actions. Writing of women, or of sex differences, they frequently switch to psychological or biological levels of explanation.
>
> (Acker 1981: 78)

An important premise of this book is that people's actions are socially constrained, although not socially determined; people make decisions which are based on an awareness of the potentialities and limitations of certain courses of action. The choices made by men and women are limited, amongst other things, by social expectations of masculine and feminine behaviour; this is not to say, however, that people passively accept their socially allocated roles.

The study of gender is, like the study of class or of race, also the study of inequality; we are interested in not only why women do not occupy positions of power, status or responsibility in the same numbers as men, but also the process by which this occurs. Whether we believe that inequality of the sexes is the result of genetic differences, the desire of men to control and dominate women, outdated attitudes and prejudices or historical struggle, it is undoubtedly the case that there is a continuous process of producing and reproducing inequality.

The use of the word 'gender' not only denotes an emphasis on the social (as opposed to biological) attributes of women and men, but also indicates a recognition of the relationship between masculinity and feminity. Acker (1981), in her review of articles published on the sociology of education between 1960 and 1979, showed that, whereas 37 per cent of those reporting on empirical research had used all-male samples, only 5 per cent had used all-female samples. Some feminists (e.g. Sharpe 1976; Delamont 1980) have attempted to redress this imbalance, by using all-female, rather than mixed samples, treating the quality of education received by girls as a serious issue, in a way that was rare before the late 1970s.

However, by focusing exclusively on girls, researchers have ignored the important premise that gender has any cultural meaning only because it is based on *difference* (Hollway 1982). As Belotti puts it:

> The superiority of one sex is based exclusively on the inferiority and weakness of the other.
>
> (quoted in Walden and Walkerdine 1982: 21)

Researching gender, then, requires an examination of the cultural creation of male dominance as well as the creation of female subordinance.

Clearly there are a number of institutions which play a part in the reproduction of inequality, whether at a material or an ideological level. The family and the media, it can be argued, both work at an ideological level in perpetuating inequality of the sexes, while firms which pay lower wages to female workers operate at a material level. However, the institution which many sociologists have regarded as central in perpetuating inequality – and also, crucially, central in potentially *eliminating* inequality – is education. From the nineteenth-century reformers who pressed for universal schooling to today's schemes for increasing the numbers of girls studying science, education has been the site of the struggle for equality of opportunity.

Education

Sociologists are not agreed on the relationship between inequality in society at large and inequality within the education system. Explanations for the failure of working-class children within the system, for example, have ranged from the 'cultural deprivation' theory (e.g. the Plowden Report 1967) to the vulgar

Marxist belief (e.g. S. Bowles and Gintis 1976) that the primary function of education is to instil in working-class pupils the docility and passivity necessary for participation in the labour force. Those who support the cultural deprivation theory tend to believe that education can play a large part in remedying social inequality, while Marxists believe that education is an essential part of the process of reproducing inequality. A common criticism of both these theories is that they simply look at the end result of education; they are examples of an 'input/output' model. However, recent Marxist critiques of education (e.g. Willis 1977; Apple 1982) have concentrated more closely on the contradictions implicit in the experience of schooling: the *process* by which inequality is created and renewed, and the cultural resistance of pupils to the dominant ideology.

Theories of gender and education have, to some extent, mirrored those on class and education: there are those who believe that inequality is caused by the differential socialization of girls and boys (in a sense, that girls are 'culturally deprived') and that this can be overcome through removing prejudice; there are also those (e.g. Spender 1982; Mahony 1985) who believe that schools both reflect and reproduce patriarchal relations.

However, it is generally recognized that gender inequality in education is in many respects different from inequality of class. Whereas the proportion of working-class students succeeding in passing A levels and entering higher education is very small, girls generally pass as many O levels as boys, almost as many A levels, and a relatively high proportion enter higher education. Statistics for 1987–8 show that in British universities, 43.1 per cent of under-graduate students, and 38.9 per cent of postgraduate students, were women (UGC 1988).

The emphasis amongst researchers on gender, therefore, has not been on increasing the participation of girls in education. Rather, attention has focused on the issue of subject choice. Many researchers (e.g. Sharpe 1976; Deem 1978) have argued that the occupational segregation of men and women which takes place after education is completed is related to the subject segregation which takes place at school. Few girls take physical science subjects; few boys take languages. Therefore, it is argued (by e.g. Kelly 1981b; Harding 1983; Whyte 1986), that reducing the imbalance is an important step in reducing inequality. The crux of the argument – the impetus of the Girls into Science and Technology (GIST), Women into Science and Engineering (WISE) and INSIGHT schemes – is that more girls must take up science subjects; *girls must do as well as boys*. It might be argued that a tacit assumption of research which examines girls' 'failure' in science is not only that girls are inadequate – not measuring up to the standard of boys – but also that maths, physics and chemistry are more difficult and more important than English, languages, history and biology. In this model, it is believed that intervention in education can bring about positive change in the balance of power in the social system.

It is fair to say, however, that while feminist educationalists have, in recent years, become more aware of the limitations of the interventionist model, the state continues to see education as an arena where social change can be promoted. Currently there is a shortage of maths and physics teachers – a shortage which will be exacerbated by the demands of the National Curriculum. Figures from the Graduate Teacher Training Registry show that applications for places on teacher training courses for physics are, in 1989, down by 25 per cent on 1988, while the 1988 figures were down by 17 per cent on 1987 (*Times Educational Supplement* 4 April 1989). The Department of Education and Science estimates that 20 per cent more students will need to be trained to teach physics, maths, technology and modern languages (report in *Guardian* 18 January 1989). Not only are science teachers in short supply, however, but also industry is facing a shortage of skilled scientists and engineers. It is not surprising, then, that the government wishes to encourage that great untapped resource – women – to take science A levels and science degrees. As a recent article made clear:

> The government . . . sees women as the key to solving the labour shortfall in the 1990s.
>
> (*Guardian* 21 January 1989)

However, it is not just a matter of encouraging women to take science A levels. Currently those women who do take science A levels and who go into higher education are far more likely to choose to study medical or biological subjects than physical sciences or engineering. Statistics for 1987–8 reveal that 45.8 per cent of medical students were women: 43.3 per cent of dentistry students were women; 53.6 per cent of biology students were women; but only 16.1 per cent of physics and 10.7 per cent of engineering students were women. Part of the government strategy, therefore, must involve ensuring that women who do choose science specialize in shortage areas (physical science) rather than in popular areas (such as medical or biological sciences).

It may appear unreasonable of any feminist to suggest that schemes to encourage women into physics, chemistry or engineering are misguided. After all, taking such subjects in higher education would apparently improve women's prospects of gaining jobs, while at the same time filling an enormous gap in the labour market. However, attempts to change the pattern of subject choice amongst women have not adequately addressed three central questions:

1 What are the educational processes which currently result in fewer women studying science than men?
2 Why is specialization in other areas regarded as indicative of 'failure'?
3 Would an increase in the number of women choosing to study physical science and engineering result in greater equality for women?

Gender and subject choice

The patterns of subject specialization shown above suggest that a fairly complex process is taking place. It looks not so much as if women are passively being forced into the arts and rejecting science, but that they are making very clear choices. It is, for example, remarkable that almost half of all medical students are women, when as recently as 1974 medical schools were operating a quota system to keep women out.

These patterns imply that it is not simply a matter either of ability or of socialization which affect subject choice. It may be easy to argue that there are too few women doing physics and too many doing English; reversing these trends, however, is an enormously difficult task, as the GIST team found out (see Whyte 1986). What I should like to suggest is that the issue of subject specialization cannot be tackled without examining our taken-for-granted assumptions about academic subjects, and their place in society.

Perhaps the first assumption is that of the demarcation lines between subjects: what makes something a 'science', what makes chemistry different from biology. As Goodson (1983) has argued, these demarcation lines have developed and changed over time; they are not absolute. One question to ask, then, is: What do we mean by science? What are its distinctive features?

A second common assumption is that the sciences, generally, are more difficult than the humanities, and that within that, physics is more difficult than chemistry, which is more difficult than biology, and so on. This assumption is hardly ever challenged; yet it is clearly the case that many scientists are as incompetent in the humanities as many humanities graduates tend to be in the sciences; it is perhaps a mark of the enormous divide we have made between the two areas that ability in one is often considered to preclude ability in the other.

The most significant – and debatable – belief about science, however, is that it is a good thing in itself. The popular media – such as *Tomorrow's World*, for example, or children's science books – tend to present science as consisting of benevolent inventions, or a series of clever tricks. Yet the reality is that very little money spent on science is spent on improving social welfare; as Rose (1986) has pointed out, 50 per cent of the government's science and technology budget in 1981–2 went on military research and development. In industry, scientific research effort is often directed at increasing profit rather than improving the quality of life (although science has of course improved the quality of people's lives in many ways). Further, it is possible to argue, as Millett (1983) has done, that because science and technology are instrumental in maintaining male dominance, women are deliberately excluded from them.

However, even if we accept the argument that the 'best' subjects are those which are most useful to industry, this does not necessarily mean that all physical scientific subjects are more useful than all humanities subjects. We noted earlier that, as well as a shortage of science teachers in schools, there is a shortage of modern language teachers. The need for industry to employ more people who can speak another language is recognized by Kenneth Baker, as this comment shows:

A new start is needed in foreign language teaching in schools. If we are to compete effectively in world markets and to communicate on equal terms with our European partners we need to increase substantially the numbers of young people leaving school with a good grounding in at least one foreign language.

(Reported in *Guardian* 17 June 1986: 32)

Baker was particularly concerned that so few boys were taking O and A levels in languages. It would seem, then, that girls, who outnumber boys by about four to one in A level French, are at an advantage; if subject choice is so clearly related to career, then those women with modern language qualifications should be occupying important positions in industry. However, that this is not the case had been pointed out by Professor Lodge, of the Department of French Studies in Newcastle University, in a letter to the *Guardian*, in which he argues that it is a matter of concern that 'A level presentations in modern languages are falling away sharply, particularly among boys'. He added:

> This would matter little if decision-making positions were occupied by women possessed of the requisite linguistic knowledge, but unfortunately for all of us, they are not.
>
> (*Guardian*, 24 January 1986: 12)

Being possessed of a 'useful' qualification does not guarantee entry into important jobs; either because women with language qualifications are not particularly ambitious (or are ill-advised) or because employers simply aren't interested in employing female linguists. Part of the problem with encouraging girls to take 'useful' subjects is that we do not know whether it makes any difference to the kinds of jobs they eventually do; and whether, indeed, these jobs would still be highly rated if women did them. Feiffer has argued

> Whatever ground woman manages to establish for herself, man abandons, denying its importance.
>
> (quoted in Richards 1982: 196)

While not necessarily accepting the fatalism of this argument, it would be wrong to assume that the balance of power between the sexes can be changed simply by persuading more girls to take 'boys' subjects': the issue is clearly too complex to justify simplistic remedies. Arguably certain kinds of jobs (such as those in the Civil Service) have historically been reserved for male Oxbridge graduates in such 'useless' subjects as history and classics: sex and class may sometimes be greater indications of a person's 'worth' than degree subject.

The significance of higher education

So far, we have looked at different views of the relationship between the education system and social inequality. However, the inequalities in higher education have rarely been the subject of close and critical attention; far from arguing that higher education serves to reproduce inequalities, commentators (e.g. Wolpe 1977) have argued merely that higher education functions to train middle-class students to take up positions of status and responsibility in society, such as civil servants, managers, teachers and doctors. Analyses tend to stop at higher education; they note that few working-class pupils or few black people or few women go on to university or polytechnic; they fail to look at what happens to those who do. This exclusion of higher education from consideration by sociologists of education must in part be due to the fact that higher education is not compulsory; it is perhaps difficult to argue that something which is a matter of choice can in any sense be repressive. It is no doubt also due to the reluctance of academics critically to examine their own institutions.

Yet finding out what happens in higher education is of utmost importance in understanding the patterns of gender inequality that exist. For example, until recently, women were outnumbered by men at postgraduate level in every subject grouping (as defined by UCCA) apart from education. The 1987–8 statistics show some improvement: female postgraduates now outnumber men in social sciences, languages, librarianship and medical studies (i.e. subjects such as pharmacy and nursing) as well as education (UGC 1988). Furthermore, women's degree results show a different pattern from those of men: in 1984, only 5.1 per cent of female university graduates, compared to 9.1 per cent of male graduates, gained first-class honours degrees. This is reversed at the opposite end, however: 11.5 per cent of men and only 6.2 per cent of women gained thirds (Universities Statistical Record). These patterns are particularly marked in the humanities and social sciences, where women are numerically stronger. We can also note that few academics are women; few high-ranking civil servants, managers or politicians are women. Despite the growing numbers taking part in higher education, women are still under-represented in the majority of jobs with any claim to status and responsibility.

Clearly something does happen in higher education; it is not enough to argue that it trains an elite and to leave it at that. It is not, as most appear to believe, the end of a process, but in many ways a beginning. If higher education is *not* an end, not an output, it may be worth looking at it as a process: a process which plays a crucial role in the creation and reproduction of gender difference. To understand this process, we have to look at the experiences of students themselves, and the meanings they give to their education.

If we are to understand the significance of subject specialization, then we must take the choices made by women seriously: we cannot assume that the student who chooses physical science is somehow 'right' while the student who chooses the humanities is somehow 'wrong'. More importantly it is necessary to understand why certain subjects have become associated with men, and others with women. It is not merely the case that some subjects have been numerically dominated by men and others numerically dominated by women; as Keller (1983) has argued, science is generally regarded as more masculine than the arts:

> To both scientists and their public, scientific thought is male thought, in ways that painting and writing – also performed largely by men – never have been.
>
> (Keller 1983: 188)

Hudson's (1972) work has also demonstrated the association of science with the masculine, the arts with the feminine, and his research will be discussed in Chapter 3. Understanding the gender-specific connotations of certain fields of learning is crucial if we are also to comprehend the process by which gender inequality is produced in education. As Becher (1981) has argued, academic subjects are not neutral, they are 'cultures', each with its own way of perceiving and interpreting the world. The aim of this book, then, will be to look at the relationship between the 'culture' of subjects and our common-sense constructions of masculinity and femininity; and the implications of this relationship for gender inequality in higher education.

The methodology

The research reported on in this book consisted of semi-structured, tape-recorded interviews with ninety-six students (forty-eight male, forty-eight female), and twelve members of academic staff, in three different institutions. In each institution, I looked at two departments, interviewing sixteen students (eight first year and eight final year) in each. Two of these institutions were universities, in which the interviews were with members of the English and physics departments. These institutions will be referred to, for the sake of simplicity and anonymity, as A and B. The third institution was a polytechnic, and the interviews were with students from a department of communications and a department of physical science. This institution will be referred to as C.

The arguments about the merits of questionnaires as opposed to interviews, positivism versus interpretivism, have been well rehearsed, and I do not propose to go into them in detail here. The philosophy behind this research is the same as Lewis's:

> If we are to explore the actual and perceived experiences of students, it may be better to work from their views rather than to try to squeeze them into some predetermined mould through questionnaires and attitude inventories.

> (I. Lewis 1983: 111)

A few brief comments need to be made, however, about why the research took the form it did.

Having argued in this chapter that the issue of gender can be discussed only if we regard masculinity and feminity as complementary, it was inevitable that the sample should include both men and women. It was intended, not to concentrate on women as an object of interest, but to compare the experiences of men and women, to look for difference and similarity.

Similarly it was necessary to move the focus of interest from the question 'Why do so few women do physical science?' to the related, but often unasked questions of 'Why do so few men take the humanities?' 'Why do so many women choose English, rather than physics, or chemistry?' 'What happens to those students who make these choices − particularly if their choice is unconventional?' To start to answer these questions entailed looking at at least one humanities subject and at least one physical science subject.

Physics was chosen as a representative subject, not only because it is studied by so few women, and is therefore a typically masculine discipline, but also because it tends to be regarded as the most objective, rigorous and, indeed, successful of the pure sciences. English was chosen, not just because the majority of its students are female, but because it is generally looked upon by commentators (e.g. P. Scott 1984), as the 'central liberal discipline'. Matthew Arnold, as we shall see in Chapter 3, regarded English as a vehicle for overcoming class divisions; in the late Victorian era, it was regarded as a sop to women demanding higher education (see Baldick 1984). English, therefore, is an example of a way in which education has been used in an attempt to effect social changes; arguably it is the only discipline (and of course this will be discussed again later) to be distinctively 'feminine'.

Both physics and English are, essentially, university subjects: I was also interested in the new tradition of the polytechnics and the emphasis they have put on applied knowledge and vocational degrees. Physical science would, I hoped, prove to be an interesting contrast with physics, being broader-based and more vocational: students took a year out in industry. Communications also had a vocational emphasis, and was essentially inter-disciplinary, covering sociological and psychological methods of inquiry. In common with English, however, most students came to the course with humanities A levels.

Interviews were the obvious method for researching the interlinked topics of gender identity and subject specialization. I was interested both in how *individuals* develop a sense of themselves through their subject choice, and in how a world-view of a discipline is constructed at an academic and departmental level. To put it more simply, I wanted to look at the reciprocal interaction between individuals and their immediate social world. The only way to do this was to allow students themselves to talk about why they chose to study their particular subject, their experience of studying it, and their hopes for the future.

The remaining chapters

Chapters 2 and 3 take a look at some of the literature available on gender and education, gender and science, and the different cultures of 'science' and 'humanities'. Chapter 2 is concerned with the different feminist approaches that have been directed towards education, and how they might help us towards an understanding of higher education. Chapter 3 looks more specifically at some traditional ideas about the value of science and humanities education, and at how these might relate to deep-rooted notions about gender.

Chapters 4–7 take up the bulk of the book, and report on the research described earlier. Chapter 4 looks at how physics students and staff construct the subject 'physics', and at the way in which this affects, and is affected by, their ideas about humanities disciplines. Chapter 5 looks at the ideas of English and communications students about their discipline, and at their view of science. Chapter 6 examines the way in which studying physics interacts with students' sense of identity, and looks at how this differs for male and female students. Chapter 7 discusses a similar process at work amongst the humanities students, and also points to certain differences between the science and the humanities students. Chapter 8 draws some conclusions from the research and makes suggestions for change.

We begin, therefore, by asking the question: what contribution can feminist theory make to higher education?

2

Feminism and Education

Introduction

This chapter will look at the different explanations that have been put forward for girls' 'failure' in education, and at some of the research that has been done in this area. It will also look at the ways in which these explanations can help us reach an understanding of inequality in higher education. Much of the work under discussion gives some consideration to the issue of subject specialization: the character of science education will, therefore, be touched on in this chapter, but a fuller discussion of this topic, and that of humanities education, will be found in Chapter 3.

Until recently, it has been easy to characterize three distinct types of feminist approach to education: liberal, radical, and Marxist or socialist. Middleton (1987) has given a useful account of how these different approaches have informed work on gender inequality in education. In recent years, however, the distinctions between these three approaches have become blurred, particularly in the area of empirical research: while there are major differences at the level of grand theory, liberal, radical and socialist feminists appear increasingly to agree about what happens in the classroom. What these approaches have most in common, however, is that they challenge a view of education which is concerned only with male experience, and which treats that experience as the 'norm'. When researchers look at schooling from the point of view of girls, it is perhaps not surprising that writers as diverse as Alison Kelly and Valerie Walkerdine can come up with very similar findings.

What *is* surprising is that so few feminist researchers in the sociology of education have chosen to look at higher education, when so much work has been done on secondary education and, to a lesser extent, on primary education. It can be argued that this failure to look at higher education may be the result of a deficiency in feminist theory about education – that feminists (and, indeed, other educational theorists) have difficulty in theorizing the role of higher education in the reproduction of inequality. This chapter will have two aims, therefore: the first will be to look at the shades of difference and similarity between feminist approaches to education; the second will be to ask whether, and in which ways, these approaches can inform our understanding of inequality in higher education.

The liberal analysis

The view of education which dominated feminist thought in the 1970s was heavily influenced by liberal explanations of working-class failure in education. Just as these explanations had concentrated on the inadequacy of working-class culture and had put forward the notion of compensatory education, so the tendency of feminists was to explain girls' failure in terms of the deficiencies of their socialization. Schemes such as Girls Into Science and Technology (GIST) and Women Into Science and Engineering (WISE) were devised as 'remedies' to girls' early socialization.

In the liberal model, education tends to be seen, to some extent, in isolation from the social structure. Education may create and perpetuate inequality; it also has the power to redress it. For example, Friedan (1983) believed that it was the 'feminine mystique' which prevented women from leading successful public lives; the education system was partly to blame for the ideology of the feminine mystique, but equally the solution for women who were trapped in their roles as wives and mothers was to return to college to obtain an education. In a sense, then, women's main problem was their own attitude (albeit an attitude fostered by the education system and the media); if only women would stop wanting to become housewives and start wanting to become lawyers or doctors instead, the problem would end.

Most liberals, like other feminists, believe that schools are partly responsible for instilling sexist attitudes into children. Delamont (1980), for example, says that:

> schools develop and reinforce sex segregations, stereotypes and even discriminations which exaggerate the negative aspects of sex roles in the outside world, when they could be trying to alleviate them.
>
> (Delamont 1980: 3)

While the EOC document on science education says:

> If girls are taught from an early age that science is a subject to be studied by all pupils, and is not 'only for the boys', then some of the problems relating to girls' under-achievement in science in the secondary school will be resolved.
>
> (Equal Opportunities Commission 1982: 4)

These statements demonstrate the two central emphases of the liberal feminist analysis. The first is the ability of the school to promote good or bad attitudes, with the implication that changing schools will change attitudes (and hence, eventually, society); the second is the concentration on girls, rather than boys. There are areas of education in which boys do badly (modern languages, for example); yet liberal feminists tend to be concerned only with the areas where girls are less successful, such as science and mathematics. There is a tacit acceptance that, because men are generally more successful in material terms than women, women could become more successful if they made the same educational choices as men.

The liberal feminist perspective in education was embodied by the GIST (Girls Into Science and Technology) project. The aim of this project was to encourage girls to choose science subjects at the age of 14; to this end, the GIST researchers went into ten Manchester secondary schools and attempted to promote a more positive image of science that would appeal to girls, partly by helping science teachers develop a more 'girl-friendly' teaching style and partly by inviting female scientists to speak to pupils about their careers. The consequence of this intervention was that in some schools, the numbers of girls opting for science increased, while in others they decreased.

The failure of the GIST initiative surely lay in the naivety of its approach: the researchers were so concerned to promote a positive 'image' of science that they brushed aside pupils' questions on the reality. For example, Whyte in her report on GIST, tells how the visiting speakers were told to 'present themselves as "rounded" feminine beings, i.e. mention how they combined home and family life with their jobs' (1986: 74). The GIST team seemed to think that they could brush aside any anxieties about the difficulties of being a woman in science by presenting a series of bright, appealing images.

However, an interesting consequence of GIST was that the experience of going into schools and seeing what happens in science lessons seems to have radicalized the researchers involved. Kelly, in particular, no longer seems to think that the problem of gender imbalances in subject specialization can be solved by making girls change their attitudes. The crucial shift is from seeing girls as the problem to seeing science as the problem; writing of an article she published in 1982, she says:

> If I were writing the article today . . . I would put more emphasis on the role of schools and teachers in dissuading girls from science, and less on girls' internal states. The article suggests that it is necessary to change the *image* of science; I now think that it is necessary to change *science*.
>
> (Kelly 1987: 2)

There has, therefore, been a significant move away from psychological explanations of 'failure' which see socialization as the root of the problem, and towards explanations which look more closely at the discriminatory practices of schools. However, this does leave us with the unanswered question of the extent to which schools reflect social practices and the extent to which they shape them. Many feminists, as we shall see below, believe that the education system is largely an apparatus for reproducing the existing social structure.

Political explanations

Radical feminist and Marxist feminist interpretations of the education system have focused less on attitudes and more on power structures. The radical feminist argument is, briefly, that we live in a patriarchy – a system in which men maintain power over women. This system of power relations is maintained both at the material level – by the military, the police, industry and so on – and at the ideological level: by the media, the family and the education system (Millett 1983). Socialization of girls and boys into sex roles is seen, not as a means of perpetuating misplaced attitudes and prejudices, but as a necessary tool in maintaining male dominance. Marxist feminism is rather more complicated in that it sees the oppression of women as inextricably linked to the class system. As Macdonald has put it:

> Both class relations and gender relations, while they exist within their own histories, can nevertheless be so closely interwoven that it is theoretically very difficult to draw them apart within specific historic conjunctures.
>
> (Macdonald 1980a: 30)

However, there is disagreement amongst Marxist feminists about whether the oppression of women is simply a consequence of an unjust economic system or whether the oppression of women is universal, but modified under differing economic conditions. In either case, education is seen as an important means of perpetuating the system of capitalist relations as well as the system of patriarchal relations.

Radical feminist perspectives

There have been two main strands to the work conducted within the radical feminist paradigm. The first is a belief that education consists of the transmission of 'male' knowledge; that is, that what is taught in schools is simply an account of male experience presented as though it were everybody's experience. It is biased knowledge, pretending to be value-free. Spender is the most powerful exponent of this point of view, arguing that:

> Men have provided us with a false picture of the world . . . not just because their view is so limited, but because they have insisted that their *limited* view is the *total* view.
>
> (Spender 1982: 16, emphasis in the original)

Spender gives numerous examples of this bias; one is that history textbooks about the nineteenth century contain few or no references to the women's movement, despite the fact that women were fighting to be accepted into the universities and to receive the franchise. Women's experience, as Spender puts it, has become 'non-data: it is rendered invisible. The role of education in a patriarchal society is, therefore, to transmit a dominant ideology: that of masculine superiority.

The second strand of the radical feminist argument is that schooling is part of a process by which the ideas and experiences of girls and women are trivialized by male pupils and members of staff. While this is a common finding amongst researchers (see pp. 16–17 below), it is the interpretation which radical feminists put on these findings that is significant. Radical feminists see the put-downs and discrimination experienced by girls as the means by which men control women – and by which boys control girls. From this point of view, women are oppressed and victimized; they are not simply the unlucky recipients of prejudice.

For radical feminists, then, schooling represents one of the ways in which girls and women are excluded from power. For that reason, they reject solutions such as encouraging more women into science; as Spender puts it

> such superficial analyses and solutions are not only insulting to women, they also ignore the distribution of power in society and the academic world, and the way in which males have appropriated and defended that power.
>
> (Spender 1981b: 110)

Many radical feminists see little point in attempting to change the education system because women are trapped in a vicious circle in which men keep changing the rules if women show any sign of becoming as successful as them. For feminists such as Spender, the only solution is a separatist one: for women to make their own education, their own rules.

Marxist feminism

Marxist feminism represents a two-pronged attack: the first on orthodox Marxism, the second on orthodox (i.e. liberal and radical) feminism. At the same time, it draws from each of these approaches, and attempts to integrate them: Hartmann's (1981) essay on the subject is appropriately entitled 'The unhappy marriage of Marxism and feminism'.

Marxist feminism, like radical feminism, regards the relationship between the sexes as political: that is, about power. However, Marxist feminists do not regard the relationship between the sexes as the only, or even the main power relationship in society. While a radical feminist like Millett can argue that 'male and female are really two cultures, and their life experiences are utterly different' (1983: 31), Marxist feminists would argue that the life experiences of middle-class women are much closer to those of middle-class men than they are to those of working-class women.

Marxist feminists are quick to point to the essentialism of much of radical feminism, and argue that while women's oppression is almost universal, it has taken different forms in different societies. Thus, under capitalism, women's oppression is not simply a question of individual men oppressing individual women, nor of men in general oppressing women in general; it takes the form of exploitation in the labour market, which has become essential to maintaining capitalism – low wages, harsh working conditions, little job security – as well as exploitation in the home and family. As Barrett (1984) has argued:

> A model of women's dependence has become entrenched in the relations of capitalism, in the divisions of labour in waged work and between wage

labour and domestic labour. As such, an oppression of women that is not in any essentialist sense pre-given by the logic of capitalist development has become necessary for the ongoing reproduction of the mode of production in its present form. Hence the oppression of women, although not a functional prerequisite of capitalism, has acquired a material basis in the relations of production and reproduction of capitalism today.

(Barrett 1984: 249)

Explaining the role of the education system under this model is rather more difficult than in the other two models. Education is neither simply about the transmission of certain attitudes nor about the perpetuation of patriarchy. Traditional Marxist explanations, such as that of Althusser (1971) or S. Bowles and Gintis (1976) had seen education as reproducing the relations of dominance and subordinacy necessary to the maintenance of the capitalist state. As we saw in Chapter 1, later Marxist explanations (e.g. Apple 1982) move away from a deterministic model towards a looser one, which emphasizes hegemony and cultural resistance. This is broadly the position taken by Wolpe (1978), in her article, 'Education and the sexual division of labour'. Wolpe's argument is that changes in the labour process have resulted in a disjunction between the skills taught by the education system and the skills (or, in a sense, lack of skills) demanded in the labour market. Consequently contradictory demands are placed on schools and colleges; for example, girls are allowed to study physical science in school, but are also channelled into subjects such as home economics which instil in them their future role as wives and mothers. Wolpe argues, therefore, that there is potential for change through struggle; there is no simple functional 'fit' between education and the demands of the labour market.

Barrett's (1984) analysis is rather more deterministic, arguing that education is explicitly the object of state policy, and serves to reproduce both class and gender relations. The reproduction of gender relations is neither outside the class system nor is it reducible to it. She notes four levels at which gender relations are reproduced in schools. The first is that of ideology, i.e. that girls and boys are socialized into appropriate 'feminine' and 'masculine' behaviour. The second is that of structure and organization: the majority of headteachers and heads of department are men, while women are at the bottom of the teaching profession. The third consists of those mechanisms which channel pupils into a sexual division of labour: that boys are persuaded to take science and technology subjects and girls to take the arts. The fourth is that of definitions of legitimate knowledge: what is often taught as neutral and objective is in fact androcentric and sexist. (However, Barrett rejects the relativism of many feminists and argues that an objective, neutral knowledge is possible.)

In a sense, Barrett's analysis is remarkable because it is so *unremarkable*. While her theoretical analysis of the interrelationships of gender and class at the general level may be controversial, few feminists would disagree with her comments about education. Her comments about subject specialization may even have more in common with traditional liberal approaches (i.e. that girls are 'channelled' into the arts) than with the approach of radical feminists who see science as inherently masculine.

Arnot (1981) has argued that a theoretical division exists between 'cultural' (what I have characterized as 'liberal' and 'radical') approaches and 'political economy' (Marxist-feminist) approaches. Both tend to present an 'overly determined view of women' (1981: 13) in that the former portrays women as 'over-socialized' and the latter regards them as 'doubly-determined' by the needs of capitalism and patriarchy. While the former does not go beyond the school – seeing the school as both problem and solution – the latter assumes that the education system is entirely successful as an apparatus which reproduces gender and class inequality. She suggests a synthesis between the two approaches which looks at the diversity of girls' educational experiences, and the ways in which shoolchildren challenge class and gender controls. I shall return to this issue of determinism a little later, but first I shall take a brief look at some of the themes in empirical research on gender and education.

Gender in the classroom

The focus of much feminist research into education is the extent to which girls are (consciously or unconsciously) discriminated against. This discrimination may take the form of bias in marking or the preferential treatment given to boys in the classroom.

The work of Spear (1984) and Bradley (1984) are examples of work which suggest – though do not prove – that markers may be biased against girls when marking their work. Recently some attention has been paid to the differences in degree results of men and women and an experiment carried out at University College, Cardiff (Belsey 1988) shows that women's degree classes improve when a system of anonymous marking is used.

Spender (1982) argues that male teachers are more likely to regard work highly if they think it has been written by a boy, although her research methodology is not made explicit. Other researchers, such as Clarricoates (1978) and Stanworth (1981), found that teachers tend to spend more time talking to boys, and that they have more difficulty remembering girls' names. Clarricoates also found that primary school teachers try to gear their lessons more towards the interests of the male pupils, because they are more likely to be disruptive: a finding supported by Morgan and Dunn (1988). It proves an interesting challenge to the Marxist idea (e.g. S. Bowles and Gintis 1976) that schools reward passivity and docility. As Walkerdine (1987) has argued, qualities generally attributed to girls, such as industriousness and diligence, are often cited by teachers and researchers as examples of girls' weaknesses in education. In other words, it seems that some schoolchildren (boys) are rewarded for breaking the rules while others (girls) are punished for following them.

The issue of preferential treatment given to boys is not, however, confined to whether their examination papers are marked more favourably or whether they are allowed to talk more in classrooms. The concern of some researchers has extended to the ways in which boys are allowed to dominate girls in schools. Increasingly, research evidence shows that, in mixed-sex schools, girls are consistently subjected to harassment, sometimes sexual, by boys, and that this harassment is either ignored or treated as harmless. When researching the GIST project, Whyte (1986) found that boys persistently intimidated girls in the science laboratories and refused them access to equipment. Kelly (1985) found instances of girls performing a service role in the laboratory – being expected to tidy up for boys, for example.

Spender (1982), Mahony (1985), Wolpe (1977) and Lees (1987) all found evidence that in mixed sex schools, girls were harassed, often sexually, by boys. Mahony in particular found that the problem was either trivialized or ignored by teachers. More disturbingly, Walkerdine (1987) recorded instances in *nursery* schools where male children were using sexual insults to challenge the female teacher: the teacher, however, dismissed it as 'normal' childish behaviour.

'Normal' is the key word here. There seems to be a sense running through all these research reports that teachers regard boys' behaviour in school, whether it be groaning in unison every time a girl answers a question, or physically harassing female pupils, as quite natural and inevitable. Teachers make use of a discourse which regards male aggression as normal: 'Boys will be boys'. The teacher cited in Walkerdine's research, for example, said that 'coming out with that kind of expression is very natural' (Walkerdine 1987: 169).

This kind of research about the treatment and academic performance of girls in mixed sex schools has led some feminists to argue in favour of single-sex schooling. Spender (1982) has put the case simply:

> By removing the group which dominates and excludes the experience of women, single-sex schools can allow women to express and validate their own experience to develop some autonomy, to build some confidence.
>
> (Spender 1982: 121)

Indeed, there is a body of evidence (Pidgeon 1967; Steedman 1980) which suggests that girls do achieve more highly in a single-sex environment. Even Dale's (1969) book which came out in favour of co-educational schooling, recognized that girls were academically less successful in such an environment. In an experiment at Stamford school (S. Smith 1984), it was shown that, whereas girls' mathematics scores were equal to those of the boys on entry in the first year, by the end of the year, boys were scoring more highly. When, however, some of the classes were put into single-sex groups, the girls in these groups started to score more highly again, while the girls in the mixed sex groups fell further behind. Deem and Finch (1986) have argued, on this basis, that women should be entitled to a single-sex *higher* education. This does beg the question, however, of the extent to which education, and higher education in particular, exists in isolation from the rest of society.

Subject choice, knowledge and curriculum

So far, we have seen that feminists are beginning to agree on what happens to girls in mixed-sex schools; there is a growing consensus in research that education is a powerful force in shaping relations of dominance and subordinance between the sexes. However, while it may be easy to accept that girls are treated differently from boys in schools, the crucial issue of *what is taught* in schools may be more complex and controversial. At the same time, most people regard what is taught in schools (either in the 'official' curriculum, or through the unofficial, 'hidden' curriculum), as the essential feature of an educational system.

Much feminist attention has been focused on the sexist bias of many of the textbooks used in schools (see Macdonald 1980a; Mahony 1982; Kelly 1985 for discussion and references). Macdonald, in her account of some of these studies, says that:

> the impression gained is one of women's inferiority, her domesticity, her lack of intelligence, ability, sense of adventure of creativity.
>
> (Macdonald 1980a: 41)

As Macdonald explains, it seems that women are either invisible in most school textbooks or, when they appear at all, they are seen performing low-status tasks. Amongst liberals, there has been a tendency to believe that remedying the gender imbalances in these books might have a positive influence on girls' educational achievement. Increasingly this is now seen as over-optimistic; as Kelly has argued, such representations are the 'tip of the iceberg'. (1985: 149). We cannot assume, of course, that girls simply accept the images portrayed of them in textbooks; a concentration on content analysis of textbooks does not tell us whether they are ignored, accepted, or challenged by their users.

The issue of curriculum and subject choice goes deeper than the portrayal of women in school textbooks, however. One of the issues that has drawn the attention of many feminists is the general treatment of women in both school and higher education curricula. Walker (1981), for example, has shown how psychology regards the male as 'norm'; any results which show that women behave differently tend to be either ignored or dismissed as an anomaly. Hubbard (1981) has pointed to the inbuilt sexist assumptions of much biology, while Lanser and Torton Beck (1979) have pointed to the exclusion of female writers and critics from syllabuses of English.

There now exist very wide-ranging critiques of male 'knowledge' in the humanities and social science subjects. However, most of these subjects tend to be studied, at undergraduate level at least, mainly by women. Given the apparent sexist bias of much humanities and social science teaching, it seems odd that it is in these subjects that women are numerous; it is the absence of women in physical science and engineering that has generally been regarded as a 'problem'. Indeed, given that the sciences are more usually concerned with the inanimate world than the animate, it would seem that there was much less potential in the physical sciences for portraying women negatively. In psychology, English, history, even biology, it is not too difficult to demonstrate a bias towards male experience. Yet girls, and women, apparently choose these subjects in preference to the seemingly more objective physical sciences, while for boys the reverse is true. The issue of male and female subject choice, then, may be more complex than we generally allow.

We might begin to explain this paradox by recognizing that not only is much of what we call knowledge socially constructed, the *boundaries* between subjects are also socially constructed. It is not simply that we can suspect the objective basis of 'knowledge' but that 'knowledge' is compartmentalized; some kinds of 'knowledge' are considered more important than other kinds, and this is communicated very effectively in schools. Measor (1983; 1984), for example, has shown that children have very clear ideas about which are high-status subjects in school, and which low-status. Bernstein has used the idea of 'framing' and 'classification' to explain this; it is an idea that is particularly potent when we discuss gender. One of Bernstein's arguments is that subject specialization,

> reveals *difference from* rather than *communality with*. . . specialized versions of the collection code tend to abhor mixed categories and blurred identities, for they represent a potential openness, an ambiguity, which makes the consequences of previous socialization problematic.
>
> (Bernstein 1971: 55)

We can argue, then, that subject specialization, in emphasizing 'difference from', can reinforce both class and gender distinctions. While classics, for example, are considered essentially upper- or upper-middle-class disciplines, engineering (in this country at any rate) has long been considered a subject suitable for aspirant working-class men. The gender divisions are, if anything, even more entrenched. Not only are certain subjects (physics, maths, engineering) considered more suitable for men than for women, but also these subjects in themselves seem to embody qualities which are closely linked to our ideas about masculinity and feminity. As Macdonald (1980a) has put it:

> The notions of appropriate behaviours for each sex is converted into the appropriate academic disciplines.
>
> (Macdonald 1980a: 38)

As Macdonald points out, some subjects change from being viewed as 'masculine' to being viewed as 'feminine', and vice versa; she argues that this is partly the result of 'pressures exerted on the school and universities by the changing pattern of employment of men and women in the labour force' (1980a: 37). A case in point might be certain subjects related to medicine, such as optics and pharmacy; the growing number of women studying these disciplines may be the consequence of the flexibility of optics and pharmacy jobs in enabling women to take time off to have children.

If we regard the curriculum as essentially concerned with *difference*, then we can begin to understand the potent ways in which gender divisions are created and renewed. It has already been argued, in the previous chapter, that we all use oppositions to make sense of our experience. In any opposition, one of the pair is likely to be rated positively, and the other negatively: for example, masculinity and femininity, science and arts. It is not enough, therefore, to say that more women should do science, or that domestic economy should be compulsory for both sexes; we have to get to grips with the ways in which 'femininity' is consistently devalued, both in society generally and specifically in the education system.

Gender and higher education

A concentration on seemingly abstract ideas like 'masculinity' and 'femininity' may seem esoteric when compared to issues of whether girls are actively discriminated against in education. However, my aim is to show that notions of 'masculinity' and 'femininity' are important in shaping students' experiences of schooling.

So far, little attention has been paid by feminist sociologists to higher education. The attitude of most feminists appears to be that, if women have reached higher education, then they are 'successful'; the only questions to be asked are why fewer women than men reach higher education in the first place, and why they are concentrated in different subject areas. Byrne, for example, says that she is not concerned with the

> intellectual minority of girls whose élite wings have helped them to fly . . . from the gutter to the university.
>
> (Byrne 1978: 15)

Wolpe, at a different end of the political spectrum, has only this to say about higher education:

> Those children who comprise the élite section of the education system are destined via higher education to fill the managerial, professional and higher executive posts of this country.
>
> (Wolpe 1977: 20)

'Elite' is the key word in both these quotes. The problem for these, as for other feminists, seems to be only how we can help women get to these positions, rather than what happens to them once they are there.

An alternative way of looking at higher education is to see it as a continuing process in the reproduction of gender relations. This is broadly the radical feminist viewpoint. Women who reach higher education are not deemed to be successful by virtue of having done so; on the contrary, higher education continues to exclude and marginalize its female students, pushing them further into 'female' jobs or marriage and family. This is the position taken by Acker (1984b) and by Rich (1979a) who argues that the university is 'a system that prepares men to take up roles of power in a man-centred society' (1979a: 127). Radical feminists (such as the contributors to Spender 1981c, and to G. Bowles and Duelli-Klein 1983) argue that higher education curricula are as biased towards male experience as secondary education curricula.

These two theoretical positions are, apparently, mutually exclusive. Surely higher education cannot be both the prerogative of an elite group of privileged middle-class women *and* a means of perpetuating male dominance. Yet neither of these explanations on their own seems to me to be entirely satisfactory. A woman who is successful in getting into higher education may feel privileged; however, her experience while she is there, and the influence this has on her decisions about her future life, may challenge this sense of privilege. As we saw in Chapter 1, the proportion of female students obtaining first-class honours degrees is smaller than that of male students doing so; Kelsall *et al.* (1970) found that the career paths of male and female graduates differed widely. At the same time, it is hardly adequate to say that higher education is concerned only with reproducing inequality; greater access to higher education has resulted in a growing number of women obtaining degrees and entering the professions.

I should like to suggest, then, that the relationship between higher education and the reproduction of gender inequality is a paradoxical one. Higher education is relatively autonomous from the state but at the same time it is not isolated from the power structures and values of society. The aims of higher education (whether, for example, it should be about the disinterested pursuit of knowledge, or about training students for the graduate job market) are confused. This confusion is very apparent in most of the attempts to formulate a statement of higher education aims and policies, from the Robbins Report (1963) to the 1985 Green Paper (DES 1985). It is also the case, of course, that stated aims do not necessarily match with practice. We cannot assume that any part of the education system works as it is supposed to; as Macdonald (1980a) has pointed out, we cannot just analyse the production of cultural messages; we also have to analyse their reception. Apple has suggested:

> Women do often partially reject or filter knowledge, or even use it to their own advantage.
>
> (Apple 1982: 21)

Education may try to produce passive and 'feminine' women, but it does not necessarily succeed. Given the confusing and contradictory messages that women may be getting on their social role, it is worth exploring the question of whether their experiences of higher education are similarly confusing and contradictory.

The small body of research that exists on female students in higher education suggests that women in higher education are faced continually with contradiction. Komarovsky's (1946) classic study found that many female students experience conflict between the experience of higher education as preparation for a career and the social expectations that women should be passive, 'feminine' and marriageable. Opposing pressures came from tutors on the one hand, and family, male peers, and non-university female friends on the other. Indeed, some went so far as to 'play dumb' when they were with male students because they knew that the men didn't like clever women. Cleverness and femininity were seen as incompatible.

Similarly Ian Lewis argues that research on female science pupils has found that

girls are presented with a dilemma between maintaining their feminine identities or becoming closely identified with the study of physics.

(I. Lewis 1984a: 110)

His own research on female undergraduate students of physics provides further support for this conclusion; many of them explicitly dissociated themselves from the male physics students and their ambitions. For these students, this was manifested by a decision not to continue with physics at postgraduate level.

Chisholm and Woodward (1980) have demonstrated that female graduates are often torn between the choices of starting a family (and taking the most convenient work to combine with family raising, such as teaching or part-time work) and using their education to enter high-status, traditionally 'masculine' jobs. Society puts pressure on them both ways.

More anecdotal work, such as that of Harris (1974) or Weisstein (1979), illustrates the difficulties of academically successful women: a woman who appears 'feminine' is unlikely to be taken seriously. At the same time, a woman who tries to shake off her 'femininity' in order to be taken seriously will be derided as unattractive, as the remarks of James Watson on the scientist Rosalind Franklin in his book *The Double Helix* (1959) make all too clear.

Institutions of higher education, like most powerful social institutions, are dominated, numerically and culturally, by men. Hacker's argument in her article, 'Women as a minority group' (1977), may prove a useful guide to understanding how higher education is experienced by women. Hacker believes that the position of women in society is analagous to that of minority groups such as immigrants and Blacks. Like other minority groups, women often accept their supposed inferior status; they use tactics of 'helplessness' and 'wiles' as a means of accommodation. The jobs they can do are limited, and they are thought to be less intelligent and more easily pleased. Some of them try to dissociate themselves from their group and 'fondly imagine' their identity to be 'different from what others hold it to be'. Like Blacks, women are seen, not as individuals, but members of a group, all of whom share certain characteristics.

This theory is a particularly potent one when we look at higher education. For, whereas women make up over half the members of society at large, in higher education they are very definitely in a minority. In certain areas of higher education – physics and engineering, for example – they make up a tiny proportion of students. In other areas, however, their position is ambiguous. In English and sociology, the majority of lecturers may be male, but the majority of students are female. When male students are numerically in a minority, do they form a 'minority group'? Is the position of women strengthened?

These questions are important ones, because they get to the heart of our concern about higher education. I have already suggested that subject choice is about 'difference'; a woman who chooses to study physics is stating (not necessarily intentionally) her difference from other women. She is making what is conventionally a *masculine* choice. A woman who chooses English, on the other hand, is making a traditionally feminine choice. What I am trying to argue, however, is that the issue is not merely one of numbers, but one of culture. Hacker's point was that women may be in a numerical majority, but they are in a cultural minority. Just because, therefore, there are fewer women in physics than in English, doesn't mean to say that they are any worse off: the opposite may be true. What I want to explore in the next chapter, then, is the question of the cultural boundaries between different subjects. Specifically I will look at what we mean by the terms 'arts' and 'science'; what qualities these two areas are seen, in society, to embody; and finally, the relationship between these qualities and the qualities embedded in our notions of 'masculinity' and 'femininity'.

3

The Two Cultures

Introduction

This chapter will consider both the idea of an arts/science division and why it exists, and two specific subjects: physics and English. I shall argue that the question of 'subject choice' is not a neutral one, and that individual school subjects can be seen to embody certain kinds of values. Further, the very notion that scholarship can be divided into two completely distinct areas, known as 'arts' and 'science', in itself implies a value judgement. To choose to study 'arts' rather than 'science' is to make a statement about the values one considers important.

The idea that the two areas, arts and science, are more than simply subject groupings, is not a new one. C. P. Snow argued that practitioners of science and practitioners of the arts, inhabit two distinct cultures; scientists, for example, have 'common attitudes, common approaches and assumptions' (1959: 9). More recently we have come to see that the concept of science or arts is a social construction; as Michael Young has argued:

> The whole 'subject choice' and 'swing from science' debate presupposes taking as 'given' the social definitions implicit in our commonsense distinction between 'arts' and 'sciences'. What 'does' and 'does not' count as 'science' depends on the social meaning given to science, which will vary not only historically and cross-culturally but within societies and situationally.
> (Young 1971b: 21)

Most of us accept unquestioningly, for example, that philosophy, an arts subject, has more in common with history, another arts subject, than it has with physics, a science subject. Yet this distinction is a relatively recent one: Isaac Newton, for example, would not have distinguished so clearly between physics and philosophy. At the same time, this division is so entrenched in our education system that a student who wishes to cross the cultural boundary and study both areas is considered something of an oddity. In this chapter, I should like to look at some of the 'social meanings' we give to arts and science today.

In the last chapter, we touched upon Bernstein's ideas about 'framing' and 'classification'. Bernstein argues that some school subjects have very tight definitions of knowledge, and clear boundary lines marking what is considered relevant 'knowledge' and what is either considered not relevant or as belonging to another subject. These subjects (which have 'strong classification') are also the subjects where hierarchical relationships between teacher and pupil are strongest:

> Strong frames reduce the power of the pupil over what, when and how, he receives knowledge, and increase the teacher's power in the pedagogical relationship. . . . The stronger the classification and the framing, the more the educational relationship tends to be hierarchical and ritualised, the educand seen as ignorant, with little status and few rights. These are things which one earns, rather like spurs, and are used for the purpose of encouraging and sustaining the motivation of pupils.
>
> (Bernstein 1971: 58)

Although this could in theory apply to any subject (history, for example, may, in certain circumstances be taught with strong classification and framing, or with weak classification and framing), it might also be seen as one of the central features of the arts/science divide.

Bernstein also suggests that students are encouraged to make an identification with their chosen subject and to form a disdain for other forms of knowledge. The English education system is a narrowing down, rather than a broadening out: disciplines outside one's own are not looked upon as worthwhile or potentially interesting, but as completely outside one's own sphere of practice; subject specialization reveals 'difference from' rather than 'communality with'.

This argument is partly illustrated by Becher (1981) who, in looking at the 'cultures' of various disciplines, found that academics showed a remarkable intolerance of each other's disciplines. Sociology, for example, was characterized by other academics as 'fragmented and pseudo-scientific, dubious in its methodology and "open to ideological exploitation"' (1981: 110). Physics was regarded as 'the extreme of pure science' but its practitioners were thought of as 'boffins living in Cloud-Cuckoo land' (1981: 111). Engineers were seen as 'dull, conservative, conformist and mercenary' (1981: 111). There was further division within each field; in physics, theoreticians were rated higher than experimentalists; in law, mere academic specialists were not as highly thought of as those who had practised the profession.

Given that most academics – and, we shall assume students – have a strong sense of subject loyalty, we have now to ask: what are the qualities that attract students to their subjects?

Subject choice

Becher (1981) showed that academics have stereotyped ideas about their colleagues working in other fields. Indeed, most of us hold in our heads a stereotyped notion of 'the scientist' or 'the artist'. Yet it is at least arguable that different kinds of people are attracted into different kinds of subjects. Weinrich-Haste (1984), for example, in a study which examined the political values of undergraduates, found that sociologists, at one extreme, tended towards liberalism and radicalism, while engineers were the most politically and socially conservative of the groups she looked at. She also found some differences between the male and female students; the women were more egalitarian, public-minded and humane than men, and she suggests that

> women are more people-oriented, and place more emphasis on community and interpersonal values, less on institutions and less on hierarchical organisation.

> (Weinrich-Haste 1984: 128)

However, she also found that differences between students of different disciplines were greater than differences between the sexes.

The differences Weinrich-Haste found between students of various disciplines were political. Hudson (1967, 1970), in his work on subject choices made by schoolboys, found personality and IQ differences between arts specialists and science specialists. After giving pupils a variety of tests, he was able to divide the pupils into two basic types: convergers and divergers. Convergers tended to be more conformist, more authoritarian in their views, have a high IQ, do badly on open-ended tests (i.e. ones which demanded a certain amount of free expression and imagination) and specialize in the physical sciences. Divergers were the opposite: liberal, imaginative, slightly rebellious, with low IQ scores, good on open-ended questions and inclining to specialize in the arts. They were also more tolerant of ambiguity and contradiction. Hudson suggests that the reason the more conformist pupils tend to choose science is that science allows the convergent schoolboy to 'specialise in work which enables him to be unambiguously right or wrong' (1967: 104). Further:

> We should recognise, too, that the ability to think in highly conventional terms may be of the greatest importance to a young scientist in his work. Far from being a fault, it may be essential that he should accept massive bodies of conventional knowledge on trust; not merely assimilating it as a chore, but thoroughly enjoying it.

> (Hudson 1967: 104)

We can already see a connection here with Bernstein's idea of 'strong classification'. We may also see a relationship between a willingness to accept the authoritative knowledge of a subject and a willingness to defer to authority in general. Certainly Hudson seems to be suggesting this.

Although most of Hudson's tests were conducted on schoolboys, he did conduct some tests on schoolgirls, amongst whom he found a different pattern:

> The relation of convergence and divergence to arts/science specialisation amongst girls proved to be far from clearcut. As with boys, divergent girls

tend to avoid science subjects, but convergent girls are equally likely to go into the arts or physical science.

(Hudson 1970: 37)

On the face of it, this finding might seem to invalidate Hudson's whole theory. However, he argues that it is an anomaly explained by social pressure. It is considered more conventional for girls to take arts subjects than sciences; as convergers tend to be more conventional in outlook, girls are in something of a double bind – they have to decide whether to follow their inclinations or to make a 'conventional' choice. Many choose the latter. However, if divergers are more unconventional, we might expect that some divergent girls would choose science, but this is apparently not the case.

Head (1980) has also discussed schoolchildren's subject choices. He argues that subject choice is related to adolescent psychological development. He suggests that choosing science is, for many teenagers, a way of delaying the usual adolescent self-doubt and questioning of social values. Science's masculine image makes it more appealing to boys who are likely to be less emotionally mature. Science becomes less appealing to boys as they get older (and to girls, it seems, at all stages of adolescence) and become interested in issues as varied as 'the meaning of life, the existence of God, ideologies, their emerging sexuality, their future career and lifestyle' (Head 1980: 289). Science as it is presented in schools, he argues, seems irrelevant to most 13–16-year-olds, and if we are to recruit more pupils into scientific careers, then science should be shown to have some relationship to the issues that concern them. In a later article (Head 1981), he points to research findings which show that pupils who are good at maths tend, on the whole, to be more conformist and obedient than other pupils.

These three studies all suggest (if do not prove) that science specialists are likely to be rather more conformist and conventional in outlook than arts specialists, who tend to be slightly more rebellious and free-thinking. This may seem surprising if we are used to assuming that girls only choose to study the arts because society 'expects' it of them; it also contradicts Snow's (1959) argument that scientists were more politically radical than the literary intelligentsia.

We shall now look a little more closely at two particular subjects – physics and English – and examine their distinctive features.

Physics

Physics has long been held as the most successful of the sciences. Most of us, asked to name some famous scientists, would think immediately of physicists – Newton and Einstein, for example. Perhaps because of its success, it has been held as a model of scholarly inquiry; social scientists have tried to emulate what they believed were the methods of physics: formulating a testable hypothesis, setting up an experiment which could be replicated, carefully observing and measuring the results, and proving or disproving the hypothesis. Physics, particularly since the work of Bacon and Descartes, has generally been thought of as an objective science, based on observable facts; in this way a body of certain knowledge is gradually built up. The work of T. S. Kuhn (1963), and others since, has of course challenged this belief; although Kuhn talks of science in general terms, most of his examples are taken from physics. His argument, now familiar to many of us, is that science, far from being linear and progressive, is dominated by 'paradigms'. Science begins as a series of competing theories, struggling for acceptance. Gradually one theory becomes dominant and ousts all the others, and scientific research proceeds within the framework ('paradigm') of that one theory. Kuhn characterizes this work as 'puzzle-solving' and refers to it as 'normal science'. Scientists working within a paradigm do not look for major discoveries; they simply try to solve the problems posed by the current paradigm. Any anomalies tend to be accommodated by the ruling paradigm, rather than challenging it. When a crisis comes, that is when a paradigm no longer seems valid, a multitude of competing theories may arise, and the scientific community is in a state of disarray. A 'revolution' occurs when the old paradigm is displaced and a new one takes over.

Kuhn argues that science education is characterized by an uncritical teaching of the dominant paradigm within a subject. Students learn their subject by accepting what is currently regarded as true knowledge:

> Except in their occasional introductions, science textbooks do not describe the sorts of problems that the professional may be asked to solve and the variety of techniques available for their solution. Rather these books exhibit concrete problem-solutions that the profession has come to accept as paradigms, and they then ask the student, either with a pencil and paper, or in the laboratory, to solve for himself problems very closely related both in method and substance to those which the text or accompanying lecture has led him through. Nothing could be better calculated to produce mental sets or 'Einstellungen'. Only in their most elementary courses do other academic fields offer even a partial parallel.
>
> (Kuhn, quoted in Edge 1975: 48)

Cooper (1984) has suggested that there is far more disagreement amongst scientists than Kuhn allows for, which may well be true. However, it also seems to be the case that science is presented in schools as a body of uniform fact with no disagreement. In an article entitled 'Political bias in school physics', Hine (1975) argues that school physics consists of a mass of incorrect and outdated ideas, presented as if they were neutral and objective, and bearing no relation to the outside world. In particular, pupils do not learn of the social and political implications of scientific discoveries. Whitty sums up Hine's argument thus:

> It suggests not only that prevailing approaches to the subject involve the selection and presentation of knowledge which legitimates the status quo and the omission of that which might challenge it, but also that the very organisation of the curriculum into discrete units militates against the asking of the sorts of questions that might indicate that the world could be different.
>
> (Whitty 1977: 44)

It is of course arguable that, as Jeevons puts it, 'a dogmatic element in teaching physical science [is] an epistemological necessity' (quoted in Whitty 1977: 45). Almost certainly Kuhn would agree with this: students must learn a rather simplified and approximate version of the current state of scientific knowledge before they can grapple with the more sophisticated ideas and evaluate the claims of competing theories. However, although this may be useful as a way of training competent scientists, it does not seem to be an ideal method of producing critical, thinking adults. Feyerabend (1974), in fact, argues that the best scientists have been free-thinkers; for example, Galileo transformed science by his ability to see beyond conventional assumptions of scientific knowledge: his science was an imaginative one, not simply a 'rational' one. Feyerabend himself believes that current scientific teaching produces an 'unenlightened conformism' (1974: 45).

Halloun and Hestenes (1985b) have found that students embarking on physics degree courses in American universities had quite mistaken notions of the meaning of terms such as 'force', 'velocity' and 'mass'. While they were able to recite Newton's laws by rote, they couldn't explain them. They were, however, prepared to justify their answers by appeals to authority:

> Galileo did the [free fall] experiment in Pisa and said they [falling objects] reach a speed limit. I guess . . . because Galileo did it, or at least if what I know about him is true, this must be true.
>
> (Halloun and Hestenes 1985b: 1,061)

Halloun and Hestenes describe this kind of response in ironic terms as 'one of the achievements of teaching passive rote knowledge' (1985b: 1,061).

It may seem curious that physics, on the face of it the most challenging and exciting of disciplines, a discipline whose discoveries have transformed the world we live in, should be taught in a way which demands little creativity or imagination. Capra (1979), himself a physicist, has argued that most physicists, despite the discoveries of twentieth-century physics, are trapped in a pre-twentieth-century way of looking at the world. Capra believes that quantum mechanics demonstrates that there is no such thing as certainty in the physical world, and that the mechanistic view of the world which dominates scientific thought should be replaced by a view of the physical world as dynamic and interconnected. Quantum mechanics, although now eighty years old, has shown no signs of transforming the school science curriculum. I should like to discuss the reasons for this a little later, but first I want to discuss the teaching of English.

English

'English' is a recent innovation. The very idea of the 'liberal humanities', as distinct from the sciences, grew up in the nineteenth century. The belief that men should be trained for a narrow role in life came to be challenged; it was argued that they should have some knowledge of the liberal arts, the 'finer' things in life. Raymond Williams puts it like this:

it was argued that man's spiritual health depended on a kind of education which was more than a training for some specialized work, a kind variously described as 'liberal', 'humane' or 'cultural'.

(Williams 1975: 141)

The central discipline of this new liberal education was to be English. English had a dual role; as Baldick (1984) has shown, it was initially used as a sop to women who were demanding higher education; in the very first intake of students of English at Oxford University, the majority of them were women. It was also seen, however, by certain middle-class educators such as Matthew Arnold as a means of subduing the masses. Arnold, like many in the middle classes frightened at the thought of working-class revolution, argued for the need to 'win the sympathy' of the working classes, for 'society is in danger of falling into anarchy' (Matthew Arnold, 'The popular education of France', quoted in Eagleton 1983: 24). Arnold genuinely believed that the transmission of a common culture could help unite the classes and promote fellow-feeling. English would reduce conflict between the social classes, while maintaining the status quo. Arnold was not the only, nor last, proponent of this view. Baldick quotes the much later Newbolt Report (1921), which said that a liberal education based on English

would form a new element of national unity, linking together the mental life of all classes.

(Baldick 1984: 95)

These do not seem like promising beginnings: English was merely to be an extra accomplishment for young middle-class women – a 'convenient sort of non-subject to palm off on the ladies' as Eagleton (1983: 28) puts it; and a substitute for a classical education for the discontented working classes. Yet perhaps it was the easy accessibility of English which made it so popular; it has grown to be the second largest university subject. At the same time, it has come to be seen – particularly by its own practitioners – as a *serious* subject. This is largely the consequence of the efforts of the Cambridge literary critic, F. R. Leavis, who provided English with a *raison d'être*. The influence of Leavis is such that it has been claimed that:

English students in England today are 'Leavisites' whether they know it or not.

(Eagleton 1983: 31)

Leavis believed that English was concerned with central moral issues and the study of literature could provide some opposition to the dehumanizing effects of modern industrial society. The study of literature could help one to become a more sensitive, more moral person. As one of Leavis's disciples, L. C. Knights, has put it:

It is impossible to indicate all the humanly important matters that literature gives us knowledge of. . . . It is through literature that we grow into a particular kind of awareness of ourselves and – an inseparable corollary – of our manifold relations with each other and all that is not self, without which there is really not much 'self' to talk about.

(Knights 1975: 133)

Studying literature, then, is a serious business; it is concerned with close examination of those authors who can bring us to a deeper (and more moral) understanding of humanity. Leavis himself was partisan in the extreme when it came to deciding which writers could be awarded the accolade of 'moral seriousness'. The 'great tradition' consisted of only five writers: Austen, Eliot, James, Conrad and Lawrence. Many other major writers – Shelley, Defoe, Sterne, Fielding, for example – were derided as 'trivial' or 'not serious'. This rather authoritarian form of elitism was usually defended by an appeal to the 'sensitive' or 'discriminating' reader; anyone who read closely and intelligently enough would be bound to agree with Leavis's judgement. Naturally enough, this lays Leavis open to the charge of 'unfalsifiability' (as Popper would put it); his unwillingness to provide a set of standards by which to judge literature meant that his own critical judgements were always irrefutable.

Leavis is not, of course, the only influence on the study of English today. As Bowen (1985) has pointed out, the contribution of I. A. Richards is often ignored, yet it is his prescription for the 'close reading' of texts which is the basis of most school and university teaching of English today. However, it is because Leavis provided a *purpose* for English that most people regard him as the central figure. After Leavis, students and teachers of English need no longer feel that their activities were trivial: on the contrary, theirs was the *only* morally serious university subject.

Yet, since the Second World War, English literary criticism (if not English teaching) has slowly changed. Perhaps English was seen to have failed in its mission; perhaps moral seriousness was not enough. It was the scientists, not the literary intellectuals, as C. P. Snow reminded us, who had 'the future in their bones' (1959: 11). It is here, of course, that we see an essential paradox at the heart of the arts/science divide. Science, as we know, has tremendous potential to change the way we live; yet it professes not to concern itself with moral issues, insisting upon its own objectivity. The humanities, on the other hand, regard a concern with moral issues as central to their meaning; philosophers, historians, literary critics, consistently make explicit their interest in morality – while the study of philosophy, history or English appears to have had little impact on the lives of the mass of people. As Bowen has said:

It is clear that Marxist literary critics . . . feel acutely their impotence as individuals to change the world.

(Bowen 1985: 36)

It is worth pointing out that this distinction is also a male/female one; whereas most important political actions that have really affected people's lives have been taken by men, it is women, historically excluded from decision-making, who have been concerned with the subjective and the personal.

Perhaps it is this sense of impotence – and the sense that English's image of 'effeminacy' or 'femininity' makes it appear unimportant – that has led post-war literary theoretical movements to espouse ideals of 'objectivity' and 'scientificity'. In contrast to Leavis's haphazard approach of determining which writers were important, and which were not, literary theory was going to be rigorously objective. Foremost among the new movements was structuralism: a literary theory which believed in the necessity of examining the 'deep structures' of a literary work. Structuralists did not believe in examining the text in relation to society – although they did believe in examining the relationships within texts and between texts – nor in examining it as a work with moral significance; the aim was simply to lay bare the universal structures which were hidden within it. Marxists too have sought credibility for their theory through claims to a scientific objectivity. Eagleton could not put it more simply:

Marxism is a scientific theory of human societies and the practice of transforming them.

(Eagleton 1976: vii)

The most recent theoretical movements in literary criticism have, however, rejected the notions of objectivity and scientificity. Deconstructionism has pointed to the inherent flaws in structuralism – that, for example, binary oppositions are not absolute, but are dependent on their social meaning – and has celebrated the idea of 'subjectivity'. Deconstructionists believe that it is impossible to reach at the 'truth' of a text, because every interpretation of a work is itself open to interpretation – endlessly. Similarly feminism has stressed the importance of subjectivity, arguing that in the past men's experience has been presented as the objective truth. Writers such as Moers (1977) and Showalter (1978) have challenged the idea of the 'canon', the Leavisite notion of a body of greater writers who have universal value, by discussing the work of many lesser-known female writers, and staking a claim for their consideration as 'great' writers.

That challenges have been made to the liberal humanist tradition by Marxists, structuralists, deconstructionists, feminists and others is not, however, to say that these challenges are widely accepted or even taught. The current consensus in English is that there is no consensus: confusion reigns. A recent article on teaching English in higher education begins:

By now everyone has heard that there is a 'crisis' in English.

(Miall 1989: 69)

One group unlikely to be aware of a 'crisis' are school pupils. In a fascinating study, St John Brooks (1983) writes of English departments in two secondary schools; one in particular, she notes, is located in the Leavisite tradition of English studies. The teachers in the two departments are possessed of a missionary zeal to improve the quality of their pupils' lives; they do not want an English education to be *useful* or vocational, but to enable the pupils to think critically about themselves, about life, and about society. As one memorably puts it:

I am not worried they'll be sold a duff car. I am worried that they'll be sold a duff life.

(St John Brooks 1983: 37)

An interesting question arising from this study is whether English continues to be regarded as a subject with a mission in higher education; and whether the view of academics differs from that of students.

Gender, subject and society

So far we have suggested that physics and English are subjects with very different traditions and qualities. In this section I want to look more generally at the ways in which arts and science are associated with ideas about gender and at the social implications of the differences between arts and science.

It is by now almost a cliché to say that science is associated with masculinity and the arts with femininity. Yet a closer look reveals that the picture is more complicated. We have already looked at Liam Hudson's early work on personality and subject choice. That early work tended to take the terms 'arts' and 'science' as givens, rather than as constructs. However, in a later book, *The Cult of the Fact* (1972), Hudson looks much more closely at the gendered nature of the arts and the sciences. He had already found that school pupils and students associated science with masculinity and arts with femininity (or effeminacy):

Artist, poet and novelist are all seen in my studies as warm and exciting, but as of little worth. Mathematician, physicist and engineer are all seen as extremely valuable, but also as dull and cold. It is clear too, that the arts are associated with sexual pleasure, the sciences with sexual restraint. . . . Yet the scientist is seen as masculine, the arts specialist as slightly feminine.

(Hudson 1972: 83)

These stereotypes have a much wider set of connotations. 'Science', 'masculinity', 'hardness', 'difficulty' and 'value' are all apparently associated ideas, while 'arts', 'effeminacy', 'softness', 'easiness' and 'lack of worth' are also related concepts. Hudson points to the fact that, not only are these terms applied by pupils to the arts and sciences, but also they are recognized to a large degree by those, like himself, working within psychology. In psychology, higher status is accorded to the 'hard' tradition within the discipline, the tradition which shows 'a preoccupation with behaviour: with the organism – its physical, corporeal presence, and what it can be seen to do' (Hudson 1972: 86). The 'soft' tradition is, apparently, concerned to 'treat people as people, and [is] concerned less with law-making and more with speculative exploration' (1972: 88). It is not difficult to see the connection between the former tradition and the stereotyped model of physical science – a model which, Hudson says, 'physical scientists themselves have long abandoned' (1972: 86). Hudson uses the instrumental/expressive distinction made by Talcott Parsons to characterize the two approaches:

The instrumental approach is one essentially concerned with the im-
personal control, the subjugation, of the environment; the expressive with
relationships between one person and another.

(Hudson 1972: 87–8)

Hudson's schoolboys saw science as masculine and the arts as feminine.
However, by this, Hudson does not mean that they see the arts as being
practised by women; rather, they see them as being practised by 'effeminate'
men. This no doubt explains one of Hudson's tests on the schoolboys, which
asked them to write a description of a scientist's wife, and a novelist's wife, not a
novelist's *husband*. In other words, the practice of discovering knowledge, of
creating works of art, in short, of making the world we live in, is seen to be
conducted entirely by men: masculine men or feminine men – but not women.

This finding is borne out by a study by Weinrich-Haste (1986) which found
that, while some subjects were rated by schoolchildren and undergraduates as
definitely masculine, and some as neutral, none was rated as definitely feminine:
a finding which suggests that the arts/science divide is not a symmetrical
feminine/masculine divide, but one which is distinctly asymmetrical.

That this distinction between 'masculine' men and 'feminine' men even exists
is interesting. We are used to thinking of 'femininity' as being something to do
with women, when in fact it also represents a set of values or behaviour which
are generally regarded with disapproval: to call a man 'effeminate' is generally
to insult him (rather more, perhaps, than it is to call a woman 'masculine'). To
what extent is it true that the sciences and the arts (physics and English in
particular) represent these different values?

Keller argues that the equation of science with objectivity is in itself redolent
of particular values, saying that:

Objectivity is itself an ideal which has a long history of identification with
the masculine.

(Keller 1983: 188)

The argument of many feminists is that the myth of the objectivity of the
physical sciences has been a way of legitimizing the abuse of knowledge within a
patriarchal and capitalist framework. Merchant (1982), for example, believes
that from the mid-seventeenth century onwards, the scientific view of Nature
began to change; instead of seeing Nature as an organic and harmonious entity,
it began to be seen as external and chaotic; the role of science was to exploit it.
Nature was likened to the feminine; science to the masculine. As Brown and
Jordonova (1982) put it:

men possessed power through their identification with scientific knowledge. Simultaneously, women were conceptualised as the passive recipients of scientific manipulation.

(Brown and Jordonova 1982: 398)

The distinction here between two different views of nature – one, harmonious,
one exploitative – is similar to the instrumental/expressive distinction used by
Hudson. Other feminist writers, such as Overfield (1981), Wallsgrove (1980)

and Fee (1983) have suggested that dichotomies such as nature/culture, subject/object, emotional/rational are harmful because they imply the superiority of culture over nature, the objective over the subjective, and the rational over the emotional. These dichotomies can be seen as a way of legitimizing both male superiority and the abuse of science. Rose (1982), for example, believes that the practice of science cannot be removed from its social context: a context both of male dominance and the drive for profit. The depraved uses to which science is often put are justified by the claim that science is 'objective'. She argues that a feminist science, which restored the personal and the subjective to the practice of knowledge, would be a more *human* science.

It is the argument of many feminists, then, that the high status accorded to science in our culture is dependent on its association with masculinity, and associated values such as objectivity and impersonality. If we accept that science is objective, then it is more difficult to challenge its practice in modern society; the scientist can always argue that his work is morally neutral. However, such a position is untenable; as Rose and Rose have argued, science today is so 'closely and directly enmeshed in the machinery of state and government' (1976b: 15), that it is impossible to disentangle the practice of science from its context in modern industrial capitalism. This helps us to see more clearly the role of science in schools; to challenge the objectivity of science in the school curriculum would be to initiate searching questions about the role of scientists in today's society. The full implications of quantum mechanics, if discussed in classrooms, might be highly threatening to traditional methods of teaching physics.

If physical science has such a strong association with masculinity, then the position of the arts, English in particular, is surely more ambivalent. We have already seen that Weinrich-Haste (1986) found that no academic subject was rated by students as 'positively feminine'. Yet we also know that English is associated with those qualities generally regarded as 'feminine' (such as the stress on subjectivity and emotional response) and that English has, since its inception, been studied mainly by women.

One of the reasons why English is, perhaps, not a straightforwardly 'feminine' subject is that most of its teachers in higher education are men, and most of the authors and critics studied are also men. Another is that a degree of tension exists in English between the ideals of subjectivity and objectivity. We have seen that since the Second World War, there have been attempts by structuralists and Marxists to make English more 'objective': attempts which, I would suggest, have not been particularly successful in penetrating the teaching of English in higher education. However, even in the liberal humanist tradition of Leavis and Richards, there is a striking paradox. This is that students are expected to respond in a subjective and emotional way to texts; yet they must also accept the 'objective' judgement of the canon. The subjectivity is limited by the conventions of the discipline; in Bowen's words, I. A. Richards enjoined students of English to 'emotionality and detachment, expression and mimesis, individuality and objectivity' (Bowen 1985: 311). Students of English, then, may be treading a tightrope between too much personal response, and too little.

Challenging the authority of the canon is immensely difficult; if a writer is great, then s/he will be in the canon; if a writer is not in the canon, then s/he can't be any good, and to try to put him/her there would be an act of mindless obstinacy. As Kolodny (1981) has said:

> The fact of canonization puts any work beyond questions of establishing its merit and, instead, invites students to offer only increasingly more in-genious readings and interpretations, the purpose of which is to validate the greatness already imputed by the canonization.
>
> (Kolodny 1981: 30)

What is frustrating about this is that the 'canon' apparently consists of works of universal and immutable value; anyone who suggests adapting it to include, say, more female writers, is open to accusations of being 'political'. The liberal humanist tradition is unwilling to admit that its own choices are political; that Leavis's intense dislike, for example, of Shelley, was based as much upon political considerations as aesthetic ones.

English, then, *is* ambivalent. It allows for subjectivity and freedom of opinion within fairly strict guidelines. Women who study the subject because they believe it to be solely about intuitive response may feel caught in this paradox.

Without precipitating the arguments of the rest of the book, I should like to suggest that attempts to make English more scientific, more objective, more masculine, are unlikely to succeed. This is because physical science can be superior as a method of investigation and scholarship only if it has something to be superior *to*. Religion lost its hold on the social imagination when it was seen to embody qualities opposed to science: irrationality and superstition. The arts now hold the position once held by religion; as long as science continues to be highly valued, then the arts will inevitably be devalued.

Summary

This chapter has suggested that our perceptions of the arts and sciences are shaped by notions of femininity and masculinity. These perceptions, far from being simple or accidental, are intimately related to issues of authority and control and the need to concentrate power in the hands of certain groups of people. Women, it has been suggested, have been historically excluded from the making of knowledge, in particular science, and this is related (not necessarily causally) to women's powerlessness. Even in the 'feminine' arts, however, women have been subject to more subtle pressures: arts, it is believed, are the domain of 'feminine' men, not women, and there have been attempts in recent years to render the arts more 'masculine'. Further, it was suggested that disciplines embody certain values and that acceptance of these values may be necessary to achieve success in a discipline.

However, it has also been argued, more optimistically, that recent develop-ments in the philosophy of science and in science itself (for example, quantum physics), and in English Literature allow for a greater freedom and flexibility, and indeed, humanity, in the education of students. Whereas it seems unlikely that these concerns have penetrated school syllabuses, it is possible, given the much greater autonomy of institutions of higher education, that they have had a greater influence on higher education syllabuses.

In the account of the research project which follows, I examine some of these issues. I look at how physics is constructed by staff and students; whether they view these disciplines in terms of the old paradigm of science as certain, objective and value-free, or whether they view them in terms of the new paradigm of uncertainty, breadth and interconnectedness. Similarly I look at English and ask whether staff and students locate their discipline within the Leavisite paradigm or whether they are aware of the developments of the past thirty years, such as structuralism and post-structuralism. We are also interested in whether the disciplines of physical science and communications, both polytechnic courses, are challenging the authority of the older disciplines and moving them in new directions.

A question related to that of perceptions of science and arts is the extent to which relationships in departments are formalized. How are students taught? Do students learn passively, by taking notes in a 50-minute lecture, or do they have more control over their own learning? Is the relationship between staff and students hierarchical or informal?

We are interested in these questions, of course, because we are also interested in gender. We wish to investigate the experience of being a female, or a male, student in higher education, and whether the experience of studying science is different from studying arts. Is the experience of higher education more or less rewarding, for example, for a female physics student than for a female English student? Is the appeal of physics the same for women as it is for men?

The chapters that follow will try to answer these questions, and address the central issue of whether women are, indeed, marginalized in higher education: whether they are, in Helen Hacker's words, a 'minority group'.

4

Constructing Science

Introduction

This chapter will look at the way in which science is viewed and experienced by those who teach and study it. It begins by looking at the ideas of lecturers, but is primarily concerned with the meanings that 'physics' or 'physical science' have for students, and the ways in which those meanings are sometimes at odds with the experience of studying those subjects. The particular emphasis in this chapter will be the contrast, both implicit and explicit, that is made between the activity of studying science and the activity of studying the 'humanities'. We discover that the contrast is based upon a particular set of values which science is believed to embody, and which is apparently lacking in the humanities. I wish to suggest, also, that in describing physics, for example, as a particular kind of subject, students are also saying something about themselves, as people: the qualities which attract them to a particular subject are also, to some extent, qualities which are central to their own self-image. This theme will be developed a little further in Chapter 6.

I also want to argue in this chapter, however, that there is more than one view of physics (in particular) and science (in general), and that there are some within the discipline who do not accept the dominant perspective of the subject, but put forward powerful alternative views. It is, therefore, with two contrasting views of the discipline that I wish to begin.

The viewpoint of staff

Physics

This section will look at the way in which physics is constructed as a discipline by briefly contrasting the views of two university lecturers, one at B university, and one at A university. The attitudes embodied by these two men were described in Chapter 3 as 'instrumental' and 'expressive'; the instrumental attitude could be said to regard physics as a useful subject, both for individuals and for society, while the more expressive, or liberal, attitude, regards the discipline as valuable for its own sake. Physics is interesting in having connotations of both: as a physical science, its discoveries (and the skills it gives to its graduates) have obvious uses for industry; while its status as a 'pure' rather than an 'applied' science gives it the appearance of being removed from the uses to which it may be put.

First, we shall look at the view of Dr L, (at the time of interview, the head of department at B), who saw physics as a discipline essentially concerned with fundamental rules and laws:

> Students come here primarily to get a degree, but also they should get an understanding of the basic laws of the universe. That's the ideal thing. We don't do any astronomy in this department, but we teach an elementary astronomy course, and astronomy of course now is just the physics of outer space; astronomy has stopped being a separate subject. It's a branch of physics now basically.
>
> (Dr L, Department B)

Dr L emphasized several times that the 'laws' of physics were absolute, and applied everywhere, all the time. His view of science was reductive; just as astronomy is a part of physics, rather than a separate subject, so is chemistry:

> All of chemistry now basically is becoming explicable in terms of quantum theory . . . we are getting, have been getting in the past 20 years, into the age where a sizeable amount of basic chemistry can now be properly understood from basic quantum theory. Once you know the thing consists of electrons and atoms, you can more or less calculate what structure it has, what properties the molecule will have. That's still got an awful long way to go.
>
> (Dr L, Department B)

The language used by L implies that it is wholly desirable that one discipline should ultimately be explicable in terms of another. He also suggests that this reductionism should be an end goal of physics; scientific discovery is not about an expansion or a reaching out, but a narrowing in. Not only are astronomy and chemistry reducible to physics; but also biology is – or would be if physicists put any effort into making it so:

> We haven't gone, in physics, seriously into trying to understand the biological aspects, but then you see biology is becoming dominated in the last ten years by the understanding of basic biochemistry of cells. The biochemistry of cells is basically just the chemistry of the larger molecules that the physicists can't yet deal with through quantum theory calculations. Give it another fifty years or so, and one should then be able to understand much more the system.
>
> (Dr L, Department B)

This view of physics sees it as a body of knowledge, or a system, which can explain all other bodies of knowledge. Chemistry is a part of physics, biology is a part of chemistry. Chemists often have to take things 'on trust' because, it is implied, the physicists are working on the harder, more fundamental problems. It is not surprising that Dr L regarded the humanities with some contempt, arguing that students go to sign on for a medieval history course in the arts faculty and

> display quite appalling ignorance of other parts of the subject – it doesn't seem to matter too much to the arts faculty or the historians, that you concentrate on something here and know nothing about important things elsewhere. In the sciences things are a bit different.
>
> (Dr L, Department B)

In order to illustrate that a reductionist view of physics is not necessarily the only one available, it is necessary to juxtapose the above quote, with the following, from Dr G, a senior lecturer at Department A:

> The reason I went into physics and what I try to inculcate is that the ideas themselves are interesting and that seems to me to be the main justification for it, so that when people try and justify scientific research by saying it's good for the economy, the country and so on, or who knows what applications are going to come of it, I'm inclined to sit rather quietly when that's said because I'm not convinced that some of the research that is done nowadays can have any practical application at all in that direct sense.
>
> (Dr G, Department A)

In one sense, Dr G's claims for physics are much less grand than Dr L's; at the same time, his view of physics is a far broader one:

> I try to justify it in terms of training the intellect to think in an abstract and critical way, so I regard it as a general education. I have on occasion told students that they're doing an arts subject, and tried to encourage them to think in those terms, because if they're constantly thinking of the job at the end of it, then I don't think they're getting the most out of it that they can do. . . . However, it sometimes depresses me, and again I'm expressing a very personal view I guess, that having tried to teach the students the subject as about ideas, they then insist on learning the subject as things to be learnt and then going off and applying their knowledge to new and more expensive ways of killing people or stopping other people killing us. So that's rather depressing actually, that a lot of students will go into RADAR and various other sorts of defence things which don't seem to me to be increasing the sum of human happiness.
>
> (Dr G, Department A)

This rather sad quote illustrates very sharply a point made in the previous chapter, which is that a field of learning such as physics, which has great power to change our lives, is usually divorced from a consideration of moral issues. This is Dr G's dilemma: that although he tries to inculcate students with a sense of the beauty and joy of the subject, and to stimulate their minds, they often refuse to think, or to be critical and regard physics in an entirely instrumental way, as a degree to be gained, which will enable them to do something 'useful', namely defence research. Dr G's emphasis on the creative potential of physics leads him to see it as an 'arts subject'; Dr L, on the other hand, sees the differences between the sciences and the arts as 'enormous'.

Dr G's belief that physics should be about learning to think in an 'abstract and critical way' is reflected in his views on teaching; it is, for example, important to him that students should have some control over their own learning. Talking of an essay that students are expected to write as part of their course, he says

> The student chooses their own subject; most of these subjects are right on the fringes of the course, or overlap several different courses, and what surprised me when I sent round a questionnaire was how much the students said they enjoyed essay-writing. And I'm sure it's because they're in charge of what they're learning – that they've chosen something interesting to them and are following it up.
>
> (Dr G, Department A)

Essay-writing is an exception, however; generally physics students, spending about 25 hours a week in lectures, tutorials and labs, have much less time than humanities students to work on their own initiative.

Physical science

The reason for the existence of a physical science course in the polytechnic is pragmatic, rather than educational. The polytechnic was originally formed from three colleges, two of which ran applied physics degree courses. When the colleges merged, it would obviously have been ludicrous to run two applied physics courses, and therefore the staff on one of the courses were kept on to teach a physical science course which was

> supposed to be an inter-disciplinary mixture of physics and chemistry, in other words, not a bit of physics and a bit of chemistry that you did in isolation, but to be integrated.
>
> (Dr H, Department C)

The first physical science course which ran was 'not very integrated'; staff feel that since the course was revised in the early 1980s, it has become more integrated. The aim, according to Dr H, is to provide students with a broader degree which will be more useful in industry. The Swann Report (1968) had argued that industry needed '85% generalists and 15% specialists'

> and we are hopefully turning out some of those generalists, people who can look at things not just from the physics angle, or from the chemistry angle, but can cope with things from both.
>
> (Dr H, Department C)

The advantage of a physical science degree over a conventional physics or chemistry degree is that there's a wider range of jobs available . . . I think they go for more sorts of jobs, it's difficult to list them, but a lot are going into computing and electronics today, but we have people – we had one student who's gone into accountancy, Royal Navy, weapons research, gas board, chemical side as opposed to physical side, video discs, hospital physics, where I would have thought the chemical aspects would be of use to them as well as the physics.

(Dr H, Department C)

The vocational aspects of the course are clearly the most important consideration when it comes to recruiting new students. Changes in the course occur because of the need to attract a great number of students; recently there has been a move to introduce a greater element of electronics in the course because

The more you can make your course look like another branch of electrical engineering, the better your chances are.

(Mr N, Department C)

The staff believe that the course is unpopular because physical science is rarely taught in schools; there is no longer, for example, a physical science A level. Teachers and careers advisers tend to push students towards single honours physics or chemistry degrees, or, more usually, engineering.

The course avoids being two separate disciplines running alongside each other through making energy and matter the core themes of the course: energy and matter are then examined from physical and chemical aspects; as Dr H puts it, energy and matter are 'pegs to hang the course on'. Because 'energy and matter are fundamental both to physics and chemistry', it can be argued that physics and chemistry are not completely different subjects, but part of one body of knowledge.

The essential difference, therefore, between this course and more conventional university courses is that it is very explicitly geared to the needs of industry, and students spend one year on industrial placement. We might also expect that, unlike university students, the polytechnic students are given an increased awareness of the social nature of science, as the CNAA has made a 'science and society' type module compulsory on science courses. However, on the physical science course, this module took the form of looking at the problems students might face as scientific managers in industry: issues like risk management, the problems of pollution, dealing with pressure groups and preparing public reports. The discussion of social problems related to science is somewhat limited; the dominant perspective is that of the company which wishes to protect its interests. It seems unlikely, therefore, that the physical science course provides any great challenge to the orthodoxy of science teaching in higher education.

Subject choice and higher education

Before we look at students' construction of science, it is important to stress that students' decision to study science was not merely a consequence of their preferring it to other subjects, or being good at it, but the result of schooling and family influences. Obviously personal inclination is very important, but personal inclination can often arise from having been taught by an exceptional teacher, or having a scientist parent who helps with homework.

As we are particularly interested in the influences on women who choose science, we shall begin by looking at the women's experiences of single-sex education. It has often been argued that girls in single-sex schools are likely to have higher educational achievements than girls in mixed schools, and in particular that they are more likely to do well in scientific subjects (e.g. Department of Education and Science 1980; Steedman 1980). More female science students (sixteen of the twenty-four) had attended single-sex schools than any other group in the sample; it may be that their single-sex schooling had been a major influence in their decision to study science at degree level. Certainly some of the female science students felt that they had benefited from a single-sex education. For example, Felicity, who had attended an independent girls' school where all the teaching staff were women, said:

> There was never any 'girls don't do science' and I'm glad I didn't have that sort of pressure on me, because I think it's a load of bosh, basically
>
> (Felicity, 1st year, A)

Although this is phrased negatively, it was clear from the interview that the school had been very influential in shaping her enthusiasm for physics. Another student said of her boarding school:

> I don't really agree with boarding schools. I think in some ways it's better, because girls are meant to get on better in the sciences in girls' schools; they're meant to be pushed backwards a bit in boys' schools.
>
> (Suzanne, 1st year, A)

The term 'boys' schools' rather than 'mixed schools' is revealing; however, this is still hardly a ringing endorsement of single-sex schools. Part of the problem is that as most women who had attended single-sex schools had not known anything else, their comments will focus on the school itself rather than the fact of its being single-sex. One physics student who had attended a convent school was full of praise for the school:

> I think the teachers did influence me a lot in their own enthusiasm for the subject; it seemed to rub off on me, you know; whenever they taught me something, a new concept or something, I'd come away feeling enlightened by it, and wanting to know more, just this curiosity for more knowledge. But that is true of a lot of subjects I did at O level.
>
> (Jane, 3rd year, B)

Another student, who had attended a girls' grammar, felt that there were important differences between single-sex schools and mixed schools. Explaining why she thought there were so few women in science, she said:

> I think it's school's fault and/or parents. I think it goes back to when you're *this* big. I think that's why so many people from our school went into scientific things – they pushed you that way, but I know from my friends

that the secondary school where a lot of my friends went to, the girls were encouraged to do typing, hairdressing, home-economics, all the rest of it. I really think that schools are at fault. That's why I'm glad that WISE thing, I mean it's about time they bloody realized – I'm convinced that once a woman gets into science she's just as good as if not better than, any man.

(Linda, 4th year, C)

This discourse of 'as good as a man' was to recur frequently in interviews with the women; certainly there were some schools which had taught their pupils to think in those terms. However, there was also severe criticism of single-sex schools from some female science students. Many, although appreciative of the education they received, felt that their schools were too strict in imposing petty regulations – a comment rarely made by students from mixed or comprehensive schools. In addition, two female science students who had attended girls' grammar schools felt that they had been disadvantaged:

If I'd done English, geography and history, I might have done a lot better, but they just didn't seem to bother about you if you were doing science – perhaps it was an old-fashioned school.

(Fay, 4th year, C)

At the male grammar school in town, they *had* to do O-level physics, but we didn't have to do it. I think they were encouraged more. [There was discrimination] not directly, but in subtle ways, like when you're choosing your options, no matter what you're doing there's always a group where you can do cookery or needlework, but if you're doing physics you have to put that down, and that means that you can't do something else that you might want to do, like history or something; you've got to make a positive choice to do science whereas it's quite easy to drift into doing history and things like that.

(Louise, 3rd year, B)

In both these cases, science departments were under-funded and under-staffed, and there was therefore more pressure on girls to do arts subjects, not science subjects. The same would not be true of independent schools, which at least are well resourced.

For most students, the decision to follow an arts path or a sciences path is made at the age of 16, when choosing A levels; for some students, it is made earlier, at 14, or, for a very few students, those who have kept their options open, later, after A level. For some science students, the decision was a straightforward one, a matter of following ability and inclination. For others, it was a hard choice to make, and different factors had to be taken into account. Clearly schools played an important, and direct, part in the actual choice of subject, as well as providing the appropriate educational stimulation. Some students, when making a choice, had been strongly aware of peer-group pressure and pressure from teachers who said that a science qualification led to jobs:

I was very all-round at school. I got virtually equal marks across arts and sciences for O levels, so making a choice at A level was difficult, but I felt a bit swayed by the fact that people said it's best to do science subjects as far as jobs and university places go; it's difficult to get on to arts courses, but it's easier to get on to science courses . . . that's really why I chose science, ultimately.

(Jane, 3rd year, B)

I found the two [arts and sciences] equally interesting, so the career edged it.

(Patrick, 1st year, A)

I did enjoy physics, but I found geography a lot easier, and I went and spoke to my careers worker at school. She said to me, 'there aren't many jobs for geographers, you should go into something more science-y', so I just drifted into it basically.

(Linda, 4th year, C)

Thus for many students, choosing science was not a simple matter of inclination or ability: many felt happy and at ease with both areas. However, schools did not like students to feel at home in arts and science: a rigid division between the two prevailed:

I liked English. At A level, I toyed with the idea of doing physics, maths and English, and if I was just doing it for pure enjoyment I would have done it at that stage. But people said to me, 'Well, the English won't be a lot of good to you if you do a science degree and you'll find it difficult to split your time between the arts and the sciences'.

(Paul, 3rd year, B)

That, at least, is a clear statement of the belief that the arts and sciences were incompatible; for one thing, the arts and the sciences are considered so different that it is difficult to concentrate one's energies on both; for another, English is not *useful* – and, therefore, by implication, worthless – to someone studying science. Almost all of the science students in the sample had taken A levels in physics, maths and chemistry or physics, maths and further maths; one had A levels in physics, maths and English, while two had A levels in geography, and some physical science students had biology rather than maths A level: these, however, formed a very small minority of the whole. There was also one student who had taken the baccalaureate – a combination of ten subjects, arts and science; she had considered changing to English in her first term at university.

For many students, the decision to study science came naturally because of family interests. A number had come from scientific backgrounds; fathers (usually) were nuclear physicists, engineers, doctors or maths lecturers, and often provided an impetus to study science through discussion of it at home or through help with homework. One first-year student, whose father was a nuclear physicist, referred constantly to him during her interview, even on one occasion prefacing an answer with 'I know what my father would say . . .'. Father had, apparently, told her she was 'too stupid' to take a degree in maths, told her she couldn't do a joint degree in physics and German because he couldn't afford to pay for the year out, and had influenced her to apply for A university because that was where he had taken his degree. At home, she would argue with him about physics:

> I don't talk to my father about physics; it's always a mistake because he gets cross when I say silly things, but the rest of the family get cross because they can't understand. Whatever he tells me seems to go in one ear and out the other.
>
> (Natalie, 1st year, A)

(Of course, Natalie wasn't silly; she was, in fact, a year younger than the rest of the first-year students, having kept a year ahead at school.) Other women mentioned their fathers as direct influences; for example:

> If I'd followed my own path, I'd probably have done something like that [arts]. But my dad was always saying, 'You're going to do sciences'. So that's why I ended up doing science and I've got this far so I can't be bad at it.
>
> (Marianne, 4th year, C)

Another said that her father had made her more aware of science,

> in normal everyday things which I wouldn't otherwise have been aware of, and he's been someone to have arguments with about science, and it's nice to have someone who understands what you're going on about.
>
> (Felicity, 1st year, A)

Some fathers seemed to have invested hopes in their daughters of the kind we normally expect to be invested in sons:

> My father's sort of said to me that if I want a job afterwards, and if I want a decent job and a job with a future, it's got to be on the engineering side of the works.
>
> (Lesley, 1st year, C)

This kind of pressure had not been confined to the women; some of the men had been encouraged by their fathers to take science, too. The women, however, were more aware of being pushed, of being expected to be unusual. Men were more likely to regard it as natural that they should take science.

Although many students were pushed, or encouraged, in the direction of science by schools or family, the physics students generally felt that physics had special qualities that appealed to them. Only one of the physics students, had, for example, considered taking a degree in chemistry. Several had considered maths or engineering, or both; maths was generally dismissed as 'too theoretical', while engineering was dismissed as 'too applied': physics was held to be the perfect happy medium – applied enough to be 'relevant' (a favourite adjective amongst both the science and the arts students), but theoretical enough to be stimulating and demanding. Engineers, it was often said, only carried out ideas that other people had thought of first. Through the use of these negatives (engineering and maths), we can see students' construction of an identity as 'physicist': a person who is not too remote from reality, but who is at the same time capable of independent and abstract thought – a point we shall return to in Chapter 6. Physics, I was often told, was a 'general degree', one which opened up a range of possibilities; it was also, many students said, 'one of the best degrees you can get'. In addition, it was held by some to combine the advantages of generality (a perceived feature of humanities degrees) with the advantages of usefulness (a perceived feature of science degrees). In the next section, we shall look in more detail at what students mean by 'physics'.

Constructing 'physics'

Physics students made sense of their discipline through a series of dichotomies which contrasted the values embodied by physics with the values (i.e. weaknesses) of other disciplines. Chief amongst these were the following:

Physics	*'Other'*
fundamental	tangential
certain	uncertain
progressive	static
infinite	finite
difficult	easy
hard	soft
concerned with understanding	concerned with rote learning
relevant	irrelevant
useful	useless

This list contains all the dichotomies, either explicit or implicit, in comments the physics students made to me about their discipline. Not all of these dichotomies were posed in terms of a physics/humanities divide. Some, for example understanding/learning and fundamental/tangential, were posed in terms of a physics/chemistry divide. Others, particularly hard/soft, have strong masculine/feminine connotations. Some (e.g. relevant/irrelevant) can be discussed only in terms of the implied criticism of the humanities, and are part of a larger arts/science contrast, and these will be dealt with in a later section. However, there are certain qualities which are seen to be peculiar to physics and these are crucial to our understanding of the construction of physics as a discipline. The first quality is the discipline's *fundamentality*:

> I think it's the big mystery, isn't it, the unknown, things like this, trying to understand fundamental concepts of nature, it's quite exciting stuff.
>
> (Simon, 1st year, B)

> I think of physics as being fundamental. The things we're doing at the moment are getting more and more fundamental. . . . I don't necessarily think that all these particle physicists are solving the world's problems – but it's fundamental in the way the world works.
>
> (Sally, 3rd year, A)

The contrast with chemistry came up frequently, and there was often more than a hint of reductionism in the comparison:

> The physics department would tell you that chemistry's only a bit of physics anyway.
>
> (Pauline, 3rd year, B)

Chemistry was regarded as a subject which was not fundamental; the issues it examines are not fundamental to the universe in the way that the issues of physics are; in this the views of the students can be seen to coincide with the views of Dr L, who said that 'all of chemistry is becoming explicable in terms of quantum theory'.

Physics was also regarded as a subject which could be 'understood'; chemistry – and subjects like French, history and so on – could only be *learnt*:

> I hate subjects where you just have to fill your head with facts. What's the point of teaching something if you can go and look it up in a book?
>
> (Ronald, 1st year, A)

> I just thought of it as learning what other people have already thought of a subject . . . physics seemed so much more dynamic somehow.
>
> (Jane, 3rd year, B)

> I think you have to know a lot [in chemistry], whereas with physics, what you hope to do is get general laws and principles that are applicable widely. With chemistry, things like organic chemistry, where you had to know every reaction, you couldn't work it out, you had to know everything that was going to happen – there wasn't a lot of understanding involved, it was mainly slogging.
>
> (Paul, 3rd year, B)

Physics is not only a more important and a more fundamental subject, but also, it seems, a more *certain* subject. One student, who had transferred to physics from medicine, explained the difference between chemistry and physics:

> RACHEL: It [chemistry] wasn't a very positive subject. You always had a few explanations for why something did something and you could never pick out which – why it did it . . . you could explain it in several ways, and it just wasn't positive enough for me.
> KIM: Is physics more definite?
> RACHEL: Yes, and more definite than medicine as well. Medicine isn't definite at all; I just call it a positive subject – you always get an answer.
>
> (Rachel, 1st year, A)

The apparent certainty of physics creates the potential for knowing about *everything*:

> The implications of it affect the whole world, it's everything, everything you do, and demonstrates how things work and why they work.
>
> (Rashid, 1st year, B)

This all-encompassing quality reveals a strong desire amongst students to understand and manipulate their environment. It is a Baconian view, rather than an Einsteinian view; students have a strong faith in the capacity of physics to provide explanations of the way the world works. It is seen as revealing certain truths about the universe:

> I think it's the diversity really, the number of things you can do in it [that appeals]. The classical thing is if somebody comes up to you and asks what a physicist does, that's the hardest question to answer. Because really, you're investigating what actually happens in life. I think that's the reason you enjoy it, because you can explain most things, most things you don't normally think of. The most surprising thing is if somebody turns round and asks you, like they did last year, 'Why is the sky blue?' and a thing a lot of people don't even think of, you end up being able to explain – I think that's the appeal of it.
>
> (Alan, 3rd year, A)

This curiosity, this quest for knowledge, which typified the attitude of many physics students, was for the never-ending mysteries of the universe:

> It's an open-ended subject. If you study a lot of subjects, they come to an end, there's only so much you can learn about them. But with physics, it can go on forever, virtually.
>
> (Gareth, 1st year, A)

> It's happening *now*, it's always progressing and it's always going on and you're never going to reach an end point, you're never going to reach a final point, whereas with something like history, I find it's interesting, but you're always going over and analysing what's happened, it's that much more backward looking, whereas science applied has got more constructive.
>
> (Felicity, 1st year, A)

Physics was regarded as an infinite subject; it was the embodiment of a search for the 'truths' of the universe, which although progressive – i.e. we are always finding out new things – is unending: we will never find out everything. Many students obviously gained immense pleasure from physics, and real excitement in finding out about the world around them; it was by no means seen entirely – or even mainly – in terms of a job-qualification. However, it is significant that modern physics appears to have had little impact on their philosophy of physics; they still construct it as a subject which is capable of revealing absolute truths. One or two found the ideas of relativity, for example, a little difficult to grasp:

> I found relativity a bit hard to understand to begin with – because if you haven't done it before, the idea that velocity is relative to everything else, I found hard to grasp, because, before, I just said, *that* velocity *was* a definite value – now you're doing it relative to everything else.
>
> (Lorna, 1st year, B)

Relativity and, more importantly, quantum mechanics, were not seen on the whole as a challenge to the idea of the certainty of physics; on the contrary, they were often presented as proof of the exciting inroads physics was making.

> It's mind-boggling more than anything else. It's just different people's ideas of what matter is made from, and how waves travel, it's really mind-boggling.
>
> (Nigel, 1st year, B)

A minority of students took a more thoughtful view of modern physics however. This is one student talking about how modern physics affirmed his Christian beliefs:

> According to classical mechanics, in theory you could write down the position and momentum of every single particle in the universe; you could therefore work out how everything is going backwards and forwards in time, obviously by highly complicated equations, but in theory, every-thing's predicted so everything's totally determined from beginning to end; but quantum mechanics says that you can never record the momentum and position of everything identically because of the Uncertainty Principle. Nietzsche, the German philosopher, adduced his argument from classical concepts – 'This proves that there's no such thing as God' – but when quantum mechanics came along, it threw all that out of the window.
>
> (Colin, 3rd year, A)

Initially Colin's argument seems unusual; the uncertanty of scientific under-standing would appear to make religious faith more difficult to come by; however, Colin argued

> If you look around there a lot more physicists who are Christian than people taking the arts subjects and I reckon it could be that the arts bombard you with a lot of different views and maybe you find it hard to crystallize to say what you want; whereas in physics we get told precisely the answer and we realize that we don't understand it totally. The standard example is that science has disproved God. An arts student may have no arguments either way; they've just heard of this mystical thing called Science, but once you've been doing Science, you realize that a statement like that just does not hold water, and so it enables faith to come far more easily.
>
> (Colin, 3rd year, A)

Colin was the only science student who touched on the relationship between science and religion. His remarks are interesting because they demonstrate a new way of looking at that relationship. Newtonian physics at one time seemed to give support to the idea that the universe was ordered and mechanistic and, therefore, divinely made; Darwinism challenged many of the basic tenets of Christianity, thereby setting science and religion in opposition and creating an important set of dualities – rationality/irrationality, reason/faith – through which we have come to construct science. Modern physics, it has been argued (by e.g. Capra 1979), supports the view, held by certain eastern religions, that the world is fluid and harmonious. Here, however, Colin is using modern physics to support Christianity, on the basis that science cannot provide certain knowledge, and that we must therefore look elsewhere for certainty. It is particularly interesting that he notes that science has come to hold, for some, the status of a religion: students of the arts, for example, might regard science as 'mystical'. We shall discuss the attitudes of the arts students towards science later; however, it is worth noting that Colin's attitude to science bore a marked resemblance to some of the English students' attitudes towards their subject. The following remark, for example, made in the realization that physics was both something less and something more than an objective body of knowledge, was very similar to remarks made by the arts students about English:

> I think it's more a way of thinking than knowledge really; because, a lot of the knowledge, I won't use two-thirds of it, but almost a way of thinking, a way of tackling problems, a way of discerning things.
>
> (Colin, 3rd year, A)

That is physics is a practice, a way of doing things, a means of doing things, a means of interpreting reality, rather than a body of fact.

As has been argued already, most students believed that there *was* an answer, that physics did provide certainty; and they did not make philosophical connections between the ideas of modern physics and the existence or otherwise of absolute truths about the universe. One or two were aware that such connections could be made, that quantum mechanics was qualitatively different:

> With classical mechanics, things tend to be all laid on a plate, there's not a lot of scope for intuitive thought.
>
> (Paul, 1st year, A)

> I enjoy the more wishy-washy concepts – I wish perhaps I'd had the chance to do a physics and philosophy option – and it seems to me that when we do things like quantum physics nobody bothers very much with the concepts that that presents – they just tend to give you all the theory.
>
> (Julie, 3rd year, A)

Julie's language is interesting; implied in what she said is a hard/soft dichotomy; philosophy is seen as being less serious, less important than 'hard' theory; she is slightly embarrassed about wanting to do something which is apparently less difficult (and by implication more trivial) than straightforward theory. Julie, because she accepts the discourse of the other physics students – the idea that physics is 'hard' – devalues her own philosophical interests. The language of the hard/soft dichotomy, as argued earlier, is also the language of masculinity/femininity, and Julie is uncomfortably aware of the devaluation of soft/femininity within the physics discourse. This hierarchy within physics was, as we saw in the last chapter, also noted by Becher (1984), in his examination of the 'culture' of disciplines.

Constructing physical science

It is more difficult to talk about the construction of 'physical science' than it is to talk about the construction of physics, because physical science is not recognized as a discipline in the way that physics is. For many of the physical science students, the term 'physical science' referred to the specific course rather than to a wider discipline; I therefore reserve many of their comments for a later section. However, there are some interesting comparisons to be made between the discourse of the physical scientists and that of the physicists. One of these is the physics/chemistry distinction which is, interestingly, maintained by the physical scientists. The students tended not to regard physical science as a unified discipline, and often complained that they disliked either the physics or the chemistry (usually the latter) aspect of the course. For example:

> I find it difficult to remember so many different things about chemistry, where at least with physics I seem to remember what things are supposed to be about . . . with physics you see it and understand it and it's stored, with chemistry . . . there are so many complicated formulae and whatever you've got to look at it again before you can regurgitate it.
>
> (Debbie, 1st year, C)

Another is that they retained some of the broader arts/science contrasts of the physicists: the progressive nature of science, for example, compared with the static nature of arts:

> English doesn't change from year to year and history doesn't change and languages are just languages but physics and chemistry are changing constantly because new things are being discovered.
>
> (Lesley, 1st year, C)

There were also differences between the physicists and the physical scientists. I suggested earlier that one element in the construction of physics was the useful/useless duality. However, this was far less significant for physics students than it was for the physical science and materials students. Amongst physics students, the intellectual appeal of the subject – its certainty, its fundamentality, its discoveries – was its most important quality. Very few students talked about their subject in terms of its social utility. Even when they did, it tended to be in flippant terms; for example, one student remarked that without physics 'we'd be in a right mess for a start'; another that 'we'd still be in the caves'. Sometimes they stressed the usefulness to their own careers of studying a science degree, and this was for some the determining factor in choosing between science and arts. Amongst the physical science students, however, personal utility was seen as crucially important, although sometimes social utility and personal utility were confused, students not distinguishing between the two. Often, it was not only the arts which were seen as less useful, but university subjects like physics: the physical science degree was regarded as one which was more useful for getting jobs in industry. This attitude – stressing the instrumental value of a degree course – is taken to its extreme in the following quote, where a student who wants to take up materials science is criticizing physical science:

I can't see physical science being as useful as a materials degree. I think it's more constructive; we're always going to make weapons of some kind, ships of some kind, boats, we're always going to drive some kind of vehicle, and we're always going to need hospital equipment.

(Lesley, 1st year, C)

Very few physical science students stressed the intellectual enjoyment of the degree course. They all thought that the value of studying the course lay in the career opportunities it opened up – what Gibbs *et al.* (1984) describe as an 'extrinsic' motivation. For example:

I think our course is quite good because of the energy situation. I think chemistry and physics students are quite a good thing to be at the moment.

(Dipak, 4th year, C)

If you want a highly paid industrial job with a lot of responsibility you've got to do a science degree.

(Linda, 4th year, C)

'Usefulness' was a key component of the physical scientists' evaluation of their discipline; and 'usefulness' referred to the capacity of the degree to get them a well-paid job. Their attitude to the course, more so than that of the physics students, was an instrumental one: the course was a means to an end.

The experience of studying science in higher education

In this section, we shall look at how the ideals and expectations students had of science compared with the reality of studying the subject. We shall also look at certain features of the learning environment of the departments which are of particular interest.

Perhaps the first thing we can note about all three departments is the formality of the relationship between students and staff: a formality which is reflected in the teaching methods. Although the nature of science teaching meant that there was far more contact between staff and students than in the humanities departments we shall look at, it was noticeable that staff were addressed by titles, not by first names. The staff were also much more formally dressed than in the three humanities departments. There was, in many cases, a reluctance to go to lecturers for help; for example:

KIM: Do you generally find the staff approachable?
NATALIE: Yeah, well, I don't know, I've never actually gone and asked any of them round here about any problem.
KIM: Do you think you could?
NATALIE: Mmm, probably. We don't – I don't know. I mean, I've got a list of all the physicists in hall, you see; I go and visit them instead . . . they're more obtainable.

(Natalie, 1st year, A)

It was commonly accepted, both in Department A and Department B, that final years could be approached by first years for help; staff were regarded as out of bounds. Some students in both departments also said that they preferred to ask postgraduate demonstrators, rather than staff, for help. Staff were often considered quite remote – even in Department B, which was much smaller than Department A:

> Some are completely on another plateau, you know, they're just not in the real world; they wander round and don't make eye-contact unless they're talking to you; they just look at the ceiling all the time when they're lecturing.
>
> (Jane, 3rd year, B)

This was seen by some as being in marked contrast to the humanities departments, a point we shall pick up later:

> If you compare it with other departments, if you talk to people who do English and stuff, and they know all their tutors by their first names; I mean, it's nothing like that here, it's all Dr So-and-So – I mean, half the lecturers, I didn't even know what their second names were, let alone their first names – maybe that's just a result of physics, nothing to do with them.
>
> (Sioned, 3rd year, B)

By its being 'a result of physics', she meant:

> It's not really a discussion. Physics is physics, isn't it, you can't really discuss . . . not in the same sense you can discuss a novel or something, you can't really discuss a formula.

As we have already seen, physics students made very strong (hierarchical) distrinctions between physics and chemistry, and between physics and other disciplines – and even between subdivisions in the department itself; one final-year student noted in B that 'on the top floor, one half is theoretical physics, one is experimental physics and they just don't seem to mix'. In the above quote, Sioned is simply acknowledging the authority of the lecturers to define what 'physics' is, and accepting that this will necessarily result in formal relationships.

However, this formality has its price. Because students felt that they could not approach staff, they often had problems about what to do when they couldn't understand the work:

> What you were saying about approachability of lecturers, I'm not afraid to ask for help, but I am reticent to ask for help more than once on the same thing, because I would hate them to think that I hadn't been listening first time round or that I was stupid.
>
> (Jane, 3rd year, B)

As understanding is crucial in physics, the difficulty in asking for help leads to problems with work; it is, as Chapter 6 will argue, a particular problem for women, who often feel isolated in the department.

The atmosphere in C was slightly more informal; this was in large part due to the physical layout of the lecture rooms, which bore a greater resemblance to school classrooms – students sat on chairs at desks and the lecturer's podium was on the same level as the desks, allowing lecturers to move about the room answering questions. Because there was a significant male–female difference in perceptions of staff on this course, we shall have more to say about it in Chapter 6. For the present, we can simply note that many of the women felt that relations between themselves and the staff were less formal than relations between the male students and the staff; the women said that they found it quite easy to 'get round' the male staff, whereas several men complained that staff were quite unhelpful. A particularly striking difference was that when the staff addressed the men, it was by surnames, but when they addressed the women, it was by their first names. It seems that the staff were inclined to regard the women as light relief from the sombre business of teaching science.

The formality of staff–student relations was reflected in the conventionality of the teaching methods used. The science students had very full timetables; these consisted mainly of lectures, with some lab sessions and problem classes or tutorials (the latter being much less frequent on the physical science course). Several students compared the teaching to school:

It's almost exactly the same . . . we get everything we need for the notes written on the board so we can just copy it down . . . so it's just the same as school, except the homework – when you do those problem sheets, they don't bother to mark it.

(Natalie, 1st year, A)

At school the teachers talk and write on the board and that's all it is here really, they talk and write on the board.

(Mary, 1st year, B)

First-year students at the polytechnic also felt the teaching to be very similar to school (or technical college) teaching; one thought that polytechnic was a 'cross between school and university'. However, a noticeable difference between school and university teaching is the lack of personal attention; and this was a particular source of anxiety for some students. For example Marie, a student at B who, in the first few weeks of term, felt herself to be getting behind with work, was concerned about the lack of help provided by the department:

A levels were so different. They were small groups for a start. My biggest A level group was twelve. You could put your hand up and ask questions, and you weren't all up at a level on him, he was at the same level as you, talking, and he knew all our abilities so he explained things more clearly to us. But here they just give you a few examples and expect you to do example sheets, it really is so difficult.

(Marie, 1st year, B)

It is interesting in that quote that the idea of being 'on the same level' is used literally and metaphorically. The staff at B are perceived as being both physically and emotionally distant.

Several other students were concerned about their inability to understand what was being taught in the lectures; a commonly expressed view was that they couldn't take notes and follow what was being said at the same time. Many students felt a tension, therefore, between learning and understanding. Despite students' insistence, as we saw earlier, that physics was a subject concerned with 'understanding', note-taking in lectures was necessary for learning and examination revision. This meant that preparation for future 'learning' could occur at the expense of present understanding; on the other hand, not to take notes, but to concentrate on the lecturer's words, would prevent students from being able to learn the work later. This applies not only to less able students, but also the cleverest: Paul, for example a final-year student at B, and the only first-class honours of his year, remarked:

> The strange thing is, quite often you do a lot of courses that you don't understand at the time, you think it's a load of rubbish, then you read through them, and just understanding them, they're really quite important.
>
> (Paul, 3rd year, B)

The student in this situation is essentially passive, not in control of his or her own education. Paul suggested a way of getting rid of this passivity, arguing that lecturers should give out notes at the beginning of lectures and then:

> They could go through them, and then they could encourage a more open thing, and people could – there could be a discussion going on in the class at the same time.
>
> (Paul, 3rd year, B)

This would certainly allow students to participate more in their own learning, and give them more chance to get to grips with complex ideas. In reality, however, the lectures allowed students almost no control; students were, in some ways, treated like school pupils; expected to listen and take notes, and accept the authority of the lecturer. As a result, some of them even behaved like schoolchildren; it was not uncommon, apparently, for students at A to throw paper aeroplanes in lectures – a rather immature (but possibly understandable) response to the frustration of endless listening and note-taking.

Most of the science students, however, accepted as inevitable that there were large chunks that they couldn't understand, illustrating Hudson's (1967) argument about the need of the scientist to 'accept massive bodies of conventional knowledge on trust'. At the same time, this is an immensely frustrating experience for the student:

> Some of the lecturers keep saying in a lecture, 'this is somehow related to something else you've done somewhere else' and I wish they'd tell us how it's related to something else because half the time we can't see that.
>
> (Dipak, 4th year, C)

Many students contrasted their interest in physics with the experience of studying it. This contrast was made by several other students. Most students, as we have already seen, were very enthusiastic about physics. Physics was perceived as exciting, progressive and fundamental, in contrast to other disciplines which were perceived as routine, static and lacking substance. Yet their experience of studying physics was far from exciting. While quantum mechanics – or 'weird physics' as one called it – was generally enjoyed, other courses seemed tedious. As Richard, a final-year student at B, put it:

> I went to all the lectures and they're easy to go to, because you're spoon-fed, they don't sit back and they don't philosophize, a lot of it, it's all material on the board, which can be a bit boring sometimes, but we've done some big course like quantum mechanics and there have been a few other theoretical ones which have been really involved but the lecturers have been really good, you can see how excited they are, and it starts spilling over to you.
>
> (Richard, 3rd year, B)

The problem is not, however, simply one of boring lectures; the few very bright students found studying physics challenging and stimulating. The problem was more one of having to absorb a vast amount of information in a short space of time. For most students, physics was no longer a subject which required thought and understanding:

> It's just proved my ability to learn chunks of knowledge, chunks of pages and books, and reproducing them the day after, then forgetting it, then you have to learn it again for next year's exams.
>
> (William, 3rd year, B)

Related to this was a feeling amongst students that they lacked independence. The most popular work was that which allowed students freedom to work on their own – projects, for example. Students felt that the need to learn large amounts of work left no time for the challenge of individual discovery.

Physics is very rarely *discussed* on the courses; the students' main aim is to get through the course and pass the examinations. This is not because they don't enjoy the subject but because of the way the courses are structured. We can see here a process that Becker *et al.* (1961) identified, whereby students embark idealistically on their courses, hoping to become good doctors (or in this case physicists), but soon abandon this ideal in favour of the short-term goal of passing examinations.

Another common criticism was that much of the work was 'irrelevant'. This word, which varies in its usage from student to student, was generally used to mean something like 'applicable in the outside world'. The criticism was often made by those who disliked the more abstract theoretical work, and who preferred more tangible ideas, which could be shown to have some application:

> I like medical physics . . . I can see some use for the theory I've learnt – there's some sort of application which is indirectly helping people.
>
> (Julie, 3rd year, A)

The comments about 'relevance' came more frequently from women than from men, and I shall argue in Chapter 6 that there are important differences between what male and female students look for in physics.

Of course, there was some opportunity for students to work independently and to discuss their work problems. While lectures were generally disliked as a teaching method, students generally felt happier about tutorials and skill sessions. However, even here there were problems. One was simply that there weren't enough of them, particularly at C:

> When I first started I thought we'd have tutorials and seminars; you get three or four students and you discuss something. We don't do anything like that; we very rarely have tutorials.
>
> (Dipak, 4th year, C)

Another, at both A and B, was that very little genuine help was given with problems; the question and answer sheets were not marked, for example, and tutorials didn't always provide the key to understanding what the work was about:

> The problem sheets are so difficult now nobody can do them and they usually just wait until the answers come out every week and usually it's just a case of copying them down.
>
> (William, 3rd year, B)

Students are often left to muddle along; the help they may need is not forthcoming, even in tutorials. Consequently many students, by the final year in particular, felt that they had lost all hope of making sense of the subject or getting to grips with the work.

So far, we have seen that while physics was viewed by students as exciting and forward-looking, in practice the teaching tended to be conventional and hierarchical, very much like school, with students being given a body of information to absorb. In higher education, however, students are expected to do far more practical experiments than in school. For at least eight hours each week, students were expected to work alone or in pairs on experiments in the laboratory, with some supervision by staff and postgraduates. In theory, this gives students more freedom to explore and find out for themselves; indeed, the final years worked on individual experimental projects. In practice, however, and particularly for the first years, what happened in labs was strictly controlled by the department. Students worked from textbooks which explain how to conduct the experiment and the sorts of results one would expect to get. As a third-year student said:

> [It was] just exercises in following instructions . . . you'd end up doing a lab before you ended up doing anything about it in lectures.
>
> (William, 3rd year, B)

One fourth-year student at C explained to me that several experiments conducted in the lab in the first term of the year could not be written up until the second term, after the theory had been presented in the lecture course, which obviously meant a tremendous backlog of work to catch up on. Therefore, conducting the experiments often involved little understanding of the theory behind them; indeed, they often involved equally little understanding about how to set up an experiment to test a theory:

If I had my choice, I'd rather be left to work something out myself; instead of it all being set up and you just walk in and take measurements, go away and analyse them, you'd have to go in and set it all up, then you'd really learn something. There's a feeling you don't learn enough from them, not in practical experience . . . you can go through the labs half-asleep.

(Linda, 4th year, C)

The point of the lab work was, essentially, to demonstrate the truth of a theory, rather than to allow students to experiment for themselves. The students do not conduct the experiments with a detached eye; rather, they are looking for the results predicted in the textbook. As one student patiently explained to me when I asked him how he *knew* what results he was looking for:

A lot of the labs are finding physical phenomena that are already well known, so if you're just validating facts that are already known you know they're wrong because your answers don't tally with the answers in the textbook.

(Paul, 1st year, A)

This practice supports T. S. Kuhn's (1963) argument that science textbooks 'do not describe the sorts of problems that the professional may be asked to solve and the variety of techniques available for their solution' but rather they 'exhibit concrete problem-solutions that the profession has come to accept as paradigms' which the student is expected to solve for himself (or herself) in the laboratory. The interesting question, of course, is what happens when labs 'go wrong', when they do not produce the result expected. On the one hand, students have the option of explaining *why* their results have turned out wrong:

a lot of the lab work done here anyway, everyone knows what the results should be, it just seems a waste of time because you know the equipment's not good enough to get the results you should be getting, so you spend most of your time writing why your results haven't come out.

(Paul, 3rd year, B)

The lack of good results is here explained by faulty equipment (an explanation also offered to me by other students); however, students gain higher marks for lab work if the results are 'correct' than if they are wrong but adequately accounted for:

Before, you might be able to say, if you haven't got the right results, you can get away with padding out your lab report and writing a lot of background, so that would bung your mark up a bit, but this year, you can do that and you still end up with a bad mark if you've got bad results.

(Stephen, 4th year, C)

The alternative to explaining faulty results, then, is to tamper with them:

It always seems to me that you've got a set of results, and if you come to write them up, and you know they're obviously wrong, you're going to get a lot more marks if you put down the right values – or what should be the right values – so you end up fiddling things eventually.

(Alan, 3rd year, A)

Alan eventually obtained a first-class honours degree, as did Paul, whom I quote again:

I know somebody here who got very good marks for his lab work and he's good on computers, and he just programmed the computers in random errors and stuff that give him set results and nice graphs, and they weren't perfect so nobody noticed them, but he fiddled them, and that way he didn't have to do any lab work if he didn't want to.

(Paul, 3rd year, B)

These two students, Alan and Paul, both very successful physicists, saw the lab work as a 'game' which has to be played. Implicit in Paul's description of another student is the idea that, although the student didn't do what was required, he got round it in such a clever and ingenious way, that he still deserved to do well in it; indeed, Paul said that 'there is less understanding in lab work than there is ingenuity'. Neither Alan nor Paul really accept that lab is an objective measure of ability; they simply see it as a set of rules made to be broken. Paul, in fact, had concluded that lab was a waste of time and his final-year project was a theoretical one, rather than a practical one. His attitude towards lab was rather blasé; he even joked about the fact that he always managed to break vital pieces of equipment. One student who was much more critical about the lab work was Mark, a student right at the bottom of his class, who later failed his degree:

The experiments are not particularly relevant to anything, they're just experiments for experiment's sake, one experiment illustrating a particular bit of theory; it doesn't do anything particularly useful, you just look at an oscilloscope and take some readings and hence you can demonstrate this bit of theory.

(Mark, 3rd year, A)

Mark, however, didn't bother to fake his results:

If they're totally wrong I don't generally bother. I don't fiddle my results really – usually it's easier to make up excuses for it being wrong than to go through and work it out to make it come out right.

(Mark, 3rd year, A)

Like Alan, Mark saw the practical work as a game, but unlike Alan he refused to play it. He resented what he saw as arbitrary and pointless rules, whereas Alan is, if anything, amused by them, and enjoys manipulating them. For some students, however, labs were not a game, but a set of rules to be adhered to. This was particularly the case amongst many of the female students, several of whom expressed anxiety about handling machinery or breaking expensive equipment (unlike Paul, who was able to make jokes about it):

As far as lab work went, I always felt very intimidated because I'd never touched anything more technical than a hairdryer, and all these boys around me were confidently plugging in their oscilloscopes, because I mean, I suppose they had their train sets and that sort of thing, and I was very scared to plug things in, in case they blew up.

(Jane, 3rd year, B)

Others felt frustrated by their inability to get to grips with the lab work:

I always seem to get the wrong results even though I'm working as hard as possible.

(Rachel, 1st year, A)

The real problem was that many students felt unable to ask for help when they were in difficulty. This was especially the case in B, where staff were considered unapproachable, and where students were expected to work individually at labs:

On the Thursdays in lab you have to work on your own and everybody's doing different experiments and it is really – I mean, I dread Thursdays, because it is really worrying.

(Marie, 1st year, B)

If students asked for help too often, marks were deducted. For Marie, this was a constant source of worry, because she had continually to choose between understanding fully what she was doing, by asking demonstrators for help, and risking losing marks, or by not asking and floundering further and further in the experiment. Thus the desire of the department to assess students (which meant that they had to work competitively, rather than co-operatively) conflicted with the desire of the students to understand the work; the apparent aim of the department – to improve the knowledge and understanding of the students – was being impeded by its other aim: to grade students. The four first-year women at B subverted this by swapping lab books; Marie said, 'We're not meant to, but we do' – as if there were some shame attached to having to ask for help. Like Jane, Marie perceived a male/female difference in attitudes to labs; when I asked her if other people on the course found the lab work difficult, she said:

I think other people are finding it difficult, but it's mostly boys and they tend to be more practical and keep calmer about it and also not worry about it, which does help.

(Marie, 1st year, B)

The difference between the male and the female experience of lab work is partly a difference between male and female upbringing; writers like Kelly (1981a) have been quite correct to point out that women are disadvantaged in science because of their lack of experience with scientific toys, machines and so on in childhood. Yet this difference is reinforced and indeed exacerbated by the women's experience of physics at university. Although departments could dispel needless anxiety by encouraging co-operation amongst students, they strengthen women's sense of themselves as inadequate by making them work individually and competitively.

Some students were more positive about the final-year work in lab than about the first-year work; as one said, 'You can do what you want; instead of being taught, you've got to learn yourself'. Projects allowed some room for genuine experimentation and discovery, although the projects themselves are decided by the department, who draw up a list from which students can choose. Despite a general feeling that project work was more interesting than first- and second-year experiments, there was much dissatisfaction with the projects; some students, particularly at C, complained that they had received very little advice on selecting a project, others that they had not been allowed to choose the project they wanted. The most common complaint, however, was that the projects weren't working; results hadn't turned out as hoped, essential equipment had proved faulty (or in some cases hadn't arrived) and students were left writing up why their project hadn't worked out. The real limitation was time; many students, although they enjoyed the projects, felt the pressure of looming final examinations and said that they were unable to complete their project to their own satisfaction and had to make the best of a bad job in order to work at other, equally pressing, aspects of the course.

Some students managed to struggle through their courses by learning as much as they could without understanding it. Certain other students simply fell behind so much that they could not catch up later on. Two students in particular, Jane and Mark, embody many of the problems encountered by those students who were not amongst the department's high-flyers.

I interviewed Jane in the Easter term of her final year at B, at a time when she felt thoroughly disillusioned with the course, though not with university, which she had enjoyed. Her problems had started before university, when she had changed schools after the fifth form. In her first school she had been considered outstanding at maths, and had obtained six grade As in her nine O levels. When she changed schools, however, the maths A level course was different from the one she'd been following at her old school, but the new teacher expected her to catch up immediately. Jane explained the difference in terms of the schools' differing perceptions of her ability:

> Because she [the new maths teacher] didn't know me, she didn't have any confidence in me . . . but because she didn't have any confidence in me, I didn't have any confidence in myself, and that is the thing that really makes me regret changing schools . . . at my first school all the teachers knew me and had confidence in me. I was doing very well in that school. I think I should have stayed at the old school where they had confidence in me.
>
> (Jane, 3rd Year, B)

Her case suggests the potency of the 'self-fulfilling prophecy'; she found maths increasingly difficult and ended up with a grade D A level. Such was her dislike of maths by this stage that she told me:

I was very disillusioned when I started doing physics by the amount of maths in the course. I got to the stage where I couldn't see the wood for the trees.

(Jane, 3rd year, B)

Jane had experienced a downward spiral such that, by the time I interviewed her, she felt completely lost. (She eventually got a third-class honours degree.) About physics as a subject she was enthusiastic; but she was unhappy about the degree course. She contrasted her experience of school physics with university physics, and she saw the distinction as a quantitative/qualitative one. This is what she says about university physics:

I find it difficult in my notes that they're all so mathematical, that you just read through lines and lines of equations and there's very few sentences in between to explain what's going on. It's very difficult to draw out any physical meaning. Trying to follow a mathematical argument is very different from following an argument that's set down in plain English, in a qualitative way. It's all so quantitative, I find it difficult to relate to.

Whereas in school:

I couldn't see how you could get a lot of maths into physics on the grounds of the experience I'd had in school. I mean, I thought they were just nice, chatty, qualitative subjects.

(Jane, 3rd year, B)

Her perception of physics as a discipline is one that is about ideas and concepts; she said that she'd always found physics much more 'dynamic' than 'static' subjects like chemistry and geography. It seems to be almost a perception of physics as an 'arts' subject; indeed, Jane told me that she had been equally good at arts and sciences but had chosen sciences because of the job and university prospects. By the third year she was beginning to regret her choice:

I'm quite an artistic person; in retrospect, I think perhaps I should have risen to the challenge and maybe applied to do a language, because I really enjoy literature and languages in my spare time. But then again, if I was forced to do them full-time permanently, maybe I wouldn't enjoy them as much. I think it's because I'm being made to do physics that I'm rebelling against it.

She concluded:

I think that's the problem with degrees, they're all very specialized, and they don't give a lot of scope for broad sort of study.

(Jane, 3rd year, B)

Jane saw her degree as a process of narrowing down, rather than a broadening out; it shut out the creative, 'qualitative' aspect of her nature, and presented her with a set of rules and definitions which she had to conform to, or reject, but which she could not challenge. Like many of the other female physics students, she rejected it and told me that she had no intention of continuing with physics afterwards.

Mark, whom I have already quoted in my discussion of the lab work, was a final-year student at A who, although he had obtained A level grades of AAAB, eventually failed his degree. He said that he found the work dull, and did as little of it as possible:

> I find it boring, it's not particularly useful – it's very academic, more so than I would have expected it to be.
>
> (Mark, 3rd year, A)

Unlike Jane, Mark did not feel that he would have been better off taking a different subject; he had decided that he was unsuited to any kind of academic work, although most of his friends were arts students. He expressed strong dislike of the department itself; it was 'pretty unfriendly'; the work was 'irrelevant'. This much is perhaps to be expected from someone who faced insurmountable difficulties in coping with the work. What is interesting about Mark, however, is that he rejects the *values* of the physics department in their entirety, as well as what he perceives as the values of academic life generally. That is he rejects the pervasive competitiveness and individualism; he was the only male physics student I talked to who talked in terms of doing something socially useful after finishing the course. Although he blamed himself rather than the department for his own failure, making comments like 'I'm just not an academic basically' and 'I don't think there's a lot wrong with the course, if you want to do an academic course', the path he saw himself as taking seemed directly opposed to the departmental ethos; stating that he didn't want to do 'anything theoretical', he told me that he wanted to train to be a nurse. Reluctant though he was to talk about it, he gave the main reason as 'it's just the sort of job that would suit me really . . . helping people, that sort of thing'. It is also, however, just the sort of career that most physics students wouldn't dream of entering, being part of a predominantly female profession, low-paid and low-status. The satisfaction gained from nursing, like that of the other 'caring' professions, comes mainly from an intrinsic satisfaction at doing something useful rather than from external recognition of one's value. It is important to recognize that in Mark's case, as in the case of some other (mainly female) physics students, the rejection of physics was not simply due to a lack of ability or application, but a clash of beliefs and assumptions about what is worthwhile and what isn't.

If we look at it another way, we can suggest that many physics students feel that they must accept what they are told by their departments and that they find it difficult to challenge what they are told. There is little space in which students can develop individually or subvert the 'knowledge' of the department. Few students said that they found the staff approachable, and some seemed just to muddle along, hoping that all would eventually be clear. Others found that the sheer workload of the course left them unable to develop outside interests, such as reading or the theatre. To do that almost seemed to entail giving up on the course altogether. For example in B, I had tried several times without success to contact a third-year female physics student who, it seemed, never looked in her departmental pigeonhole where I left the notes. It turned out, when I asked another student about her, that she spent most of her time organizing the Drama Society and almost never came into the department. In the event, I interviewed someone else, but the incident is an indication of the fact that a science degree and artistic interests are often perceived as incompatible. In this sense, a physics degree can indeed be a narrowing down rather than a broadening out. This is how one physical science student put it:

> It [being at polytechnic] has broadened my outlook, and it's also narrowed it – science-orientated. You tend to keep to that sort of regime. I wouldn't say it was exactly narrow-minded, but you've got a position, you're given a position to hold and you get it rammed down you that 'I am now an applied scientist'. I don't feel like one, but I'm supposed to be, well, a physical scientist, so you get that sort of identity thrown at you. So you accept it, because you don't know what else to accept.
>
> (Matthew, 4th year, C)

Consequently many students who find themselves unable to accept this defi- nition of themselves, who have difficulty in constructing an identity as 'physicists' or 'physical scientists', find that they are outside of the department, that they are gradually less and less successful in getting to grips with the subject.

Science students' perceptions of the humanities

Given that the meaning of 'arts' and 'science' is dependent on the differences between them, it is necessary to look at scientists' perceptions of the arts, and vice versa. It has already been argued that physics is constructed through a series of dualities in which physics is rated positively, and other disciplines, chiefly the arts, are rated negatively.

One of the dualities noted was that of hard/soft; another was that of difficult/easy. These were articulated more often when students were invited to talk about the arts than when students simply talked about physics. The mention of the word 'arts' often brought out feelings of resentment in physics students about the apparently easy time arts students had of it:

> More work has to go into a science degree than an arts degree . . . I see arts students' timetables, an English student comes in for two hours a week, and he's home for the rest of the time. I just think we do a lot more work than they do.
>
> (Dipak, 4th year, C)

A first-year physics student told me that he had thought of transferring to an arts subject, maybe psychology, in the first few weeks, because:

> I thought it'd be a lot easier because arts students get about ten lectures a week . . . we had thirty lectures a week, or something like that.
>
> (Rashid, 1st year, B)

The same theme recurred frequently; because arts students had few timetabled hours, science students tended to assume that they did little work, although one first-year physical science student did note that most of her work was done in lectures and labs, while many girls on her corridor had a lot of background work to do outside timetabled sessions.

In addition, science students thought that arts students had freer relationships with staff, and this resulted in an attitude of some disdain towards the arts:

> Some of the courses I know, lecturers go drinking with the students and everything, but they're all older, suits and ties and things, there's nothing wrong with that, you just know them to be a lecturer and get on with the work rather than thinking, 'we had a nice drink last night, didn't we?'
>
> (Debbie, 1st year, C)

Implicit in that quote is the idea that science is more serious because of the more formal nature of staff–student relationships. Physics and physical science students had a strong sense of the hierarchy of different disciplines; Debbie, for example, described business studies (which she had originally hoped to study at university) as a 'soft option'; a first-year physics student at A described astro-physics (a course also run by the department) as 'watered-down physics'. The language of 'hard' and 'soft' subjects – which can extend into the discipline itself, as in the derogatory description of astro-physics – reveals a perception of academic study in which subjects are tiered, with 'hard' sciences at the top and 'soft' arts at the bottom. The harder the subject is, the more work students have to do, and the more formal are relations with staff. Subjects in which it is possible to have fun are not serious subjects.

Students also showed an impatience with the intangibility of the arts:

> Languages and stuff seem to be boring. You're just looking at words every day. With physics, you find things about the environment, you know, things you wouldn't normally think about.
>
> (Stephen, 1st year, C)

> Physics is more or less talking about actual things in life. That's the difference between arts and science, because you've actually got something there you can look at and study, so you're talking about facts, whereas in the arts side it's all airy-fairy and you're beating about the bush a lot. I'm not one for doing things like that. I'd rather have something there that I can look at and take hold of ideas, and actually get to grips with something that's actually there.
>
> (Nigel, 1st year, B)

The language used by Nigel is particularly revealing: 'airy-fairy', 'beating about the bush', 'get to grips with'. It reinforces the idea of science as more relevant, more concerned with reality and more certain. It shows a desire for an orderly and methodical way of examining the world, and a dislike of detached contemplation or philosophical and intuitive ways of understanding reality.

The most common criticism of the arts and the most strongly expressed, however, was that they are 'useless', that is not so much that they are useless to society, but that they are useless to the individual. This criticism was expressed most often by physical science students, but it was also made by physics students; for example

> There's a friend of mine doing Anglo-Saxon, Norse and Celtic – what on earth is she going to do with that afterwards? She's going to have to work in a museum for the rest of her life!
>
> (Natalie, 1st year, A)

Several science students seemed to believe that there was very little that an arts degree qualified graduates to do. Often, it was argued that science degrees qualified students to enter 'general' jobs such as management as well as specialized scientific ones, whereas arts students could apply only for the general jobs. On more than one occasion the view was expressed that 'physics is the best degree you can get' – because employers looked on it favourably. In this emphasis on personal success and achievement we can see a strong thread of individualism in the physics students' world-view; they are keenly aware of competition between individuals both in higher education and in the labour market. Physical science students were particularly harsh in their indictment of the 'uselessness' of the arts:

> I'm not into education for education's sake. It's a waste of taxpayers' money. I couldn't motivate myself to do it just for the sake of it.
>
> (Vicky, 4th year, C)

> I think it's a lot more worthwhile doing a science degree because a lot of arts degrees don't lead anywhere because then you have to find a job . . . they're not leading to a career of any sort . . . I feel they're a little bit of a waste of time . . . the course I'm doing, I'm gaining knowledge which I can use; which, I mean, you can't really use a history degree unless you're going to be an archaeologist or an historian or a teacher.
>
> (Debbie, 1st year, C)

> It seems that if you've done an arts degree, apart from social science, then really you're in line for jobs that science students go for as well, whereas arts students can't go for science degree jobs so you've got more scope to apply for. My tutor was saying to me that when he did his degree twenty odd years ago, he knew everything there was to know about chemistry, but because it's growing, because it's new, you've always got to keep up with it, whereas history doesn't change, does it, apart from you add a bit on to what happened last year; with chemistry it's constantly changing, you've always got something new to learn, you never stop really.
>
> (Fay, 4th year, C)

A feature of all these quotes is that they conflate the social and the personal; Vicky, for example, argues that the arts are 'a waste of taxpayers' money' and then says 'I couldn't motivate myself to do it'. The idea that education should be functional for the individual is confused with the idea that education should be functional for society. Debbie uses three ideas common to the science students: one, that science degrees are more useful in enabling students to gain jobs; two, that a degree is a process of 'gaining knowledge' which can be applied; three, that the knowledge gained in a degree such as history can be applied only in limited ways and therefore a limited number of jobs is open to the history graduate. Debbie's view of knowledge as a body of fact means that she does not regard the acquisition of skills, ways of thinking about and approaching problems as an important part of learning and does not, therefore, consider their potential usefulness in jobs. Neither does she consider the possibility that there are reasons for doing degrees other than as qualifications for jobs; therefore humanities degrees are a 'waste of time'.

Like Debbie, Fay starts from the premise that the point of doing a degree is to get a job, as we can see in her statement that science students are able to apply for a wider range of jobs than arts graduates. Obviously if one does not start from this premise, then the point about the wider range of jobs is no longer relevant; the belief that degrees are taken in order to get jobs is so much part of the physical science students' taken-for-granted ideas about education that it remains implicit rather than explicit. Fay's other principal assumption is the same as Debbie's: that learning is about the acquisition of a body of knowledge. When learning is viewed in this way, students often regard science as progressive, and the arts as static; science as infinite and the arts as finite. It is this belief that enables Fay to say that her tutor had at one time known 'everything there was to know about chemistry' and that 'history doesn't change . . . apart from you add a bit on to what happened last year'.

The perceptions that most science students had of the arts, then, are grounded within a discourse which regards education as primarily functional, believes learning to be concerned with the acquisition of knowledge, and views the relationship between different types of knowledge as hierarchical. It would be wrong, however, to suggest that all the science students disliked the arts. Physics students were more tolerant than physical science students; amongst the physicists, women were more tolerant than men. It was noted earlier that some physics students had had difficulty choosing between science and arts at A level, and these students, like those who had interests such as reading or music, were usually more broad-minded than those who had always regarded themselves as scientists; for example

> In a way, long-term, something you do in science is possibly going to be of more value, but it's very necessary, I think, literature and things like that are very much part of your life, you'd go mad without them, I certainly would; so I don't think you can really assign values like that – it's just where your personal interest and qualities lie, what you're best at.
>
> (Felicity, 1st year, A)

> I see education as far more than just training you to go out and do a job, and I think the whole learning process, whatever you're learning, matures you

into being capable of taking responsibilities and learning other things, and I think arts subjects do that just as well as science subjects.

(Julie, 3rd year, A)

Even those who, like Julie and Felicity, were tolerant of the arts, were clearly aware that sciences were generally perceived as superior; Julie, for example, noted that 'arts subjects do that *just as well*', while Felicity went on

I don't look down on arts students, though I do moan about their empty timetables, but then, someone doing a German degree, no way could I do that, I have the greatest respect for them.

(Felicity, 1st year, A, my emphasis)

A physical science student showed a nice awareness of the science/arts hierarchy when, talking about her brother who was doing a Fine Art degree, she said

He thinks I think I'm better than him because I'm doing a science degree and he's doing Fine Art.

(Linda, 4th year, C)

These students were aware that they were being magnanimous towards the arts; very few conceded that the arts might have more to offer than sciences. One who did made the same point as many arts students:

I think university just trains you to think and to prove to an employer that you can apply yourself for three years; perhaps because in the sciences you learn things that will be relevant in your career, but as a training for an individual I don't think it is any more worthwhile. In some ways, in fact, it's a bit less worthwhile, in that you tend not to think about social matters, people's characters and things like that.

(Patrick, 1st year, A)

Another expressed the same view:

Only from your own personal practical point of view is it [physics] more worthwhile, getting a job at the end . . . but I think a lot of people who come to university and do a degree job that isn't related in any way and what they should get out of university is social skills, and enjoyment, they should enjoy the course, so they should do the course they want to do, I think, in as many cases as possible.

(Paul, 3rd year, B)

It has already been noted that some science students had made the choice between science and arts on the basis that it was easier to keep up with arts in one's spare time than it was to keep up with science. It is perhaps interesting that some of them, because of the volume of work, had had difficulty keeping to this, and that those who had – Natalie, for example, who played a trumpet in a band – found some tension between their course work and the time they wanted to devote to their hobby. The attempt to bridge the arts/science divide was, in many cases, doomed to failure, with the result that students felt forced to make a choice between their coursework and their outside interests. For some of the students, science demanded an all-or-nothing commitment.

Conclusion

We began this chapter by noting the importance of certain ideas of science amongst both lecturers and students. The most prevalent view was that physical science consisted of a body of hard, certain and fundamental knowledge. Amongst physicists, there was a belief that physics was essentially about *understanding*, while other science subjects such as chemistry were about the rote acquisition of 'facts'.

The less common view of physics was that it was concerned with exploration, breadth, uncertainty. The challenge of physics was not its certainty, but its lack of certainty. Whereas the holders of the former view of physics made a strong distinction between arts and science, the holders of the latter view saw affinity between arts and science. Most students, in fact, not only made a distinction between arts and science, but also believed in a hierarchy of different disciplines, with 'fundamental', 'useful' subjects like physics at the top and 'wishy-washy' humanities subjects at the bottom.

From the picture drawn by its students, physics can best be seen as a highly organized, tightly structured set of rules which its students are expected to obey. The heavy workload and the difficulty of the work itself meant that a high degree of conformity was required of all but the most able students. Lab work, for example, was a matter of getting the 'right' answer; failure to do so resulted in loss of marks. Some students were reduced to learning their work parrot-fashion in order to keep up to the standard, while at the same time lacking any real understanding of what they were taught.

Many physics students, and almost all physical science students, had an instrumental attitude towards their degree courses. Higher education was seen by them primarily as a means to an end, not an end in itself. Those students who did not have an instrumental or single-minded attitude towards studying physics or physical science were the least successful. Mark and Jane, for example, who rejected the implicit values and beliefs of the discipline, both did badly in their degrees. There were others, such as Marie, who had hoped to gain a greater understanding of a subject they loved, and found themselves bogged down in a process of constant marking and grading, passing and failing.

Using Bernstein's terminology, we can characterize physics as a discipline which has 'strong frames' and 'strong classification'; it is a subject in which 'the educational relationship tends to be hierarchical and ritualised, the educand seen as ignorant, with little status and few rights'. (Bernstein 1971: 58). The same can also be said of physical science: despite the apparent breadth of the course, students felt that they had little control over their learning.

To say that physics and physical science have such strong boundaries is not simply to make a statement about the disciplines. It is also something which has important consequences for the people studying those disciplines. We have already seen that some of the less successful students had suffered a blow to their self-esteem as a consequence of the rigid rules on learning. There is a strong demarcation in physics between those who have succeeded and those who have 'failed'; quite a lot of firsts and thirds, and not a great concentration in the middle. There is a great pressure on students, therefore, to conform. It is precisely this need to conform that causes tensions and difficulties for women studying physics. If, to be a successful physicist, one has to conform to a certain code of behaviour, what are the implications for women who, by definition, do not conform to our conventional ideal of 'physicist'?

Scientists characterize the humanities as uncertain, vague and irrelevant. The next chapter will look at how humanities students characterize their own discipline, and at the extent to which the characterizations match. It will also begin to consider the extent to which humanities students' sense of themselves is affected, adversely or otherwise, by the experience of studying their subjects.

5

Constructing Humanities

Introduction

This chapter will follow the same pattern as Chapter 4, but this time it will look at the views and experiences of students in English and communications. It will look at the parallels between the humanities students' viewpoint and the science students' viewpoint, exploring similarities and differences. In particular, it is concerned with the question of symmetry – whether the experience of studying humanities is a mirror image of the experience of studying science, or whether there is an asymmetry. Of especial interest is students' perception of science and scientists: is their view of science, like the scientists' view of humanities, limited and partial?

The central question, however, is: what does it feel like to be a humanities student? We are interested in the relationship between studying a subject, and students' sense of identity: the way in which the beliefs we hold about an academic discipline affect our sense of who we are. For humanities students, as for science students, the values that attracted them to a subject were values which were also important to them as individuals. In some of the comments which follow, we can see that students are discussing more than a subject which they happened to choose to study at college: they are discussing issues which are central to their lives.

As in Chapter 4, however, we shall begin by looking at the 'official' view of English and communications.

The viewpoint of staff

English

I began Chapter 4 by contrasting two views of physics, which I loosely characterized as the instrumental and expressive view. This section on English will take broadly the same shape; I do not propose to discuss the theoretical debates in English (such as those between structuralists and liberal humanists) but to discuss instead the *purpose* of English: what the teachers of English think is the point of teaching it. Again, the easiest route is to take opposing views, though I am aware that one could probably detect many shades of opinion amongst teachers of English in universities. Of the four lecturers I interviewed, three could be broadly described as 'traditional' in their views, while one might be described as having a 'radical' viewpoint in so far as she challenged the conventional wisdom of English studies.

The difference between the two viewpoints is not really the instrumental/expressive one that we found in physics. The traditional view in English sees the subject as a 'practice', a set of skills for reading and analysing texts, which students acquire during the course of an English degree. One lecturer, asked what he thought students should gain from an English degree, said:

> Skills, certainly. Knowing how to read, I suppose, knowing the varieties of reading which are necessary and available is perhaps the most important thing.
>
> (Mr R, Department A)

The other view of English sees it as a means of enabling students to think in a critical and intelligent manner:

> What I'm interested in is people thinking. And in a sense it happens to be English language and English literature that I teach, but I don't really think I'm teaching that, what I'm doing is helping people to think, hopefully, and have ideas and excite them about ideas and think about themselves and the way they live.
>
> (Dr S, Department A)

While these two viewpoints may not at first sight appear to be strikingly different, they do in fact embody two quite opposing ways of approaching the discipline. Whereas the second quote implies independent thought, 'skills', in the first quote, refers to a discourse, a way of doing things; it implies a 'right way' of studying English. In a similar vein, Dr M in Department B said that the first year is concerned with 'settling in and acquiring practice, and acquiring a certain body of common reading which can then be appealed to or built on in subsequent years'. We can look a little more closely at what this practice, this right way, is.

The dominant idea in the liberal ideology of English is that of 'universality'; great literature is universally 'great' for different peoples in the world and at different times in history. This ideology is reflected in the content of the courses which, in both institutions, consist mainly of individual 'great' writers. The successful reader is one who can transcend her social background to make a sympathetic adjustment to a writer whose norms and values may be those of a different age. This is how Mr R, talking about Milton, put it:

> It's a useful way of getting a perspective on the present, to realize that people think and feel in such different ways, in totally alien ways, that are

completely unsympathetic, which is why feminism is an interesting development, because the ability to read something written in a totally
patriarchal tradition, and to make the sympathetic adjustment, giving him
his due, recognizing that he couldn't have thought what you think, because
people didn't think like that then. . . . And what do you say, do you say, 'I
don't agree with what that man says, it's a bad book, I don't like it or I
won't read it', or do you say, 'it's probably useful for me to try to make the
imaginative judgment to see things the way he sees them, to see the way the
world looks like from his point of view, and I may reject that, but at least
one ought to have some tolerance and some understanding', and it seems
that that's where the study of literature meets life.

(Mr R, Department A)

This is interesting because it disguises *who* is making the sympathetic adjustment. The tradition of writers represented in most of the texts studied on the
course is that of the white, male, Christian middle class. It is those who do not
come from those dominant traditions who have to make the sympathetic
adjustment. To put it more crudely, those students who are male, white,
middle-class and Christian, will very rarely have their views challenged or have
to make sympathetic adjustments as a consequence. The idea, too, that 'people
didn't think like that then' is significant; we do not know, of course, how many
people at a certain point in a history were (for example) feminists, who were
prevented from writing about their views, or whose writings have been forgotten
or lost. Arguing that we should criticize literature only on 'literary' grounds
rather than on political or personal grounds ignores the difficulty of making
boundaries between the purely literary and the political. The assumption is that
of I. A. Richards: that it is possible to disengage oneself from one's own
prejudices, beliefs, experiences, indeed, one's own historical and social location,
in order to shape a purely aesthetic or literary response to the text. The term
'universal' is in itself interesting. While the writing of male white middle- or
upper-class Christian writers is considered to have 'universal' relevance (and is
thus put on the curricula of university English departments), the work of writers
outside that tradition is considered of 'local' rather than 'universal' relevance
(hence terms such as 'woman writer' or 'black writer').

Another feature of the traditional liberal humanist ideology is the emphasis
on close reading of individual texts and the lack of emphasis on theory. There
was a 'critical approaches' course at A, but no theory at all at B. At A, the
'critical approaches' course is taught by a variety of lecturers; each specialist
lectures on his/her favoured critical approach. Thus the department's structuralist lectures on structuralism, the department's feminist lectures on feminism,
and so on. The different approaches are thus seen to be distinct, but perhaps not
in conflict; each approach is seen as an area of specialism, rather than as an area
of commitment. I asked a lecturer at B why there was no theory course:

My experience is that students of literature, and teachers of literature, too,
I would even put myself in that category, are not very good conceptually,
they respond more to actual texts in a sort of affective way, or quasi-

sensuous way. When you start talking about arguments in literature, conceptualising, generalising, a lot of people get rather lost, one would have to admit that. So I mean, maybe they need a course in theory all the more for that reason, I don't know, I think a lot of them would have real problems with it.

(Dr M, Department B)

Again this is the language of Richards and Leavis: the sensuous response to the text, the words on the page. It is surely only in English that an academic would admit to finding 'conceptualizing' difficult. By refusing to include theory, the department is, in effect, refusing to declare its own theoretical standpoint: it must *have* a standpoint, for it is impossible to judge or measure the correctness of someone's 'affective' or 'quasi-sensuous' response; yet English departments do examine and judge people's performance, just like any other department. We need not devalue subjective, affective response to understand that subjective response is partly determined by theoretical (if unacknowledged) preconceptions.

Dr P was asked what effect the growth of English literature all over the world, and the advent of modern literary criticism, had had on English teaching in universities:

Well, I think academics are quite good at resisting what they don't want to deal with you know, so in many departments, it's not had very much. People are quite good at covering things up; they say, I don't know very much about literary theory, you talk to so and so down the corridor; or Well, I don't know African writing, but So-and-So does, and then people offer options on them, that to some extent is what we do here, within a framework of a fairly traditional English structure . . . people manage by excluding what they don't want to deal with, really.

(Dr P, Department B)

What is so interesting about this is the way in which it both resembles, and differs from, Kuhn's account of changes in 'paradigm'. On the one hand, there is certainly a resistance to change and to new ideas; academics appear quite happy to continue teaching the same old syllabuses as if there had been no 'explosion' (Dr P's word) in English studies; at the same time, there is no resistance to allowing other people within the same department to teach quite different things to students, and to do quite different types of research. There is a great tolerance towards a multiplicity of paradigms, provided those paradigms never challenge the mainstream in any serious way. Thus, as in A, matters such as Literary Theory or non-mainstream areas of literature (such as African literature) are considered 'specialisms' which need not interfere with the traditional way in which English has been, and is, taught.

Dr P makes it very clear that one must accept that certain pieces of writing are superior to others; but the criteria for judging superiority are, interestingly, not very specific:

What I think is happening, I find this interesting, people are rejecting the idea of the aesthetic, and I'm not quite sure why; I don't know whether they think it's elitist or whether they've got no taste of their own, or what, I don't know, but people read poems not as poems which convey aesthetic emotion, which is the way I tend to think about poems ultimately, but simply as ideological statements and political texts, or at least, things that give you some understanding of the way people thought or so on at the time. . . . If you take out the idea of the aesthetic, you're just left with communication. Then people, for some ideological reason, people might say, well, you know, you can't say one form of communication is better than another, so that say, I don't know, I suppose, a kind of feminist belief is better than *Paradise Lost* or something – well, it might be more acceptable to some people for various reasons, but I say some writing is more rewarding, ultimately some things are better than other things. If you say, how do you know they're better, then how do you know one football team is better than another, it plays better, gets more results, you know, and people respond to that.

(Dr P, Department B)

He concluded:

In terms of institutional study, there is a dislike of what I think is rather sourly thought of as high culture and high art, and in favour of communications, which can be awfully boring and not terribly rewarding. But yes, it is going on, and certainly in polytechnics.

(Dr P, Department B)

The idea that certain analyses of literature reject aestheticism is, in fact, a fairly crude parody of the Marxist and feminist positions. However, the belief that good poems are like good football teams, in that they get 'better results', is undoubtedly novel. Certainly *Paradise Lost* does get 'better results' for some people; Sylvia Plath gets 'better results' for others, while Catherine Cookson gets 'better results' for even more people. People from different backgrounds, different eras and with different levels of education will inevitably respond in a variety of ways to the same texts. Dr P's argument is that in a piece of 'good' writing, there are certain qualities, above and beyond the techniques s/he uses to communicate an experience or belief, that make that piece of writing intrinsically superior to other pieces of literature. If one asks the question, 'Who decides what is a piece of "good" writing?' one is back to Leavis's statements about the 'morally sensitive' reader. Dr P's argument disguises the reality that, as has been pointed out by writers as diverse as Spender (1981a) and Eagleton (1983), only a small group of people, historically, have participated in deciding which literature gets the best 'results'.

Whereas the liberal view emphasizes the universal qualities of 'good literature' and claims that there is an objective standard by which that literature can be judged, one alternative view, as expressed by Dr S, is that our responses to literature are necessarily subjective. This is what she said about her 'women and literature' course:

I try and make women's history clearer, because obviously they've done history A level so they've probably learnt about wars and all the male sort of things, so what women were doing and thinking and the way in which that has been suppressed; as much as possible I like to teach by not putting very much of what I think across but trying to get other people to produce it . . . also encouraging them to share as an experience and personal responses and talking about things one wouldn't normally talk about in the department, the emotional side of things, in quotes 'irrational', 'intuitive' and all of that, and valuing that . . . try and make it a space where people can say whatever they want to say; I suppose value things that would not be valued elsewhere.

(Dr S, Department A)

In Dr S's view, the discourse of the emotional is devalued in the rest of the department, and she tries to bring it to the fore. She sees this course as explicitly challenging some of the accepted norms of the rest of the course. It is intended to be non-competitive and less about following rules than allowing people to express their own feelings and ideas. Perhaps the inherent problem with this is that 'women and literature' is labelled as 'subjective' and 'trivial', and therefore becomes marginalized: it is not allowed to challenge the mainstream ideas of the English degree.

Clearly each of the English departments contained a multiplicity of views within its staff. Curiously however, the three traditional lecturers with whom I discussed the matter insisted that the plurality made no difference to assessment of students' work; in the words of Mr R:

As far as examining goes, or marking essays, I assume that most of my colleagues take the sort of line that I do, that what we're looking for is not a particular interpretation of something, but an ability to get to grips with texts, to produce an argument that's logical, coherent, well-written and is supported from the texts.

(Mr R, Department A)

This view was also the one put forward by Dr P and Dr M in Department B. However, Dr S had a different view:

They [theoretical differences] are not resolved really; they continue as quite big arguments; and there are quite big camps really of those who believe in theory and those who believe in scholarship, I suppose; and we pretend that you can just muddle along and it doesn't matter, but the crunch comes at things like marking exam papers, because if you've got a student who's heavily into theory, writing for a marker who's heavily not into theory, then they tend to say things like 'oh, he's just read Terry Eagleton, so blah blah blah' or 'she's just read Cate Belsey and regurgitated that' so someone can get a bad mark because they've written for the wrong person.

(Dr S, Department A)

This statement points to an alarming rift in English, and suggests that degree classes can be determined by whichever side wins the battle in a particular examination meeting. However, while most teachers of English in our universities believe, or appear to believe, that there is an unspoken consensus about what constitutes 'quality' in the practice of English, then this rift will remain unresolved. The divide in English studies seems to be between those who want to bring the rift out into the open, and those who prefer to pretend that it doesn't exist.

There is, therefore, a continual tension between the claims of the departments to objectivity, and their emphasis on subjectivity. Despite this tension, there is also a refusal to examine curricula or practices: student failure, therefore, is the fault of the student's inability to make the necessary sympathetic adjustment to the requirements of literary judgement; not the failure of the departments in setting those requirements.

Communications

The communications course, in many ways, is as much a social science as an humanities subject, although many of the staff come from English literature backgrounds. It is concerned with the ways in which people communicate (with particular emphasis on the mass media), in both a practical and an academic sense. Lecturers I spoke to saw the course as chiefly concerned with the development of critical skills combined with promoting an understanding of the vocational areas on which communications has a bearing:

> I think any student going through higher education is getting something from it if they come in as some measure sceptical, in some measure critical, that they're not prepared to take things at face value. If you are encouraging them all the time to consider propositions or arguments and then what evidence has been marshalled in support and the like, then you want them to come out like that. . . . We don't pretend in any way to professionally train students [but] they are expected to understand something of what professional training would consist of. . . . What we would be dealing with are more of the implications, or this is how, for whatever reasons, it has come to pass that people write journalistic stories in this kind of way – might there not be other, better, more adequate ways of writing journalistic stories? Those kind of questions . . . it makes them, should they become practitioners, better practitioners.
>
> (Mr E, Department C)

Despite the clarity of this statement of intent, staff still regard both the course and the discipline of communications as emergent, rather than complete:

> Our general philosophy about the area hasn't changed. We still think that communications arguably, whilst still emerging as a discipline, is best approached from a range of disciplines. So it's still, if you like, at the

beginning, a multi-disciplinary exercise which progressively becomes inter-disciplinary.

(Mr D, Department C)

Unlike English, which is an established discipline, communications is still in the process of finding a language and an identity; it is not yet a discipline in itself. Having said that, it is beginning to gel as a discipline; Mr D said that staff rarely discussed the aims of the course now, there being a 'general assumption that the ground rules are more or less the same [as when we started]'. He added:

> I wouldn't say there's a consensus, but there are various consensuses, that's the plural, which overlap, which aren't in opposition, about what communications ought to be about.

(Mr D, Department C)

The awareness that there is not a discussion about what communications is, and that perhaps there should be, is rather different from the viewpoint of some English lecturers, who believe that English is established as a practice and therefore has no need of a debate about its development as a discipline.

The multi-disciplinary/inter-disciplinary nature of communications can, however, make it very disjointed, particularly in the first year when sociology, psychology, and so on, are studied as separate subjects between which little connection is made. In the second and third years the course comes together as it concentrates on communications as a discipline, taking the discourse of sociology and psychology much more for granted.

Communications, as taught at C, is more overtly theoretical than either of the English courses. Despite the many points of contact between the study of film or media and the study of literature, despite the fact that there exist theorists such as Barthes who have made important contributions to the study of film and the study of literature, it is only on the communications courses that such theorists are studied. Most of the English practitioners were not concerned to look at literature as a method of *communicating*. The teaching of communications demands that students approach the subject in a way that entails thinking, not just about individual ideas or issues, but about the relationship between those ideas and also the social location of those ideas. It is assumed that a text, or a film, is not something which has a set of meanings which can be extracted from it, but something whose meanings exist only because they are part of a wider social world; people can find meanings only if their world shares some common meanings with that of the text. For example, a question on one of the communications examination papers asks:

> How is masculinity constructed in any of the films you have studied this year?

This question is interesting not only because it suggests a world wider than that of the film itself, but also because it focuses on the issue of 'masculinity'. This provides a contrast with many of the English papers which had the occasional question on 'Discuss Rossetti's/Dickens's/Browning's representation of women', but never had anything on an author's representation of *men*. The response of Dr P to communications, it will be remembered, is that it ignores the aesthetic, that it is so obsessed with 'ideological statements and political texts' that it can no longer make a distinction between good and bad. In fact, the 'aesthetic' is discussed on the course, but as a problematic rather than as a response to literature.

Interestingly Mr D denied that communications was more inclined to encourage students to question conventional wisdom than subjects such as English, saying that 'I don't think academic subjects do . . . take things for granted' and that English looks at how writers are 'situated socially and economically and culturally'. He believed that communications was only different in that it offered some vocational skills. His claims for communications were, in fact, much more modest than the English lecturers' claims for English.

Essentially, what the communications course does is to bring to the fore issues which had hitherto been considered marginal; it brings the perspectives of a variety of disciplines to bear on one subject. To a greater degree than any other discipline – maybe even than sociology – it is concerned with the social construction of meaning, with dispelling certainty about knowledge.

English departments are apparently tolerant of competing ideas and para-digms; lecturers, however, argued that assessment of students was more concerned with assessing students' grasp of a discourse, their ability to *practise* English, than with judging the validity of their opinions. In communications, given that the course deals with a variety of political relationships, disagreement between staff would have to be more overtly ideological; the course itself is easily open to charges of left-wing bias. It doesn't give the impression of staff muddling on regardless: differences in theoretical perspectives are made explicit. The extent to which these differences should be made obvious to students is less clear:

> What you're trying to do is indicate to them how best you might be able to work your way through those controversies to be able to make some statement of policy or some recommendation and the like. . . . There's no point, I don't think, in that kind of pretension to an absolute objectivity, and some of my colleagues in the department do, and I think that's regrettable, and I don't think it serves any useful function.
>
> (Mr E, Department C)

There's a much greater sense here of tolerating plurality and diversity than there was in the English departments, although obviously there *is* conflict amongst staff about the extent to which such plurality can be tolerated. Students are encouraged to challenge orthodoxy, to be critical. Having said that, it would presumably be very difficult for a student who held particularly strong right-wing views to survive on the course. There is a sense in which the challenge to convention can become a convention in itself; it is easier to say that a multitude of views will be tolerated than to put it into practice. Indeed, both the lecturers I spoke to felt that some of their colleagues were less tolerant of dissent than they were; we shall see later that some of the students felt this too.

Subject choice

In Chapter 4 we found that many students chose science because other members of their family were scientists. Others felt that, if they were equally capable at science and arts subjects, they should choose science because it would give them a better chance of a career. Some of the female students thought that their single-sex schools had encouraged them to take science.

None of these factors appeared to operate for the humanities students. They didn't feel that their families had encouraged them to take an arts degree rather than a science degree (although, of course, their families had usually encouraged them to enter higher education). Neither did they feel that a humanities degree would give them an advantage in their career, except in so far as English was a good 'general' degree. The nine female students who went to single-sex schools did not feel that schools had encouraged them to take humanities. Indeed, none of the students thought that their schools had encouraged them in this direction, although it may be that there were indirect pressures operating on girls in mixed-sex schools to choose arts rather than science.

Some of the women who had attended single-sex schools *did* experience a pressure to take science – a pressure against which they rebelled:

> I went to an all-girls' school and the headmistress was terribly into competition with the all-boys' school, and we all had to be into chemistry and physics, and go to university, and be career women and be successful and dynamic and not get married and all this sort of thing and it just didn't agree with me at all.
>
> (Vera, 3rd year, C)

When an all-girls' school tries to mimic all-boys' schools in this way, rebellion can take the form of asserting traditional 'femininity': some of the female students – Vera was one of them – said that they had rebelled against the authority of single-sex schools by having lots of boyfriends, wearing jewellery and make-up with school uniform and so on. The schools produced exactly the opposite result to that intended; because they define themselves as being in competition with boys' schools, as having to reach a 'masculine' ideal of achievement, they reinforce common-sense notions of 'masculinity' and 'femininity'.

Rebellion cannot, however, be the only reason students chose to take English or communications. Ten of the forty-eight arts students interviewed had at least one science or science-related A level. Of these, three had biology A level only, five had maths A level, one had biology and chemistry, and one had both maths and physics, but had low grades and had later taken arts A levels at night school with excellent results (he had seven A levels in all). In addition, one communications student had an HND in engineering and had worked for several years as an engineer. This suggests that for those students the decision to specialize in arts had not been a simple or straightforward one.

Those students who had not taken scientific A levels were often very negative about their decision to specialize in arts – not because they put a low value on the arts, but because they apparently felt that other people did. Several of them, particularly the women, defined their decision in terms of lack of ability in science:

> I've always really enjoyed English; it was my best subject at school . . . chemistry lost me on the equations. I suppose I could do them, yes, I just didn't have the confidence to be able to work them out quickly enough. I don't have a terribly scientific mind, I don't think . . . I suppose in a way English is a bit self-indulgent.
>
> (Diane, 3rd year, B)

One or two were more spirited about their dislike of school science:

> There were no people involved, personalities and things that you can latch on to. It was just test-tubes and experiments, and also I wasn't very practical either; I used to blow things up. It just wasn't about people or what I understand to be about life and things, I just wasn't interested remotely . . . it just didn't interest me at all. I just can't stress how much it didn't interest me, it really did bore me rigid. It wasn't just a mild distaste for it, I really hated it.
>
> (Jennifer, 3rd year, A)

The theme of science's lack of involvement in people – its lack of 'relevance' – recurred again and again in my interviews with arts students. It is significant that some of the students, both male and female, favourably contrasted biology with the physical sciences:

> I couldn't see the point of it. I couldn't see the point of knowing what reacted with what and what blew up. In chemistry, I used to have such a mental blockage. I liked things that I could see around me, and relate to, rather than pure fact. That's why I liked biology.
>
> (Helen, 3rd year, C)

> That's why I did biology O level rather than physics or chemistry, because biology is studying something that is actually happening in the world, studying life, whereas physics is just machines, and bits of chemicals, it didn't really turn me on as much.
>
> (Simon, 1st year, A)

Biology is, therefore, contrasted with the other sciences as a more 'relevant' discipline, more 'human'; more like English, in fact. As Saraga and Griffiths (1981) have argued:

> Biology . . . with its concern for living things, appears more personal and alive, and closer to the everyday world of values and emotion, which women are expected to inhabit.
>
> (Saraga and Griffiths 1981: 85)

This is certainly borne out by the remarks of some of the female arts students. However, biology was also perceived as more 'human' by some of the *male* arts students; this preference was not the result of social pressure, but the consequence of an interest in people and in life over an interest in 'things'. In other words, students of both sexes articulated a preference for biology which was based on a rational and coherent set of values, rather than a response to sex-stereotyping.

Although some students framed their decision to study arts in the context of an inability to understand science, they were generally more positive about their decision to study English at degree level. The main reasons given for studying English were that they were good at it; that they enjoyed it; that it was a good 'general degree'; and that it was concerned with 'people'. The following comments were typical:

> It was something I had an obvious talent for at school, and the one I enjoyed by far the most.
>
> (Ben, 3rd year, A)

> It broadens your outlook I think – I think it makes you feel an affinity to people in the past – just like a general human condition – people were having the same conflicts and worries thousands of years ago when they were writing all these poems that we're doing now.
>
> (Joan, 1st year, A)

Joan's perception of English is of a subject which creates links between people; which allows for the possibility of a common understanding. She hopes that she will be able to gain some insight, through the study of literature, into the spiritual – or at least emotional – world of human beings; physics students wanted to gain insight and understanding of the physical world. This contrast, although apparently obvious, is crucial to our understanding of the social contruction of arts and sciences.

The response of the communications students was more mixed, however. Most students wanted to enter the media, but they did not all enter the course for that reason. Many had specifically chosen a polytechnic course because they thought it more 'relevant' (not just in the vocational sense) and more interesting than traditional university subjects such as English and sociology, and had chosen the course in the face of school pressure:

> At school they kept saying 'Do an English degree', but I was so sick of doing things like Shakespeare; it was all theory and that's why I like this; it's things that you can see around you, so it's easier to understand.
>
> (Helen, 3rd year, C)

> Everybody seemed to think that I should go in for a redbrick university at least and do something totally irrelevant like history.
>
> (Ken, 3rd year, C)

It should be said, too, that the choice was a genuine one; many of the communications students had excellent A level grades and would have had no problem in getting into a university. Communications was consistently described by the students as more 'broad-based' and more related to everyday 'reality' than subjects like English, which was perceived as consisting of 'irrelevancies' such as medieval literature. The development of critical awareness was considered as complementary to, rather than in opposition to, the aim of getting a job. Helen, for example, was very keen on becoming a journalist, but that was not the most important aspect of the course:

> It makes you think a lot, not only about the media, but about politics, and about what goes on in the world, not just burying your head in books. . . . Before I used to tend to shut myself off, thinking because it doesn't affect me, it doesn't matter. I think it does make you think about other people and other ideas that are going round.

> (Helen, 3rd year, C)

I have since seen Helen's name on the byline of an article in a national magazine, so she had obviously begun to succeed in her ambition, though only a minority of graduates of the course do enter journalism afterwards. There is some degree of tension, too, in that the course encourages students to adopt a very critical attitude towards the profession that most of them want to enter, although this had not deterred them from wanting to do so.

None of the arts students said that they were encouraged to take arts rather than sciences by their parents. On the contrary: Martin, who had switched from engineering to communications, had fallen out with his father over his decision, while a woman studying English had frequent arguments (albeit friendly ones) with her immediate family about the respective values of arts and sciences (all her family – mother, father and sister – were scientists.) Some students, therefore, had to resist pressure from families, while those students who chose science were supported and encouraged by their parents. Obviously there were other influences on students' decisions; the fact that most of the arts students came from middle-class backgrounds and had highly educated parents was in itself a major factor in their decision to carry on to higher education at all. But the choice of subject was less influenced by the school or by parents than in the case of the science students.

Constructing English

Like the physics students, the discourse of the English students consisted of a number of dichotomies in which English was rated positively and other subjects, particularly science, were rated negatively. However, the dichotomies of the English students only overlapped partially with those of the physics students. Those that did were the dichotomies of relevant/irrelevant and certain/uncertain; like physics, English was perceived as being more about 'real life' than other disciplines; unlike physics, it was regarded as 'uncertain', but this, interestingly, was regarded as a virtue, not a deficiency of the subject. However, English students also made use of a number of other ideas not present in the discourse of the physics students:

English	*Science*
broad	narrow
flexible	rigid
tolerant	intolerant
individualist	conformist
moral	amoral

Obviously not all the students made use of all these dualities; and not all of them saw science as 'narrow, rigid, intolerant', and so on. Some students, as we shall see later, adopted a 'live and let live' attitude towards science and some had scientific interests. However, whereas physics was often seen in opposition to chemistry as well as to the humanities, there was no counterpart amongst English students whereby history, say, represented values which were in opposition to English. Where English was thought of in terms of 'difference', it was always in terms of difference from science.

The dualities listed above represent a different set of values and priorities from those held by the physics students. Let us examine the first of these: 'broad' and 'narrow'. English was perceived as a subject which was not tied to one area, but which covered many different subjects:

> I think with a subject like English you can cover a lot of other areas of learning, subjects like psychology, sociology and even science in a way, but it's with an art form, so it's much looser, and yet in a way in literature you'll cover subjects like sociology and that but you're not tied to theories, it's much more interesting.
>
> (Geraldine, 1st year, B)

> There's a certain attraction about English . . . it's like a Jack of all trades in many respects because you're reading literature, the source of all knowledge, as it were, or a good proportion of it; you've got to dabble in virtually every subject, you've got little bits of everything I think, and it's a broad subject, that's why they call it a general degree.
>
> (Ben, 3rd year, A)

'Breadth' as used by the English students had more than one meaning. Partly it meant being able to study a lot of different subjects – such as psychology, sociology, history, philosophy – in one discipline. But also it meant 'tolerance' – understanding that other people have different viewpoints without any one view necessarily being 'right':

> I've learnt a lot more about the way people think, the way people's thoughts are put down in literature, and I think that helps you in life generally, just some knowledge of how people have reacted to different situations.
>
> (Lee, 3rd year, A)

> [I've gained] an improved capacity for understanding or analysing things, just a more varied approach or a more varied way of thinking . . . because you're just reading someone's personal viewpoint all the time, so you have

to jump about a hell of a lot . . . you read Wordsworth one week and his view on the imagination and Nature and then you read Blake or somebody who'll argue the opposite, but also take things from it and so you just get flexibility.

(Daniel, 3rd year, B)

Students felt that they gained from being given access to a variety of ways of looking at literature, and at life; this recognition that there is more than one perspective on a subject and that many people have different views led to a celebration of 'uncertainty' – a belief that a multiplicity of viewpoints was better than a single 'truth'. One student, when asked what he felt he had gained from the course, replied:

I can't say any great philosophy of what to do with my life or something – quite the opposite actually. I'm less certain than when I came here I think . . . English is very good as a touching stone for everything; you can do what you want with it, look at it historically, or become more politically aware, look at it through language, it's all different ways of redeveloping your notion of what reality is.

(John, 3rd year, A)

The idea parallels that of Colin, the physics student who saw physics as a 'way of thinking, a way of tackling problems'. John sees English as a process, a way in which we can look at and interpret the world; although many science students saw arts subjects as static, because they are not a growing body of knowledge, John sees English as fluid, ever varying and ever changing. He rejects the idea of the imposition of any one point of view; when talking about his favourite authors on the course, he gave a more precise example of what he meant:

I suppose I'm interested in books in which you don't feel you're getting any unified reading laid upon you – I don't like Lawrence at all because I feel there's a sense of imperatives about him which I don't like at all – someone like Virginia Woolf I'm much more interested in, the way she uses language.

(John, 3rd year, A)

This pluralist ideal was echoed by other students:

I like working with ideas, and I think I like the idea that literature doesn't tell you anything which is true, it doesn't make any claims, or even when it does it knows that it's lying, that's how I like things anyway, and I like things to be ambiguous, I don't like the lie of science which claims that it is true when it isn't, because even science is just based on ideas, as is literature. None of it is proved, it's proved until something else is discovered.

(Terry, 3rd year, A)

This rejection of authority, this assertion that there is no absolute truth, when contrasted with the physics students, claims of certainty and objectivity for their subject, matches the divergent/convergent pattern that Hudson (1970) found amongst the science and arts specialists in his sample. However, whereas Hudson saw this as a reflection of personality differences, the English students in my sample held an *intellectual* attachment to notions such as breadth, pluralism and so on. Whereas the physics students believed their subject to be objective (and therefore more important), English students valued their subject for those qualities most devalued within the physics discourse: subjectivity and individuality.

> I know people are really into maths, but they have lectures where they learn most of the stuff and they have a tutor . . . but they don't have a seminar where they can sit down and discuss it and say *this* is my point of view, this is how *I* feel about it, this is how *I* react to it, and I think I enjoy the freedom of that, it's very much *me* reacting to it, and it's not that that's right and that's wrong, it's me as well.
>
> (Jean, 3rd year, B)

The word Jean uses – freedom – is important in the idea of individuality. The English students very much disliked being tied down to a single viewpoint; an important part of doing English was the freedom to disagree with the established point of view:

> It's not so much being taught, it's more just developing yourself, so if you've got a completely opposing idea to what your tutor does, then it's perfectly all right, they make you feel it's all right; it's hard to do that at first, but then you learn to, you learn to form your own opinions and teach yourself – English is a teach yourself subject really – although you discuss it with tutors and that, you have to formulate your own ideas and your own opinions in the end.
>
> (Kate, 1st year, A)

> I don't like going by standard opinion. If I know what the standard opinion is, I'll try and look round it to see if there's another way to interpret it.
>
> (Sharon, 1st year, B)

These four concepts – of breadth, tolerance, uncertainty and individuality – are all interrelated; they were all seen as innate characteristics of the discipline, which did not exist independently of each other. There was a fifth strand, however, running through the answers of some of the students, which indicated, for many students, the *value* of the subject, and that is its moral (in the Leavisite sense of the word) aspect. Many students clearly believed that English was a subject which dealt with moral issues, and it was important for that reason. This is one first-year student, for example, enthusing about the subject:

> Somebody said to me once, 'English is studying the soul of people' and I thought that was really good, because it *is*, and you can understand people more, and you can understand History more, the history of what happened, and people in situations, and understand things that are connected with the modern day . . . it's got history in it, sociology and psychology.
>
> (Kate, 1st year, A)

Kate is arguing that English gives the student empathy, an insight into the lives and minds of other people; another student expresses the same opinion:

> What I like about it, I think, is that it does reflect life and you can read something and it gives you a different viewpoint on things that perhaps others before you have experienced.
>
> (Joan, 1st year, A)

English, then, gives students the opportunity to engage with human issues, the experiences of a variety of people; it gives them access to a variety of ways of interpreting and understanding the world. For this reason, many students felt English to be a more moral subject, which enables them to relate to the experience of other human beings. Time and again, students said that English was more relevant because it was about people, rather than about things. Just as many of the science students said that physics was about studying 'life' or 'the world as it really is', so the arts students argued that the arts were about *reality*:

> I think arts are relevant to the world today . . . you actually learn something about life, whereas science, it might get you a job, but you haven't really learnt anything about what's happening in life, have you?
>
> (Simon, 1st year, A)

> English has more room for feelings in it . . . I think maths and that are much more schematic sorts of subjects; they seemed to me to be much less connected to the real world. Maths seemed at the time to be very abstract and it was very hard for me to connect it to the real world.
>
> (Anthony, 1st year, A)

There is a very strong feeling, then, amongst these students that English is more in touch with reality; that anything more abstract is divorced from 'life'. In Chapter 3 we noted Eagleton's comment that 'English students in England today are "Leavisites" whether they know it or not'. This assertion is borne out by much of what the English students said to me about their subject. Their stress on the breadth of the subject – the fact that it could encompass so many disciplines and therefore, by implication, was superior to them – and their belief in the subject's relevance to society and people's lives, and their emphasis on the moral questions the subject raises, reflect Leavis's own views of English as a practice which, in the words of Knights, 'deepens our humanity'. English has to be the most important subject because it is the only one which involves students in thinking about moral problems, and the only books worth studying are morally serious ones. That this vision is derived directly from Leavis is not, in fact, something that would be clear to most of the students who held to it. Contrary to the claims of lecturers in B, who argued that students picked up literary theory as they went along, most students were quite unaware of the multitude of critical attitudes that could be adopted to the study of literature; and those who did, with a few exceptions (one or two Marxists, for example), either rejected the alternatives in favour of liberal humanism, or were very naive about the nature of those alternatives.

It should be noted, however, that there is an important difference from Leavis. Leavis was particularly authoritarian when it came to discussing the issue of which literature was worthwhile and which not; the students in my sample were strong in asserting their right to their own opinions, and in rejecting the imposition of a uniform point of view. Having said that, very few of them seriously challenged the right of the departments to define the syllabus or the content of the course. The few who did, those who recognized liberal humanism as a single approach, and who chose not to subscribe to it, saw the study of literature as serving a different purpose. Anthony, a first-year student at A, said:

> Most arts tend to become part of ruling-class ideology, really, they tend to support an élitist sort of social structure and one reason, as far as I'm concerned, for doing English, is to subvert that, but how far it can be done is debatable.
>
> (Anthony, 1st year, A)

The wry recognition, at the end of that quote, of the impotence of the individual in the face of the social order, illustrates Anthony's awareness of the gap between his view of English and the dominant view. Later we shall examine the tension between the stated ideals of freedom of opinion, and the need of the department to maintain control over what is taught and believed (pp. 95–98).

Constructing communications

The communications students' construction of their discipline was similar to the English students' construction of theirs. In particular, they emphasized the breadth of their subject and the fact that it encompassed many different areas:

> Whatever you learn about a particular subject you learn a lot more about the ways of thinking about any subject at all. . . . On a course like this, whatever you learn is disproved the next week, so concrete knowledge-wise it hasn't given me much, but it's given me lots of ways of approaching problems.
>
> (Mark, 3rd year, C)

> The course has made me much more socially aware. I think how much I've done that I really wouldn't have known about if I hadn't done this course. Most of the things we've done seem to be of relevance to some other area – media, sociology, psychology, political processes . . . there's a lot of things I look at now in a totally different way.
>
> (Ken, 3rd year, C)

Simon's view coincides with that of certain of the lecturers quoted on pp. 78–80: he sees communications as a practice rather than as a body of knowledge.

Similarly communications students saw the discipline as subjective, individual; they felt free to make up their own minds:

> Everything's interesting, it's not facts, it's your own view. Nothing's right or wrong, it's all debatable which is good.
>
> (Rebecca, 1st year, C)

Like English, the discipline was regarded as more 'relevant', in the sense that it discussed immediate issues concerned with the lives of people. It is worth quoting Helen's words again:

> It makes you think such a lot, not only about the media, but about politics, and about what goes on in the world, not just burying your head in books. Before I used to tend to shut myself off, thinking because it doesn't affect me, it doesn't matter. I think it does make you think about other people and other ideas that are going around.
>
> (Helen, 3rd year, C)

Communications was seen as a vehicle for understanding all sorts of important social issues. The issues it is concerned with, however, are more immediate than those dealt with by English; whereas English students often thought that studying the views of writers in the past could help them to a general awareness of the problems of humanity, the communications course was much more concerned with the here and now. The Clive Ponting trial in 1985, for example, was discussed on the media policy course and used as a focus for discussing a variety of political and social issues. Many of the communications students believed that communications was a more 'relevant' subject than most university disciplines, as can be seen in a phrase used by Helen in the above quote: 'burying your head in books'. The students tended to be anti-academic and regarded traditional university arts subjects such as English or history as elitist and remote. In this, they bore some affinity with the physical science students: they believed in the practical relevance of the discipline to everyday life. In addition, they felt some extrinsic motivation in doing the subject; they stressed the intellectual aspects of the course, but also its importance in getting them jobs:

> I wanted to do something that wasn't totally academic with a bit of practical work. I'm good at languages and communications seemed logical. And I'm interested in the media, and I think there's a growing market there and a lot of job opportunities.
>
> (Sandra, 1st year, C)

> It's a broad-based degree. It's got so many facets to it – all the areas it covers are areas that vaguely appeal to me as areas I'd like to go into afterwards. It's basically that I can go into virtually anything afterwards.
>
> (Harry, 1st year, C)

However, the communications students' emphasis on breadth, individuality, freedom of opinion, and the importance of social issues, meant that their world-view resembled that of the English students far more than it did that of the physical science students.

The experience of studying English and communications

Probably the major difference between the initial experiences of the arts students and the science students in higher education was that the arts students spent far less time in the department. Science students spend up to twenty-five hours a week in tutorials, lectures and labs: most of the work they do is timetabled by the department. The English students, however, with only approximately ten hours timetabled, found that they were expected to do a great deal of work on their own. This in practice meant two things; one, that the arts students had to adjust to independence and self-discipline in work; two, that relations with staff and other students within the departments were perceived as of less importance.

Some students commented positively on the staff in the English departments. One student who had transferred from management said:

> I get on with most of the staff, I'm quite impressed 'cos you know, you get the feeling that it's efficient and that they do actually care about the students, which I didn't find when I was doing management.
>
> (Geraldine, 1st year, B)

This opinion was not held universally; indeed, one student at B complained that some of the staff 'exude an air of authority'. However, students generally seemed unconcerned about the attitude of staff; it was accepted that staff and students kept themselves to themselves. As at A, students and staff didn't generally mix informally; the department's common room was never used, except for departmental seminars. In neither English department could it be said that staff knew the names of all the students, but this is to be expected given the few timetabled hours. In short, English is a far less *social* discipline than physics; students and staff work individually rather than in groups.

Staff–student relations were noticeably less formal on the communications course than on any of the other five courses. Staff tended to dress casually, and students were on first-name terms with them. The contrast can be illustrated nicely by Martin, a first-year student who had come into communications from an HND in engineering:

> They [the staff] are completely different from anything I've known before. I know I keep going back to this diploma I did, but that's all I can compare it with. That really was a teacher–pupil relationship . . . you were taught *at*, you were referred to by your surname, and you called them 'Mr X' or whatever. You never saw them outside the lecture socially, you didn't even see them in the refectory, it was them and us. You come here, and the lecturers here are far more accessible. They treat you as adults, as opposed to students or pupils. You feel as though you could go and speak to them on any subject . . . they seem a lot more intelligent and aware than the staff at the college I was at, definitely more approachable.
>
> (Martin, 1st year, C)

This view of the staff had general accord. Students talked freely with staff, and in some cases mixed with them outside of the course time. There were criticisms of some members of staff, but these centred around intellectual differences or a dislike of certain teaching styles, rather than a feeling that they were un-approachable. The numbers on the course were comparatively small, and the atmosphere was generally friendlier than on other courses. In addition, it was noticeable that students tended to stick together much more outside of course hours than on the other courses, where students were more likely to have friends from other departments. At the opposite extreme to physics Department B, the communications course too suggests that hierarchical relationships between teacher and pupil are weakest where the boundary lines between types of knowledge are most blurred. Communications was taught as an inter-disciplinary subject, covering a wide variety of areas and, as we shall see shortly, students often felt free to challenge staff's definitions; by no means was the authority of the staff beyond question.

As we have seen, the major problem for first-year science students in coping with their new courses lay in having to deal with taking in large amounts of information; they had to become adept at note-taking and at understanding what they were being told. In particular, they found it difficult to do this without receiving any individual attention or advice on work. In the English depart-ments, the basic problem – that of getting to grips with new teaching methods and coping with the volume of work – was the same, but the form of the problem was different. The difficulty lay in knowing exactly how much they were supposed to do. For example, students are usually given long reading lists in lectures; reading all the books would be an impossible task; on the other hand, it is difficult to know whether to read one, two, three or maybe none of the books. One of the first things the first-year student has to do, then, is to come to terms with independence, and to decide upon the balance of work necessary. There was, indeed, some surprise at the amount of work involved:

> Everyone says that English is a doss degree, Mickey Mouse, you don't do any work or anything, but there's a lot of reading.
>
> (Gary, 1st year, B)

Some of the first-year English students I spoke to had not yet got to grips with the work; they were either working much too hard, or not hard enough. Many students felt uneasy at the lack of guidance:

> There's one lesson per week on things like Marxism and Structuralism, and it just isn't enough to cover it in depth. They give you a huge booklist and ask you to go away and read them but there's no way you can and there's no way most people do. Most people just go away and forget about it.
>
> (Anthony, 1st year, A)

First-year students on all three course, at A, B and C, commented on the difficulty of adjusting to lectures; one student at A said that he found it difficult to concentrate for more than twenty minutes, a student at C said that she found herself still taking down notes on one point as the lecturer was moving on to the next point, while another, Gina, complained that most of the lecturers 'just talk at you' and that 'the person who's doing the tutorial doesn't know what the lecturer's been saying'.

However, there was far less anxiety amongst arts students than amongst the science students about lectures. Science students were genuinely worried about getting behind with the work, whereas the English and communications students regarded lectures as a chore rather than as a source of particular difficulty. There were even some students who enjoyed lectures, or at least some of them. Martin, quoted earlier, said of the lectures in C:

> I have a guilt complex because I'm actually going to lectures and enjoying the lecture and it's almost like going out and talking to friends about something you really enjoy. I'm finding that a little bit difficult after six years of doing something I didn't really want to do.
>
> (Martin, 1st year, C)

The idea about 'guilt' is perhaps useful in shedding light on the attitudes of some of the science students to the arts: a belief that if education is fun or enjoyable, then it can't be any good; as Hudson (1972) argues, the arts are associated with pleasure and effeminacy; and for that reason, are also believed to lack value. Generally students felt fairly relaxed about lectures, although some first-year students had difficulties of adjustment; final-year students were much more blasé about the course – those who got bored with lecture courses or who disliked the teaching, simply didn't turn up:

> A great deal of the third year is theory, critical practice and literary theory and all the rest of it, and if you want that you can go and read a book . . . you need lectures in the first year because you know absolutely nothing about what's going on and you need a lot of lectures based on the social background and history . . . but by the third year, you don't really need lectures.
>
> (Terry, 3rd year, A)

> The lectures are fairly arbitrary – it's very much a case of, you've got one man's opinon of Jane Austen and it virtually turns into a reading list. . . . Quite frequently I will skip lectures because they're not compulsory, and in some cases they're completely superfluous.
>
> (Ben, 3rd year, A)

Skipping lectures was a much more frequent occurrence amongst arts students than amongst science students, who were rightly afraid of falling behind if they missed lectures. The confidence that third-year students felt about missing lectures however, the fact that they felt able to learn on their own, is an indication that they have gone through the process of becoming an 'English student'; they have been successfully socialized. A major part of becoming an English student is learning to cope with independence, learning to understand what is required, getting the balance right.

Tutorials and seminars were also new to first-year students, and these were regarded more favourably than the lectures. Students enjoyed the opportunity to express their ideas, and it was felt, too, that tutorials and seminars were more like the classroom teaching they were used to. Many also said – again there are parallels with the science students – that they would prefer to have more tutorials, because that gave them an opportunity to discuss their ideas.

One problem for many students in tutorials and seminars was that of overcoming shyness. Many found it difficult, especially initially, to say very much:

> To start with one or two of them were quite intimidating. I'm fairly shy and I'm OK now but the first term I know the report at the end said she does not talk enough in seminars, and this sort of thing. Because the one seminar, we had an awful lot of clever people in the seminar, and the people have actually changed about a bit now. And there's people I feel are more on my level, and I'm more able to talk and say what I feel without feeling too stupid about it. Seminars were quite a big shock after school, but now I've settled down.
>
> (Carole, 1st year, B)

Given the fact that, as many students pointed out, seminar discussions often include long silent pauses, the student who is prepared to talk a lot is at an advantage:

> If you say a lot, and you're quite talkative and outgoing, you'll get quite a lot of attention from other people in the seminar.
>
> (Gary, 1st year, B)

This advantage is increased for male students; arguably male students often make an impression both because of their maleness – and therefore unusualness – and their talkativeness. In this respect, seminars are particularly important because, unlike physics or physical science, English and communications do not examine or grade their students very frequently; whereas physics students are assessed weekly on lab work, and may often have written tests or problem sheets, and thus gain some guide as to how they're doing, in English, a person's performance in a seminar may be the only indication, apart from occasional essays, of that person's ability. As Deem (1978) has suggested, students may be selected for postgraduate research on the basis of their performance in seminars. Students who were shy, who found it difficult to talk in tutorials, often worried that their real ability was under-estimated, that tutors regarded them as less intelligent because they were not very vocal. Conversely the student who is simply a good talker may have an unfair advantage over the quiet but studious worker.

Like the physics students, the response of English students to their courses was mixed: some enthusiastic, some critical. Where they differed, however, was that most of the critical science students ended up with poor degrees – thirds and passes – whereas many of the critical English students came out with upper seconds. This suggests that English departments are more able to accommodate dissent and disagreement.

So far, it seems that the English students had a greater degree of freedom and control over their learning than the physics students. Some felt that coming to university had simply given them plenty of opportunity to read; one student, for example, who had never read much at school said he had turned into a 'literature junkie' since coming to university.

However, not all students were happy with their English courses. Their criticisms centred around the belief that courses were less intellectually stimulating than they had hoped, and that there was not enough room to develop individual interests and pursuits. Given that, as we saw earlier, most English students celebrated individuality of opinion, breadth and range of ideas as the central virtues of English, it is not altogether surprising that criticism of their departments centred around the departments' lack of tolerance, breadth and so on. Yet here we have a certain paradox. Both the English departments were essentially pluralist in that members of staff held differing critical viewpoints; A, for example, had a renowned structuralist critic on its staff, as well as Marxists, Leavisites and feminists. Despite this, students were not trained in a variety of ways of reading a text, but were taught in the liberal humanist tradition of close reading of set books. Students rebelled against this, not by demanding a greater understanding of critical theory, but by a strong assertion of their rights to give *individual* opinions. Individuality was held to be the one freedom above all others; the most commonly expressed belief about English was 'Anyone's opinion is as good as anyone else's; we're all entitled to our different viewpoints'. For example, one third-year woman in B, who regarded herself as a feminist, talked about how a seminar course she'd done which was taught by 'radical' left-wing tutors was different from the rest of the course:

> They did like it much more if you wrote quite personally or quite originally and just weren't afraid to put down your enthusiasm on paper and just wrote how you felt and what your gut reaction to a book was, which is just as valid actually, as much as anybody else's, as much as a critic which you read from sixty years ago (which is always male by the way).
>
> (Alice, 3rd year, B)

Here freedom of expression, the right to show gut emotional responses to literature, is seen as a radical challenge of the status quo. More intellectual, 'objective' approaches are seen as both sterile and reactionary. As another student said:

> This routine of what is good literature, and this is how it all is don't challenge it, this is the way it's got to go, this is what the authorities say is good literature and therefore you study it, because they're the people who've got their finger on the pulse of the world, which is annoying, profoundly annoying, because I'd listen to someone who didn't give a damn about Shakespeare. . . . I think it's perfectly in anybody's rights to say that, if they have an informed opinion. I just hate having things rammed down my throat.
>
> (Robert, 3rd year, B)

He went on:

> They think they've got it all sorted out; this is it, these are the absolute
> truths, you're here to learn and we are the people who are going to teach
> you.
>
> (Robert, 3rd year, B)

The rejection of the idea of absolute truth leads to the idea that everyone's
viewpoint is equally valid – if, of course, they have 'an informed opinion'. (That
qualification is always present, of course; for if everyone's opinion is equally
valid, what is the point of studying English as an academic discipline at all?) For
Anthony, a student at A, the problem would be resolved by allowing students to
pursue their own intellectual interests, rather than following those of the
department. He said that the course should be

> more geared to what the student requires. If I'm interested in psycho-
> analysis or something like that, then I should be able to read more on that
> than on something that doesn't interest me and be able to go to tutors who
> are particularly interested in that field and talk with them rather than
> having the same tutor who's interested in a particular type of criticism.
>
> (Anthony, 1st year, A)

Curiously, considering Anthony's Marxist beliefs, this prescription is very
similar to that of the head of Department B, quoted earlier, who argued that the
department contained a number of specialists in different areas who co-existed
harmoniously.

A common criticism was that English departments were very insular, and
that they had been teaching the same texts for years and years. Students
particularly disliked having to take Old English and Medieval Literature when
they could have been reading novels. As one student wryly put it:

> An English degree has to prove that it's a genuine degree, and the only way
> to do that is to make people suffer.
>
> (Terry, 3rd year, A)

The feeling about the English department at A was summed up by Jennifer:

> It's very trendy, it's very self-conscious, very narrow-minded. I think they
> can only see as far as the English department and there's no world outside
> and I think, particularly English departments are like that. It's very
> enclosed and there are a lot of impossible boffin-type figures.
>
> (Jennifer, 3rd year, A)

Jennifer sees the department is narrow and inward-looking, stifling rather than
stimulating. Her comment, when I asked her if she felt she'd gained anything
from the course, was interesting:

> It's probably made me more analytical. I'm able to sit back and analyse
> things. It also means that I've read virtually every book that any sort of
> faintly intelligent person is meant to have read, I've just read them all. I
> haven't enjoyed many of them, but you know, you just read everything. It's
> probably made me a more observant person, and a more aware person of

what's going on, but it hasn't made me work harder and it hasn't given me self-discipline, which is probably what I came for.

Elsewhere Jennifer said that she was disappointed that the course had been, in a sense, so easy; that there had been no 'mind-blowing theories' which she would 'have to work really hard to understand'. She is demanding the kind of rigour which physics students felt they had too much of; she felt that she'd been allowed to be lazy. She didn't feel any commitment to the degree or what was studied on it; a similar comment were made by a student at B:

> The last thing I want to do and which I've had to do for the past three years is sit down with a book I couldn't care less about and talk about issues I couldn't give a damn about either.
>
> (Robert, 3rd year, B)

In other words, lack of 'relevance' was a key criticism of many students: relevance was, after all, what many of them sought in their degrees. Some felt alienated by what Robert described as 'the fast food machinery process by which you get a degree'; there was no time for genuine contemplation of the 'real' issues. For many students, their degree course had been counter-productive; their real enjoyment in literature had been lost in the process of using books to get a qualification. One of the reasons students gave for wanting to take an English degree was that it would make them more 'broad-minded'; yet several felt that exactly the opposite had happened.

However, there were certain important differences between the students at A and the students at B. As has already been noted, A ran a critical theory course in the first year, while B had no such course. The third-year students interviewed in A were more aware of alternative ways of teaching the subject than the third-year students in B. Much of this is to do with the fact that students in A take a compulsory lecture course in literary theory in the first year, and have the option of taking a seminar course in theory in the second and third years, while the students in B do not take such a course. A student in A, for example, had a good idea of the different critical stances of members of the department:

> [the department is] fairly diverse really, there's no dramatic conflicts, there's very much specialists in various subjects. *X* is a big Leavisite, and I mean, that doesn't go down well with my tutor who thinks Leavis is terrible whereas someone like *Y* of course is very much involved in structuralism, but there's no heavy bias, the tutors are very good, they restrain their own views quite well . . . there may be hidden conflicts in the staff room but we never come across them.
>
> (Ben, 3rd year, A)

Most students in B, however, if I asked them about theory or the critical perspective of the department, looked at me blankly or misunderstood the question. The consequence was that their criticisms of the department were less specific and less articulate than those of students in A.

The attitude of most of the students, however, even those who were critical of their department, is not so very much at odds with the attitude of the departments themselves. Most students subscribed to a kind of democratic liberalism whereby the individual studies literature through a combination of emotional response and detailed analysis of the text. A common complaint, for example (whether it had any basis in fact, I do not know) amongst students was that they were marked down on essays because their view did not coincide with that of the lecturer. Despite the plurality of views amongst the teaching staff, students were taught, and expected to work, within the liberal tradition: thoughtful, affective response to the texts was encouraged. The reason that conflict exists between some students and lecturers is that, within that liberal framework, the staff – or *some* of the staff – have the power; despite the liberalism, a student's opinion can never be as valid as that of the lecturer. Students are free to hold differing opinions from lecturers, but not to the extent that they can challenge the basic premises of what is and is not worth studying or how it should be studied.

Communications students were notably more enthusiastic about their course than the English students were about theirs, although there were several sharp criticisms. Communications was felt to be intellectually demanding – even difficult – in a way that English wasn't. All final-year students, for example, mentioned the 'Ideology' lecture course, some finding it rather too abstract, but most finding it a challenge:

> 'Ideology' is a very complex, involved subject, but I really like it because it's something which really gets you thinking in a way. Sometimes it tends to swamp you, there's no solution to it, you'll never find an answer to 'What is ideology?', but all the debates are going on, although they're very complex, you'll get a lot of satisfaction if you can master some of the stuff. I really quite enjoy that.
>
> (Ken, 3rd year, C)

In many other ways, the case of the communications students is very different from that of the English students. Although communications students were likely to have similar opinions about the merits of their subjects as the English students did about theirs – breadth, personal involvement, 'relevance' and so on, their criticisms were somewhat different. The chief reason for this is that the course concerns itself very deeply with concepts such as 'Ideology' and the political nature of knowledge; students are taught, from the first, to challenge received notions of (for example) the purpose of the media, and to question taken-for-granted assumptions about class and gender. This is not to say that all students have a highly developed awareness of these issues, but at least there is an attempt to get students to think for themselves. This does, however, lead to many contradictions and ambivalences in the course. One student who had described himself as 'left of centre' felt uncomfortable about what he perceived as the extreme left-wing nature of some of the teaching:

> Sometimes you feel obliged to agree. I don't know whether it's because of power relationships, you know, they are more knowledgeable than we are,

sort of thing, because they're older, even though they try and treat us as equals to a large extent, there's still these sort of power relations implicit within the relation. And you think, I can't say what I really think, because I'm just going to get jumped on – not just by the lecturers but by other people on the course . . . I don't think – because the establishment, the convention, is towards a right-wing sort of viewpoint pretty well, this course tries to outline the inadequacies of that particular regime, and I think by its very nature, by trying to do that, obviously it's going to be dissenting from that convention, from that conventional view. So I think that's why you tend to get the left side really, the dissenting view because the left view is the dissenting view in British and American politics.

(Charles, 3rd year, C)

The point is that on this course, the dissenting view has become the established view, and to dissent from that is just as difficult as it is to dissent from the usual establishment viewpoint. Yet the course itself lends tools to the students with which to criticize its own paradigm; the student quoted above, for example, uses the phrase 'power relations', a phrase which is really borrowed from the Marxist discourse of the communications lecturers. So whereas the English students were sometimes rendered inarticulate in their attempts to criticize their departments, the communications students were provided with a language of criticism by the course itself. None the less some students were uneasy about the course, and tried to distance themselves from it politically:

Politically it's a bit lefty, but I shouldn't say that, I'll get into trouble! . . . there's a lot of Marxism in it . . . I've got to detach myself from it, thinking I've got to learn this, you know, Marxism, it's a subject we're learning rather than – because people don't ram it down our throats, it's just that most of the theories are Marxist theories.

(Helen, 3rd year, C)

Some of the students explained to me that there was a rift amongst the course lecturers which led to opposing viewpoints being presented. Unlike the English courses, which tolerated a multiplicity of opinions, there were two main factions, it seemed, on the communications course. On the one hand, there were lecturers of the 'old school', who held a fairly straightforward belief in the relationship between base and superstructure, who believed that the media were obviously biased in favour of the ruling class and were in fact ideological weapons used by the ruling class to deceive the working-class. The other faction, however, using the ideas of post-structuralism, believed that to view the media solely in terms of bias was simplistic and that, as one student put it, 'you can't analyse a text, you can only analyse a reading of a text'. According to this viewpoint, one can neither assume that the media are simply and eternally biased in favour of the ruling-class ideology, and neither can one assume that audiences are blank slates, easily duped by what they see on television or read in the newspaper. The small number of students who had noticed this division (or who mentioned it) favoured the latter viewpoint; as one student put it:

> He [one of the lecturers] was telling us, and I think he's still telling the first years, things which are patently now not true, theories that have been chucked out of the window . . . it's not his teaching it that is bad; he's teaching it as gospel which is bad.
>
> (Mark, 3rd year, C)

The language again is interesting; neither is able to use language which suggests the absolute correctness of one view over another; but both imply that the logic of the orthodox Marxist view is old-fashioned or out of date or immature ('theories that have been chucked out of the window', 'now not true', 'teaching it as gospel'). There is, therefore, in communications, as in English, an uneasy tension between the idea that the opinion of each individual is equally valid, and the idea that, in order to progress, some versions of the truth have to be shown to be more valid than others. This is made more complicated in this case by the fact that the version of the truth subscribed to by these two students was that there is no one truth ('you can't analyse a text, you can only analyse a reading of a text'). The students resent the fact that any theory can, in fact, be taught as 'the truth'. This dilemma – the absoluteness or relativity of truth – is nothing new in literary theory; in fact, it has plagued debates in the arts and the social sciences since their inception, but it is a debate which, until recently, had not affected 'science' – and for most science students, as we have already seen, it is still not a relevant debate.

Arts students' perceptions of science

Most of the arts students were strongly aware of the hostility towards the arts felt both by society in general and other students in particular. Very many of them were defensive about their subject, and several of them mentioned having arguments with other students (usually engineers) about the value of studying English or communications:

> As soon as you tell somebody that you're doing an arts degree the first thing they think is you're a dosser, just not doing anything, just lazy, wasting your time. I just don't understand it because it's not like that at all.
>
> (Kevin, 1st year, B)

> When I came here I was quite surprised at the amount of rivalry there was between different students. One night we were in our common room, and a couple of third-year engineering students came in and they said, 'You're just wasting time, you know, doing a Mickey Mouse degree, you might just as well be doing drama and theatre studies or something, film studies, something like that, what job can you get at the end of it?'
>
> (Gary, 1st year, B)

The two criticisms arts students said they received from scientists were that arts degrees didn't involve much work, and that arts degrees weren't useful. The response of the arts students to the former charge is that arts degrees demand a lot of work; not timetabled work, it is true, but independent work in one's own 'free' time – reading, using the library, writing essays. As one English student commented:

> In science subjects you get lectures and you get told everything and taught just about everything, and it's just a question of learning it. I know everyone says English is a dossy subject, and you just get one seminar a week and one tutorial a week, but the science people get spoon-fed much more than we do.
>
> (Kate, 1st year, A)

Science students, of course, said that physics involved understanding, whereas the arts involved 'learning'; but it is undoubtedly the case that much of the timetabled science work was 'passive' – sitting in lectures taking notes, carrying out pre-set experiments in the lab.

Students answered the criticisms about English's 'uselessness' partly by arguing that getting a job was not their principal reason for doing the subject, and partly by arguing that, as Gary, a first-year student at B, put it, any degree should demonstrate 'a capacity to absorb things, a capacity to learn, a capacity to just analyse; it shows you have some sort of mental capability'.

The English and communications students did not spend all their time on the defensive, however. Many felt antipathetic towards science and scientists; indeed, the very mention of 'science' produced a surprising number of invectives against scientists, as we shall see shortly. The arts students' criticisms were the ones we might expect, given their earlier comments. Science was, first, regarded as too certain, too definite:

> With science, it's so final, absolute, empirical, positivistic, there's a right answer and there are an infinite number of wrong answers, but with the arts and economics to a certain extent, there's right or wrong answer really, it's what you feel, what you think and you can put forward a view of your own which may or may not agree with the general consensus, but which is just as valid.
>
> (Charles, 3rd year, C)

This certainty is hampering, leaving no scope for original thought or individuality:

> They're all working at something that's already been proved, so they're just experimenting on something that's been proved and is a theory whereas on arts courses you make up your own answers and your own theories – there *are* theories that have been made, but they're debatable . . . it seems pretty pointless to me.
>
> (Rebecca, 1st year, C)

Many arts students wanted the freedom to think out ideas for themselves, to have control over their learning, rather than to learn a predefined set of ideas. The consequence of having to think for themselves, according to some of the students, was that arts students were much more broad-minded than the scientists:

I prefer the liberal environment of arts subjects because the sort of people who come to do arts subjects are usually the sort of people who do have broad minds, rather than – the worst thing I've noticed here is people in my kitchen just talking numbers and calculations and theorems and equations, it just drives me up the wall.

(Robert, 3rd year, B)

I think English, arts degrees in general, demand a bit more original thought than a science degree – though I'm so biased it isn't true – though I do tend to think that artists at university are more open to ideas and tend to be better company.

(Jennifer, 3rd year, A)

By 'broad-minded' and 'original', the arts students tended to mean, 'more interested in people', and the most common criticism of science was that it was about things, not people, and was thus remote from reality. Science was perceived by many of the students as inhuman and irrelevant to 'real life'. Scientists, therefore, were commonly seen as anti-social. A number of respondents regarded science students as boring and unfriendly:

I think arts students tend to be a lot more amiable than a lot of the science students. You can spot a science student a mile off round here, they're horrible people.

(Simon, 1st year, A)

I do think that there is a different temperament between arts and science students, I'm pretty sure of it. And these terrible stereotypes: we're supposed to be terribly arty, and then you get engineering students who are a classic stereotype – weird and introverted and strange, and they do exist, just as much as the arty English student exists. Stereotypes are perhaps wrong, but there's always a precedent for them.

(Daniel, 3rd year, B)

Another student recalled his first day at the polytechnic:

We came up to the union the first night and everyone around us was engineers; you could tell, it was that kind of leather jackets, Motorhead albums, greasy hair, and they were all talking about sprockets and engines, really really boring, and I thought, 'Oh no, they're all going to be like this!' but all the communications people were really different – they stuck out because they talked about more interesting things.

(Harry, 1st year, C)

For the arts students, however, it was not simply a question of scientists being interested in different things or being introverted. There was a strong feeling that science students were conformist (because they were not encouraged to think for themselves) and immature, as the following diatribe indicates:

There is a running joke that the typical science student, the typical engineering student, is wearing one of those duffle coats with hoods that look like a snorkel, an Adidas bag, flared trousers, long hair ('cos he's nine times out of ten a bloke), long hair, slightly greasy, glasses and a few spots, and nine times out of ten that's what the stereotype is like because they are those sort of people who are interested in science and don't take good care of their appearance or, boys, being away from Mummy for the first time, don't know they should wash their hair twice a week; they all eat beans on toast or go to the cafeteria – the cafeteria's full of people at breakfast times who are science students because they don't know how to cook their own breakfast.

(Susan, 3rd year, B)

Susan's image of scientists excludes women; indeed, none of the arts students talked about female scientists – neither about their impressions of them nor about friendships with them. Ben, a third-year student at A, during a discussion about staff–student relationships, mentioned a male friend who did mining engineering, and the comment he made indicates the masculinity of the world inhabited by the students:

there's about twenty in his year and I mean, they scream obscenities at their lecturers and throw things at them, and if I did that with mine – well, I wouldn't dream of doing that, you know, they're very much the teacher figure.

One of Dale's (1969) arguments in favour of co-educational schools was the civilizing influence girls would have on boys; one wonders whether the same argument might not be equally valid in higher education.

It will by now have been noted that, for many arts students, the word 'science' always conjured up images of engineers, who were the focus of much of the hostile feeling towards science. Engineers were held to be the model of instrumental, narrow-minded and conformist thinking; arts students never mentioned physicists or chemists when asked about their views on science. This distinction between engineers and other scientists may have some grounding in reality when it is remembered that the physical science and materials students (whose discipline was applied rather than pure science) were more instrumental in their attitudes towards education than the physicists.

Those arts students who saw scientists as conformist, immature and anti-social believed this to be a direct result of science itself; because the teaching of science involved so little questioning and debate its students were unable to develop normal communication skills. They saw scientists as shut up in a world which was remote from everyday concerns; one criticism was that scientists lacked a sense of the aesthetic:

Science is basically an aesthetically-lacking subject. The people who do it have got no appreciation of aesthetic principles. People who have done it have got very little interest outside the field.

(Harry, 1st year, C)

It's just dead . . . there's no soul to it.

(Jack, 1st year, B)

However, the final indictment of science, amongst the arts students, is that it is 'amoral'. We have already seen that many arts students talked about English as a 'moral' subject, one which raises serious issues. For them, science is incomplete because it ignores those issues. One communications student, for example, complained about the science students amongst his friends:

> I mix a lot with the computer crowd and a lot of engineers – I don't know whether it's mere prejudice on my part, but they seem to be so insensitive, politically and morally.

> (Mark, 3rd year, C)

When asked whether this insensitivity was a direct result of studying science, he said:

> I'm sure of it. I'm absolutely sure of it. There's no reason why they should all be sexist racist fascist bigots. They're not – but it seems like that sometimes.

His explanation for the attitudes of the scientists again stressed the conformist nature of the disciplines:

> All their lecturers wear suits, and they all work solidly all day and very little in the night. It's like the work thing, the work ethic is ingrained into them, and when they come out it's pure relief.

It is curious that the issue of whether lecturers do or do not wear suits appears to have so much significance. Dress is a potent symbol amongst arts and science students of the differences between them, representing formality, hierarchy and conformism on one side of the divide, and informality, freedom and individuality on the other.

Not all criticism was directed against scientists, however; some more thoughtful criticisms were made of the nature of science itself. George, an English student, gives an account of the moral failings of science:

> I don't find that sort of definite theory all that interesting, and there are areas of physics which I just cannot make sense of. I don't particularly see the point of Newton's Third Law and when I was doing maths, I discovered the point of Newton's Third Law; it was to solve problems that had no solution any other way. . . . There are various aspects of most of these sciences which don't seem to make any sense to me and the point of actually studying them doesn't make a great deal of sense to me. Because I think in the end that science, when carried through to its extreme limits, doesn't do a great deal of good in the world, and though there are areas in which it does do good, in farming and medicine, I would point out that a lot of money in science goes into warfare and things which aren't quite so useful, and I think scientists, in the study of science, lose sight of the more important things in life which to my mind are the aesthetic things, moral values if you like, and for those reasons that's why I stay clear of it in the end.

> (George, 3rd year, A)

This quote, like some of the others, seems to indicate an insuperable divide between arts students and science students. Their whole ways of thinking about life, about what is important and what is trivial, about what constitutes knowledge, seem to be completely at odds. Yet there were students who didn't experience a divide, who seemed tolerant of differences, or didn't see the differences as being very great; one student with A level mathematics, for example, loved the linguistic element of her English course because of its 'logicality'.

There were, however, some students who took a more philosophical interest in science. Terry, for example, a third-year student at A, was particularly interested in the debate about the truthfulness of knowledge, and made the following criticism of science:

> I think what science does is, it pretends that it's right, it pretends that it's logical, that to be logical is correct, that it's *proven*, you know, 'we've used a model to prove it', but the model is only based on a preconception, which is based on previous ones. There's no truth in it; I think science is as truthful as religion, in absolute terms.

For this reason, he saw the division between arts and science as based on a false premise, the greater truthfulness of science; as he put it,

> both [arts and science] are equally valid; they're both equally nonsensical and both equally true. Literature tells you truth which science can't, and vice versa.

In these criticisms of science, Terry is pointing to the similarities between arts and sciences, rather than the differences; both are ways of looking at the world and interpreting it. Another student, Russell, saw parallels between arts and science, particularly in what he saw as the aestheticism of science; discussing some work he'd read on Einstein, he said:

> he [Einstein] says there's no place in the world for ugly maths; maths is to be beautiful, simplistic, harmony, beauty; you could have the Theory of Relativity in another form and it would be mathematically ugly, there would be too many statements of proof whereas you could only have one; the point of maths is to get things down to as simplistic a level as possible, and in that idea and that methodology there is an aesthetic and once you see that, then that changes a lot of things to do with how we see knowledge.
>
> (Russell, 3rd year, C)

That this kind of reflection on the philosophy of science should be undertaken by arts students, often ignorant of basic scientific principles, rather than by science students, is ironic. Yet another student, John, a final-year student at A, was also interested in the ideas about artistic and scientific knowledge. Like Terry, he saw the arts and science as basically similar, divided only by false social assumptions about their roles. John had himself attended a boys' public school, and was very aware of the subject choice restrictions imposed on pupils; one pupil at his own school, for example, had studied biology, maths and English A levels, and had had to go to the girls' school to study the English because the school couldn't accommodate the unusual subject grouping. Like several other students, he noted that this division was also common at university:

> It's rife . . . this ridiculous notion of science students denigrating arts students. I know people who say English students never do any work and so are doing a jokey degree, a Mickey Mouse degree or something like this; it's all nonsense really, a ludicrous division. And the notion that science students are useful and arts students aren't, it's prejudice that has built up.

John himself admitted to possessing an inadequate grasp of science, but was undertaking a linguistics project on Einstein's use of language in the Theory of Relativity. This is how he explained it:

> The reason for reading the Einstein is to look at the concepts he comes up with in terms of space and time and see how this bears on traditional thinking of what is reality – like he breaks down the notion of never-ending space and defines this in terms of a metaphorical presentation of a person being in a train, this sort of thing; so I mean I'm studying it for how he redefines things using these metaphors.

This project is a clear attempt to break down the usual barriers that exist between arts and sciences and to look at science aesthetically, using methods usually applied to literature. John, however, regards the barriers as social, rather than real:

> I see it all as different forms of knowledge, and to present life in terms of fiction and to try to discuss what's going on in the atom, are all different forms of exploration and expansion, there are overlaps in all of them.

This insight into the affinities between arts and science is, however, more accessible to English students than it is to physics students. Although physics is traditionally seen as a more liberal, more 'arty' science than, for example, engineering, many of the physics students, as we have seen, saw physics as a subject which was about logic, consistency, the one road to the Truth; a subject which imposes one idea about knowledge, rather than admitting several different ideas. The English students (although, as we shall see in the next section, they complained about the authoritarianism of their departments) had far more freedom to think what they wanted than the science students. If knowledge is to be about 'exploration' and 'expansion', then any dogmatism about the precise nature of knowledge has surely to be removed. In moving away from dogmatism, John was atypical; yet there were other students who were thoughtful and articulate about their subject and the boundaries between it and other disciplines. There were more students, however, particularly in physics, who had ideas but found them difficult to articulate – perhaps because they were in the process of breaking away from a predefined idea. There were also many more, of course, who were willing to accept the traditional ideas about their discipline and its aims.

Conclusion

In this chapter, we have seen how the arts students' view of their discipline contrasted with the scientists' view of the arts. It is true that both groups saw the arts as uncertain, but for the arts students this was something to be celebrated, not denigrated. They relished the fact that their subject was neither certain nor immediately applicable; they enjoyed the scope it allowed them for individual thought and feeling, and disliked the idea of having to learn a truth pre-determined and discovered by others. When they criticized the courses they were studying, it was because they felt their departments were imposing certain views on them about the nature of literature and how it should be studied.

Unlike the majority of science students, who hungered after 'definite' and 'certain' knowledge, which could give them some control over the physical environment and over their own lives, the arts students saw higher education as an opportunity to become familiar with a range of different ideas and beliefs. They were highly pluralistic; few were dogmatic. Some regarded the teaching and practice of science as alien to the values they themselves held; they perceived it as a discipline which wrongly attempted to pose a single view of the world on others without regard for alternative opinions, ideas and practices, or the moral consequences of that view.

Few of the English students, however, were aware of current debates in the discipline, and were therefore ignorant of the multitude of ways of looking at texts. Their own attitude to the discipline emphasized 'freedom of opinion' and their criticisms of courses centred around the lack of such a freedom. Their idea of freedom was, however, narrow in that most of them simply wanted to exercise a greater amount of choice within the liberal humanist framework. Com-munications students were rather more sophisticated in that they had access to ideas not available to English students, and were able to criticize those ideas. None the less, many of them felt that there was not enough room for disagreement, and were unhappy about the 'bias' of the course.

However, the arts departments were able to accommodate dissent in a way that the science departments were unable to. Students were free, to some extent, to disagree with the views of their lecturers, and students were tested and graded much less frequently than on the science courses. The final degree classifications of the arts students fell broadly into upper seconds and lower seconds, so that students rarely 'failed' or 'succeeded' as spectacularly as the science students.

In these two chapters, then, we have demonstrated that there are two cultures – at least two cultures – in the disciplines of physics, physical science, English and communications. The differences between these subjects are not simply differences of what is studied, or how it is studied; they are differences of world-view: the students and practitioners of these disciplines really do look at the world in a different way. What an English student thinks is important in life is quite at odds with what a physical science student considers important.

Understanding these differences is crucial if we are able to say anything about the significance of gender in education. The majority of physics and physical science students are male, the majority of English and communications students female. Not only that; the experience of being a male or female student on a course dominated by one or the other sex is affected by the culture of the subject studied. Put another way, we can say that the 'culture' of which we speak may have distinctively masculine or feminine qualities, and that these qualities may reinforce or contradict a student's sense of his or her own 'masculinity' and 'femininity'. This is the possibility that we shall explore in the next two chapters.

6

Gender Identity and Science Students

Introduction

We have already argued that gender identity is neither infinitely malleable nor biologically determined, but something which develops and changes in response to circumstances. Gender is a social construct, but it is also an inextricable part of an individual's sense of identity. Segal (1987) has talked of 'the over-riding significance we each attach to our sense of gender identity'; this chapter will look at the ways in which this identity is constructed and reconstructed for students through the experience of studying physics and physical science.

Chapters 4 and 5 examined the construction of the arts and the sciences in higher education. It was found that science, and physics in particular, was constructed as hard, certain, concrete; the arts as uncertain, broad, adaptable. It was suggested that these constructions are closely related to our constructions of masculinity and femininity. The issue, then, is whether there is confusion and tension for women and men in constructing their identity through a discipline which has been socially defined as 'masculine' or 'feminine'. Chapter 2 noted Hacker's (1977) argument that women are treated as a 'minority group', and it was suggested that, as women in physics were numerically a minority, it would be possible to examine whether or not they were also a 'minority group'. One aim of this chapter will be to examine whether the female science students have a sense of themselves as a minority group, and whether this affects their sense of gender identity.

Chapters 4 and 5 provided some evidence in support of Weinrich-Haste's (1984) findings that subject conformity is stronger than gender conformity. This chapter, along with Chapter 7, will examine the proposition in more detail.

This chapter falls into three main sections: the first section looks at how physics staff view gender; the second looks at the relationship between male students' sense of identity and their subject; and the third looks at female students' attitudes towards their subject. It will be argued that the issue of gender and subject is, for the female students, a problematic one; for that reason, the third section is rather longer than the second section.

The problem of women

All six lecturers interviewed were agreed that the absence of women in physics was a problem. One of the lecturers, the admissions tutor in Department A, said that attempts were made (through, for example, inviting most female candidates for interview) to get more women in the department. Department B was also apparently keen to get more women in:

> Well, we've tried very very hard to get extra students. We managed to get one lady into our electronics course last year. . . . I think the problems must be in schools. We just don't get the applicants. . . . We must have about five or six altogether in a class of seventy. I can't remember when we exceeded 10 per cent. . . . Half our female graduates go into teaching, but less than 10 per cent of the men.
>
> (Dr L, Department B)

This attitude is unpromising: the problem is seen to lie wholly with the schools. A lecturer in Department C also essayed a fairly conventional explanation:

> One question I often ask people on the course when they come just to see round, is do you do anything yourselves, thinking back to my own time when I used to play with meccano and that. I get the usual answers about motorbikes and that sort of thing, which is fair enough, because we quite often find people in the lab whose fingers are all thumbs and I'm sure that's because they're not used to doing delicate things with their hands. Now I always think that the equivalent for the ladies who come is in fact whether they do sewing or that sort of thing, which is just as delicate on the fingers, just as precise on the fingers as playing with little nuts and bolts. Now whether in that is the answer, that they're not used to mechanical things even though their dexterity is good, I don't know. It could be that we're going back years and years in their life to how they're conditioned when they're young. . . . when they don't have meccano and mechanical toys like that.
>
> (Dr H, Department C)

Obviously it is true that boys generally have more experience of playing with mechanical toys than girls, and that must have some influence on their development of scientific skills, and practical laboratory skills in particular. Dr H's explanation is only unusual in its combination of perception – that a skill like sewing is of equal utility to a scientist as mending motorbikes – and datedness – that men mend motorbikes and 'ladies' sew.

Dr G of Department A had given some thought to the processes involved in women opting out of science. From the experience of his two daughters at a local comprehensive school, he was first able to argue that 'it's a multi-stage filtering process . . . some of the teachers tending to push them [the girls] away from technical subjects'.

The second problem is that of peer-group pressure:

There's a strong social pressure on girls not to take scientific subjects. And the boys will tell the girls, 'You can't be any good at physics', and so, if they are any good, they come home extremely jubilant, saying 'I showed them up'. And so, I think that happens already at O level and then again at A level, and it's not an absolutely forbidding pressure, it's just that at each stage you have a fraction of the girls who might have carried on into a scientific career.

(Dr G, Department A)

This view tends to support the research of people like Whyte (1986), who have argued that boys intimidate girls in the classroom, particularly in science lessons. Girls have to prove, not that they are capable, but that they are as good as boys. Dr G's daughters are able to compete and assert their equality or superiority (when a girl does well in physics, it is therefore much more loaded with significance than when a boy does well); but it is, no doubt, more difficult for those girls whose fathers are not university physics lecturers. Note also that Dr G has suggested that there is a 'filtering process' which takes place *at each stage* of the education system: O level, A level, degree and Ph.D. He goes on to identify a further barrier:

I think there may be also apart from, shall we say, society's pressure, an image has got something to do with it, that the jobs that physicists go into, an awful lot of them are defence-orientated, in various ways, and there may be a feeling that therefore it has that male, slightly violent image, at least in the terms of the jobs he can do, but whether that's true or not I don't know. . . . So I think there's all sorts of pressures which are all having their effects, and there's very little we can do about it. I think we're all sexist here among the staff, in the sense we want more girls.

(Dr G, Department A)

Physics, then, has an image of being 'male' and 'violent', which deters women from entering it. Dr G also felt that the introduction of co-education had had an adverse effect on the numbers of girls doing science; a very high proportion of the female students were from single-sex schools.

Up to this point, Dr G has explained the lack of women in physics mainly by reference to schools; schools discourage girls from taking scientific subjects; boys make fun of girls' supposed lack of ability to do science. Obviously, however, these will not suffice as attempts to explain the lack of women continuing with physics *after* degree level. After all, Dr G noted that:

My impression is that the girls are all looking at teaching and biophysics, and the boys much more into other areas. I suppose that's either their or society's view of what women are good at.

(Dr G, Department A)

When I commented that few of the women seemed to go into research, he agreed, noting that 'we've got just one girl research student in the department at the moment' and that this was partly due to the fact that if you look at the distribution of the girls over the class list, there is a tendency for quite a fair fraction of them to be fairly much straggling with the course.

Thus we have moved from an explanation which lays the blame on the immediate environment (i.e. schools and fellow pupils) to one which notes that women don't achieve as highly as men at degree level. However, there must also be an explanation of why women don't do as well:

It may be that there is a real difference between the minds of males and females, but men do tend to prefer abstractions more. Maybe so, I don't know. It does seem to happen at least, in what we see in how they achieve at the moment; the blokes manage to cope better with the abstractions and actually are attracted to it, but whether that really is an intrinsic difference or not, I wouldn't know.

(Dr G, Department A)

The difficulty faced by Dr G in trying to find an explanation is that, while understanding the *social* problems facing girls in schools, an admission that those problems continue at university would appear to be an acceptance of a cricitism of the department. Therefore while recognizing that women face obstacles at every stage, it is far less easy to explain why women drop out at the hurdle of higher education than it is to explain why they drop out at the schools level. Dr G's tentative suggestion that there may be an intrinsic difference between the minds of males and females is a way of avoiding the issue of women's experience of physics at university.

What none of the lecturers appears to have considered is how the *experience* of studying physics might be different for women and men. The next two sections examine that experience.

Male science students

We saw in Chapter 4 that physics was perceived by students as distinctly different from other disciplines – not only the arts but also certain science subjects. Physics was constructed as certain, fundamental, useful and progressive. It was argued that this construction of physics was achieved through emphasizing its difference from other subjects.

Self-identity is also shaped through emphasizing difference. Male physicists construct their identity as physicists, both by contrasting the work of scientists with that of arts students, and by pointing to the differences between physicists and other scientists: mathematicians and engineers. They see doing a physics degree as a process by which they learn to be a particular sort of person. For example, the arts, as we noted in Chapter 5, were seen as 'airy-fairy', soft, intangible: the kind of person who did physics was hard-working, a realist. One student said of his physics exams:

I think exams is where you learn everything. You might do nothing in the rest of the year, but in that period you get so pressurised, that that's when you really grow up, and that doesn't happen so much with arts students.

> (Edward, 3rd year, A)

Physicists are also tougher, more in touch with reality:

> Sciences are more use in everyday life . . . you can tell if someone's making up something if you've got a reasonable basic understanding of physics and maths. You don't necessarily get fooled.
>
> (Ronald, 1st year, A)

The male physicists also made distinctions between physics and maths, and physics and engineering, and, within physics, between applied physics and theoretical physics. They said things like 'maths is too theoretical for me' or, as one student said of the differences between physics and engineering:

> There's a lot less learning work in it, there's a lot more variety in the subject, the scope in physics is vast; also engineering involves a lot of work which would cut down your social life a lot.
>
> (Patrick, 1st year, A)

The male students often made distinctions between physics and maths on the one hand:

> Physics is the most fundamental science and maths – we have trouble with maths – whatever maths is, wherever maths fits in, because maths is totally divorced from reality and physics ties it down.
>
> (Colin, 3rd year, A)

and physics and engineering on the other:

> I'm not an engineer because I'm not practical but I like the way physicists think, I suppose. I like the theory bit of it, but I'm not a theoretical physicist, I'm an applied physicist and I like physics because I like playing with maths as well as doing lab work. If I was doing an applied degree I wouldn't get that.
>
> (Edward, 3rd year, A)

These distinctions reveal a process amongst students of interpreting their attitudes and abilities in a way which allows them to build up a self-image of 'physicist' and hence an image of themselves pursuing a certain career. The distinction was carried further: some students, like Edward, saw themselves as 'theoretical physicists' or 'applied physicists'. This distinction was directly related to the kinds of futures students saw for themselves:

> I believe this university's theory-biased. I think that places considered the best physics departments tend to be theoretical, and so this has been quite a well-established physics department, tending to be more theoretical; and so you can go for an interview for a job, and your head will be filled with quantum mechanics and you'll be no good for them to employ you.
>
> (Edward, 3rd year, A)

However, Edward's position, that the content of the course should be more applied and hence, more directly related to the kind of job he wants to do, is not accepted by all students. Alan, for example, wanted to work for British Aerospace in a job where

> You are actually doing what they call the fundamental research; rather than just developing a problem, you actually develop it from the very basics.
>
> (Alan, 3rd year, A)

Alan disliked the applied work on the course. Or as Colin put it

> I wasn't too keen on the more lab-orientated things because I like something where I can sit down and like maths, if you turn the handle you can get the answer, get the right one, but you can set up an experiment perfectly and it still wouldn't work.
>
> (Colin, 3rd year, A)

We can see this building up of identity in Paul, a final-year student at B. He was one of only two final-year students undertaking a theoretical project; he said that he was disenchanted with lab work. However, he also disliked pure maths:

> I argue with pure mathematicians that it's a waste of time unless there's some application because what I'm interested in really is just understanding things, I think, and with maths you don't as much understand it as derive from what you've assumed to start with, you have to make some assumption and this is consistent with it, this is mathematically correct, whereas with physics, you have to see what's going on and work the other way, get the assumptions if you like, go as deep as you can and find out what you have to assume, to get results. That's the difference, I think. That's why I'm interested in physics more, it's more applied than maths.
>
> (Paul, 3rd year, B)

Physics was central to Paul's life, and for him, the extrinsic value (doing physics as a means to an end) and the intrinsic value (doing it as an end in itself) merged:

> I'm lucky in that I've been here doing what I want to do. You find that most people who are doing a degree, it doesn't really matter that it's physics, it just so happens that physics has a good value on the job market; but that means that I've enjoyed it.
>
> (Paul, 3rd year, B)

He intended, after his degree, to do an M.Sc. in theoretical physics, before doing a Ph.D. He then wanted to work in industry. For Paul, doing a job simply meant continuing with what he enjoyed doing already; he wanted to work

> somewhere like BP where they've got a big project going and you can work on theoretical aspects.

In ten years' time, he hoped he would still be a research scientist in industry, 'involved with the problems myself', not 'organizing other people to solve problems'. Paul has a very clear sense of identity: he already sees himself as a 'physicist'; he makes no distinction between what he is now and what he will become. The same is true of most of the other male physics students, most of whom had a clear image of themselves as physicists. Their attitudes towards physics tended to be instrumental: not so much that they were doing a physics degree only because they wanted a job out of it as because they did not distinguish between being a student physicist and a qualified, working physicist. Physics dominated their lives; as one first-year student put it, 'Physics is *the* subject for me at the moment'. Thus the intellectual content of the degree was not differentiated from the use to which they intended to put their degree; when students talked about their future careers, for example, it was often in terms of continuing with the aspect of physics they'd enjoyed most:

> I would like to stay in physics, this area; I don't particualrly fancy doing industrial research or anything like that. I'd prefer to do pure physics, but that's difficult, it depends on how good I am at it. I don't know yet.
>
> (Tim, 1st year, B)

They embarked on the courses with a clear idea of what they wanted to do, and why they wanted to do it; they often left with a future career mapped out. They tended to measure other academic disciplines only in terms of their extrinsic, rather than their intrinsic, value. When students were asked about whether the sciences were more worthwhile than the arts, the answer was often couched in terms such as the following:

> Yes. I think there's more chance of getting a job in physics, or a physics-related subject, because there's a shortage of scientists and technologists at the moment.
>
> (Adrian, 1st year, A)

Adrian was a student who exuded self-confidence; he had a clear idea of what he wanted and how he was going to get it. His interest in physics was inspired by the film *Star Wars*; in ten years' time, he said, he wanted 'a big house, a big car, lots of money'. He had come to A through a process of careful planning; first he had eliminated from his list all those universities which had more arts students than science students. Then he had gone through the physics courses of the remaining university prospectuses ticking off the elements that most appealed to him; the course with most elements he put top of the UCCA form, the next course he put second and so on. (This had backfired slightly; A was fourth on the lists, but at the interviews for his first three choices, he decided they were 'dumps' and accepted A's offer.) Ronald, another student on the same course, had also planned his future carefully; he wanted to move into engineering after graduating and said that he intended to choose his final-year specialisms according to the demand on the job market at the time.

Although the male physics students had developed a clear identity of themselves as 'physicists', the physical science students did not make such fine distinctions between their own discipline and others. Partly this is because physical science was a second choice for many students and partly it is because it is less clearly defined as a discipline in its own right. Physical science was seen entirely as a means to an end: not an end in itself, like English, nor even part of an end, like physics. Physical science was consistently seen as more practical, more applied, more useful in helping students to get a job; a strong separation was made between doing the course and having a scientific career. Part of the reason for this is that the course is so broad-based, students have little sense of themselves as 'physical scientists' in the way that physics students regarded themselves as 'physicists'. Physical science students tended to prefer those aspects of the course which they found directly useful – such as computing – and were intolerant of coursework which was not directly related to scientific skills; one student, for example, talked about the 'risk evaluation' part of the energy studies module:

> [It was about] how do you evaluate somebody's life in terms of how much money you spend on safety and so on, which I thought was thoroughly boring and not very relevant . . . we could have spent the afternoon doing proper work.

> (Matthew, 4th year, C)

The same emphasis on extrinsic value was true of students' assessment of their industrial training. Generally they evaluated its worth according to how useful they felt it would be for their future career.

Many male science students had interests outside physics; in the main these were sports such as rugby or athletics, although some – about four – expressed an interest in painting. None mentioned an enjoyment of literature or theatre; few, surprisingly, mentioned music. Some clearly carried science into their outside lives, through an interest in computers, for example. Generally the outside interests – sport, for example – were not regarded as conflicting with the demands of the course. However, those who enjoyed art and painting did regret that they had no time to pursue that interest while they were doing their degree. Doing a physics degree was seen as a full-time occupation; Alan, a third-year student at A, regretted the fact that he had so little time to keep up with current affairs.

For these men, the physicists and the physical scientists, self-image was concerned with the particular nature of one's abilities and the sort of job one could do with them; it was rarely concerned with one's identity as a *man*, as opposed to a *scientist*: the two were one and the same thing. There was, as we might expect, no conflict between the two. One can see this deeply ingrained idea of 'male as norm' carried over into language, in this quote from a student talking about his old further education college (which he had attended after leaving his boys' grammar school):

> It [the college] is dropping now because they had a woman headmaster come in and she's – not being sexist or anything – she just wasn't very good. The standard went, and of course with comprehensives coming through –

not that I'm against comprehensives – but with grammar schools, you had the cream basically, that kept the rate up, they're not quite the same now.

(Adrian, 1st year, A)

It is the curiousness of the term 'woman headmaster' rather than 'headmistress' or even 'woman headteacher' which is striking, and which belies his assertion that the headteacher's sex didn't matter. The unconscious slip is probably more revealing than any number of conscious qualifiers about 'not being sexist'.

Not unnaturally, most of the physics students wanted careers that needed a physics qualification – scientific research jobs in industry, for example. Four of the eight men intended to do Ph.Ds after finishing; all four of those men said that they hoped for a career in industry either after completing their Ph.Ds or instead of Ph.Ds if they failed to get a good enough degree. One (Paul, already mentioned) intended to do a Master's degree in theoretical physics, and then do a Ph.D, and after that take up a research job in industry. Two wanted simply to go into scientific research posts in industry; only one man intended to do a job not directly related to physics – Mark, the student who wanted to be a nurse. For some students, doing a Ph.D was simply part of the natural progression in being a physicist:

I've not made up my mind what I want to do with regards to a job. And I've quite enjoyed this year, I've really enjoyed the lab work and I'd like to carry on.

(William, 3rd year, B)

Many students had a remarkably clear vision of their long-term futures, and these tended to be highly materialistic.

I'm assuming that I'll get a Ph.D . . . and then I'll probably want to make some money so I'm going to go to the USA for five years, so perhaps nine years, ten years [from now], probably married with two kids, living in London, working for somebody like Plessey.

(Edward, 3rd year, A)

What I'd like would be a job in the States with a big company, and the proverbial nice house and home to go with it. Certainly something scientific. I can't see myself going into something like R and D – certainly something that uses the physics.

(Ronald, 1st year, A)

I've not really thought what I'll be doing in ten years time. I presume I'll have entered the rat-race like everyone else and worked me way up the ladder.

(Patrick, 1st year, A)

Even allowing for the cynicism in the last quote, the physics students had very conventional and materialistic ambitions; almost all the first-year students, for example, wanted to obtain jobs in industry. One, Rashid, was slightly unusual in that he wanted to become a teacher; however his attitude towards the job was highly instrumental. When asked why he was doing a degree in physics, he said:

So I can get a job. You can't become a teacher unless you've got a degree.

(Rashid, 1st year, B)

When I asked him if he'd always wanted to be a teacher, he said

No, not always. It's just, I like an easy job.

There was little sense of doing something for the enjoyment of it; he also told me that he'd considered changing to psychology in the first weeks of term because he thought it would be easier. His comment on the respective value of the arts and sciences was:

It depends on what arts subjects you're talking about. Some I think are totally useless and some I think are useful. English literature I don't feel is useful, and history, I suppose, you can apply it to today, and physics you can apply it; I think it's worthwhile, it's all around you, and without it you'd be back in the caves.

(Rashid, 1st year, B)

In Chapter 4 we noted that Mark, who wanted to be a nurse, rejected the perceived values of physics. It is perhaps significant that he rebelled, not simply through turning his back on physics, but by choosing such a low-status, traditionally feminine, 'caring' occupation; clearly the very subject of physics was associated, for him, with individualism and a desire for personal achievement and financial success. However, it must be noted that Colin, also a third-year student at A, had managed to reconcile (without apparent difficulty) a career in physics with social commitment. Although at present sponsored by GEC, and intending to do a sponsored Ph.D after completion, he saw himself in the future working in a university behind the Iron Curtain; he said that it was 'too easy to get into comfy suburbia, with a Ford Cortina and two point four kids and half a mortgage'. Whether Colin's is a realistic ambition it is hard to say, but he, unlike Mark, experienced no contradiction between being a successful physicist and being socially useful.

The future plans of the physical science students were slightly different from those of the physicists. Perhaps surprisingly, given the vocational nature of their degree, some of them had not made a final decision on what career to pursue. None of them had applied for Ph.Ds. Two of the four final-year students expected to go into scientific jobs in industry; one hoped to go into medical physics; one intended to go into management. Of the first years, three simply said that they wanted scientific research or engineering jobs in industry, while the fourth said: 'Don't know . . . somewhere where there's money'. Paradoxically because the course is so explicitly vocational, there is a less urgent need for students to decide exactly what they want to do. Their visions of the long term are, however, similar to those of the physics students:

I'll probably be abroad, . . . the next ten years are really the beginning of what's going on . . . it would be nice to be, say, somewhere up the higher echelons of management of whatever I'm doing.

(Matthew, 4th year, C)

In ten years time, I'd like to have a house, a car, a steady job which would be in the region of £10,000 to £20,000 – that should be nice and comfortable.

(Stuart, 1st year, C)

I'll be doing some job possibly connected with management rather than research, and I'd like to travel around, not in England, elsewhere. I suppose I'll be doing some sort of job connected with science – not so connected with science as research – I'd rather be connected with the production side rather than research.

(Jeremy, 4th year, C)

There is one student, Richard, whose own history of developing a personal identity through studying physics can be used to highlight the beliefs and attitudes of the male physics students. His attitude is 'instrumental'; he sees physics as a means to an end, a way of bettering his chances for a career, although he also loves physics for its own sake. In some ways he is typical of most of the physics students, but he was more explicitly instrumental than the others, almost to the point of self-parody. Further, class plays an important part in his sense of himself, and he uses his class background to highlight certain of his beliefs and attitudes.

Richard is from a working-class family, and retains a strong Liverpool accent. His mother works as a cleaner and his father is a Labour councillor on Liverpool city council, or, as Richard put it, 'he's a trouble-maker'. Before that, his father worked in a factory until it was closed down. Both parents left school at 16, with no education beyond that. Richard went to the local grammar school, where he did well, gaining twelve O levels in a variety of subjects; he chose his A level subjects with an eye to the job market. Having gained grades of ABB, he came to B University. As the eldest child, he is the first person in his family to enter higher education.

Richard is obviously a very able student, and his enthusiasm for physics seemed boundless. Here he is, for example, talking about the relativity and quantum mechanics courses:

I get really excited about some of the sub-topics. Some parts of physics aren't that interesting, I mean, I do have favourite areas, and when you go through some of the notes then, like the quantum phenomena things and mechanics where it's all physics on a microscopic level you can't see in our scale of the world and then you start studying strange effects that happen and it's really quite funny, and you think, wouldn't this be funny if you could bring it up to our level; and I read a few silly little books about it – there is one by someone which was called 'Mr Tomkins in Wonderland' and it's like trying to imagine if a person got shrunk into a microscopic world and seeing these microscopic effects, and relativistic effects, it's all really interesting – it's hard, and you think what is the point of doing it, all this big work by Einstein, you know, there was questions of whether he should have got a Nobel prize, because what benefit is it to mankind, but it's really, like, good to think about, isn't it, because if we could do this, or if that happened to me, so I do get some subjects we've done which have been really good.

(Richard, 3rd year, B)

Richard's mind worked incredibly fast and, as is obvious from this extract, he had no difficulty moving from one idea to another and back again. In the above quote we see a very old-fashioned working-class respect for intellectuality, combined with an unease about the value of studying something that's not really useful. Although most of the time he seemed to take the view that doing a degree was all about getting a job and making a success of one's life, he occasionally veered towards a belief that all intellectual pursuit was worthwhile. For the former attitude, expressed at its most potent, this is what Richard had to say about the difference between his background and attitudes and those of the middle-class students in the university:

It's a funny upbringing, because you come here and everyone's so liberal, and I'm very conservative natured in me ways. I don't really know what me politics are because back home everything's just socialist stroke communist, you know, me dad's like that, and I come here and I can see a different view, but then a lot of people here are from, like, much different backgrounds and they feel much more humane and aware [*said ironically*] and things like that, and I just go Uuurgh! you know, because I don't want to know. Success is all I'm interested in, and success is spelt with a dollar, that's what I believe in. I just want to make money. I believe I can do it; I'm really going to push to get on.

(Richard, 3rd year, B)

His view about gaining jobs had, apparently, changed at university:

People say I'm narrow-minded, but I reckon in the opposite sense of what I was when I came here. I used to think, 'Oh, you'll never get a job, no, things are really bad' and I was always arguing the case the way the Socialist Workers do, but now I think the opposite way, I believe that if you just keep on working, and climbing, then you will be able to get success. Apart from all the knowledge I've learned in me subject, I've got a different outlook on life from when I came here. I look at things in a different way.

(Richard, 3rd year, B)

Richard firmly believed that it was possible to get on in life by working hard, despite the evidence of his own family to the contrary. ('It's horrific the amount of money my father's bringing in, I'll probably be earning double or more next year.') His immediate ambition was to work for the CEGB ('I'm very pro-nuclear power'). Despite his appetite for success, however, he was different from some of the other physics students in that he maintained a degree of respect for education for its own sake – although some of its manifestations evidently puzzled him:

It's wrong that people mock and laugh at the arts things when people are doing history of art or higher degrees in really specialized things, like there's a girl I know who's doing what happened to women in the French Revolution, and I mean, when she told me that, I just cracked up, but you know, you recognize then that you must be fairly clever or something to get the money to do that, but then I argue like it's totally useless and all things like that for a lot of them, but then, it's true really with physics, in that what good is some of the quantum mechanics and the theoretical stuff. It's just pure research, some of it, and can't be applied. . . . So I always think that I couldn't imagine meself doing an arts degree, but I think it's wrong that people cut back on the arts, I don't support that, because a world full of scientists would be incredibly boring.

(Richard, 3rd year, B)

Richard's view of the world is a social Darwinian one in which people compete for success, money and power. People who chose not to compete are free to do so, but couldn't expect any reward for it. His personal vision is a purely individualist one; he hoped to succeed as an individual, regardless of anyone else. His reply to the question 'What do you see yourself doing in ten years time?' was remarkably blunt:

Power is my main aim. Power and money. I always see meself getting more involved in politics. I'd like to see meself getting involved in local government. I reckon I could – I like the idea of selling meself, and things like that – I could see meself, modelling meself on what people want to see and doing it just to promote me own interests. I'm very selfish, I'll admit that. I'm only interested in Number One, really. It's just to get on and earn money and that, maybe when I have earned money in five or ten years, I'll be bored and want to do something different . . . I'd like to think that in 10 years' time I'll be earning a salary that is equivalent today to around £18,000 – and having real prestige – and then maybe do something completely different.

(Richard, 3rd year, B)

The extraordinary thing about Richard is his self-awareness. Earning a lot of money and being successful are not taken-for-granted realities for him as they are for many of the middle-class students. He has thought quite hard to come to the conclusion he has done; having considered the alternatives, indeed, *experienced* the alternatives, he has consciously taken on a set of right-wing middle-class attitudes as the best way of achieving what he wants. He is at once atypical of the physics students – in that he is both working-class and very self-conscious about his own attitudes – and extremely representative of them, a more articulate exponent of what the others believed implicitly. While many others regarded physics as a means of getting good, well-paid jobs, none of them would have characterized their attitude as 'selfish': selfishness for Richard is a political philosophy.

The female science students

Women's construction of their identity was very different from that of the men. They did not, generally, think of themselves as 'applied physicists' or 'theoretical physicists'; in one sense they did not see themselves particularly clearly as individuals. The female physics students were clearly aware of themselves as an homogeneous group. Women generally sat together during lectures; they were conscious of being in a minority. This does not necessarily mean that they were a minority group, but they knew that they were 'different', as the following quotes indicate:

> There aren't many girls doing the course, we're singled out much more easily, they know our names, but they don't know all the boys.
>
> (Debbie, 1st year, C)

> I felt a little bit self-conscious [at first], but it wasn't as if you were the only one, there's about twenty of us out of a hundred, so you didn't stick out that much. I think I might have been a bit worried about it if there'd been three, but it was quite nice, I quite liked it.
>
> (Melanie, 3rd year, A)

> We're really outnumbered, but we get on with the boys all right, we have to really.
>
> (Marie, 1st year, B)

> It didn't seem unusual or anything – just every now and again when you looked around, and you notice it's only your row that's got girls on it, you know, and all the rest are male but you don't notice it really.
>
> (Mary, 1st year, B)

Several of the women mentioned being 'singled out', saying that staff learnt women's names before they learnt men's names and that skipping lectures was harder because lecturers noticed if there was a woman missing (if, say, there were only four women instead of five). Although some women are used to being a minority, those from single-sex schools have to adapt rapidly to this new situation:

> The only thing I'm not used to is having man teachers and boys in the classroom, and I'm finding lessons less relaxed than they were in school; it's a lot more serious, 'Let's get down to it', but I'm finding the people not as friendly as at school . . . and I think that gives it a cold atmosphere.
>
> (Lesley, 1st year, C)

> I was surprised at first because I thought there'd be a lot of girls on it because it isn't quite physics, that there'd be a lot of girls like me who weren't sure enough of themselves to try physics.
>
> (Donna, 1st year, C)

> I can remember the first day I walked in, this big massive room, full of people. I got there about five to nine, and it was absolutely packed, and I

can just remember walking – I had to walk right to the back of the room – and getting redder and redder as I walked up, and I thought, O my God, there are all these lads and no girls, and I was sitting there spotting the girls and there's only five of us on the whole course.

(Linda, 4th year, C)

None of these women regarded themselves as victims of discrimination in any way; all denied that being a woman in science was more difficult than being a man in science. Yet they all registered surprise, awkwardness and embarrassment at their conspicuousness in the course. Being conspicuous is not in itself a disadvantage; indeed, it could be advantageous – women might experience preferential treatment as a result of being in a minority. However, Donna thought that 'there'd be a lot of girls like me who weren't sure enough of themselves to try physics'. Physical science is, for Donna, less rigidly defined as a masculine preserve; she thinks it might be more open, less difficult maybe than physics, and therefore more likely to be studied by women. She introduces the element of uncertainty; she suggests that she herself lacked the self-confidence to take physics. She thinks that other women might also lack that self-confidence, implying at the same time that men do not lack confidence. There is a sense, then, amongst these women, of intruding on a masculine preserve, of being slightly unwelcome. This is reinforced by the comments of Debbie, a first-year student at C, talking about her male peers:

I find an awful lot of them, if you speak to them, it's 'Aah, a girl spoke to me', you know. When you think we've been here for six months now and some of them, I've said 'Hello' to them once or smiled at them, and they've looked at me like *this*, and I've thought, 'I won't bother again'. But in the lab, and computing, when you're sitting at the terminals, asking questions, that's a good way of making friends with the blokes ('cos the girls naturally are friends whether you're the same type of people or not, the girls all chat to each other), but I find you've got to make an effort with the blokes, to say, 'Mmm, I can't do this, can you help me', sort of thing.

(Debbie, 1st year, C)

Debbie is here developing a strategy to cope with a particular problem, in this case the problem of feeling excluded, of not having friends. There is not, as might be imagined, any deliberate deviousness in her strategy; she is simply aware that her male peers find a woman who is obviously a 'woman' (i.e. someone fairly helpless and not very good with computers) easier to cope with than someone who is both a 'woman' and a 'scientist'. From Debbie's comments, it would seem that the idea of a 'female scientist' is outside the frame of reference of many of the men on the course. Debbie resolves the contradiction of being both a woman and a scientist by becoming more 'feminine', and stepping into that frame of reference. In this way, men's idea of what constitutes 'femininity' is strengthened, rather than weakened, by their interactions with female science students. (It must be noted that when Debbie was interviewed, she appeared to be neither helpless nor stupid, but lively, intelligent and self-confident.)

Debbie also says, significantly, that 'the girls naturally are friends whether you're the same type of people or not'. This remark was borne out by the fact that most of the women in Debbie's year sat together, as a group, during lectures. (The exception was Donna, who sat with the men, of whom she said 'I don't think of them as the opposite sex': an attempt to identify herself with the dominant group.) The implication of this is that these women see themselves primarily as *women*; that the fact of having femaleness in common is more important, at least in the context of the science class, than that they get on with each other or have other interests in common. This impression is strengthened by the initially puzzling remark of a female student in University A:

> In a way it's easier for girls [to make friends] because there are only twenty girls so you can pick them out more easily.
>
> (Felicity, 1st year, A)

It is, of course, just as easy for the eighty men on the course to pick each other out as it is for the twenty women; there is also no immediately apparent reason why the women shouldn't be friends with the men. What this student seems to be saying is that the fact of having gender in common, and more particularly, of having a minority gender in common (and thus a collective identity) is more important than other shared interests or personalities. This attitude is surely part of a defence mechanism; it suggests that some of the women at least are gathering together in the face of an unwelcoming environment. Obviously some of the women do make friends with the men, but there are certainly barriers; a first-year student at B explained to me the nature of friendships on the course:

> There are, on my floor, another two girls who do physics, and there's only four girls who do physics; anyway, there's three of us together, so we stay together a lot, and we get on with all the other people who do physics, but it's sometimes a bit difficult because you don't know how they're going to react – some of them have got girlfriends and if they see you talking it can be a bit bad really.
>
> (Mary, 1st year, B)

Thus male–female relationships are seen not to exist outside the realm of the sexual: there is a rigidity in the male–female distinction in which the barrier of gender is more important than the common ground of physics; women are perceived as women first, and physicists second. This is explained in greater detail by Fay, a fourth-year student at C, who recalls her first weeks on the physical science course:

> It was funny really, because when we first met the lads, they wouldn't swear or anything, they were really nice; and then, after about two or three weeks, they realized that you weren't any different to them, and just went back to normal, but the first weeks were really strange because they were so nice it was unbelievable, and you wondered what you were doing, they'd hold open the door, they wouldn't swear, if they swore they'd apologize, but after a few weeks they realized we weren't any different.
>
> (Fay, 4th year, C)

Fay makes it clear that she doesn't see her own position as a female scientist as odd, but that the men are odd because they can't accept the idea of female scientists. The easiest thing for them to do is to treat them as 'women', thereby normalizing them to some extent, fitting them into predefined categories. They may even have been exaggerating this categorization, because it is at least arguable that they do not treat other women in this deferential way. Fay concludes by saying: 'they realized we weren't any different' – a common assertion from the female physicists and physical scientists. The assertion that, whatever problems they may be facing, they 'weren't any different' was, for many women, a fundamental part of their identity and self-confidence. To admit to being different is also to admit, within their frame of reference, to being inferior ('I don't think of them as being the opposite sex'): an assertion of equality and of sameness with their male peers is a way of establishing their identity as scientists who are 'just as good as the men'. Marianne, also a fourth-year student at C, uses the same discourse of 'being as good as men':

> It doesn't bother me because I'm in less of a minority here than when I did my A levels . . . I realized that you can keep up with the lads anyway. I mean, it would bother me if I felt stupid and if every time I said something they laughed at me, but because I know I can keep up with them it doesn't bother me at all. . . . One of them I knew [at sixth-form college], I really felt like 'stupid woman', you know, every time you said something or did something wrong in the lab, there was a comment. But the lads here are great. They treat you just the same.
>
> (Marianne, 4th year, C)

Here the power relations are taken for granted. Just as science students were able to say, 'I don't look down on arts students', female science students are aware of the magnanimity of men in treating them 'just the same'. Marianne is aware of the vulnerability of women in the dominant discourse; she has to earn her right to be treated 'just the same' by proving that she 'can keep up with them'.

If Debbie uses femininity as a strategy to get herself accepted, Lesley, a woman on the same year of the same course, tries to get herself accepted not as a woman, but as a serious scientist which, for her, meant taking on masculine traits and values. She talked at some length about another woman on her course, who she felt was too 'feminine':

> One girl seems very quiet and she's not got any confidence in herself, she's just hoping for the degree, whereas I'm hoping for honours . . . I don't know whether she's doing it because it's idealistic for a woman to start on this industrial sort of course, and she seems too feminine to me to be on this course. She gets dressed up every day, she gets her clothes on and her tights, and her make-up is always done immaculately; and she seems a bit too flighty, too girlish, you know, to do something like get down to cutting bits of metal up on a big machine.
>
> (Lesley, 4th year, C)

Later in the interview she mentioned this woman again, saying that she'd be better in a job where she'll be admired for what she wears, a nice secretary or a manageress or something like that . . . because if we face what we're looking for in the future, job-wise, we're going to be in a dirty great factory, or somewhere where it's going to be dirty because it's basically manufacturing materials.

(Lesley, 4th year, C)

She concluded

I think you've got to – especially with it being so male-dominated – sort of leave the skirt behind, and say to them, 'my brain's just as capable as yours'.

(Lesley, 4th year, C)

Particularly significant in Lesley's description is the language she uses to make explicit her rejection of femininity. In each of the above quotes she talks in terms of clothing: 'she gets her clothes on and her tights'; 'she'll be admired for what she wears'; 'leave the skirt behind'. The criticism Lesley makes of clothing, although intended literally by her, is also metaphorical; it suggests that femininity is something which can be removed, discarded, in order to change the sort of person one is. Femininity, or womanhood, is equated with triviality: Lesley's class-mate is 'flighty', 'girlish'. Lesley implicitly rejects the idea that womanhood is an integral part of someone's make-up; indeed, she perceives the male as the 'norm' by which others must be judged. For Lesley, then, to be taken seriously as a scientist means leaving behind girlish things and taking on masculine values and attributes. Lesley has to be *as good as a man*; she implicitly accepts male superiority. Women cannot become equal with men unless they, figuratively speaking, become men themselves. When I asked Lesley who had been the greatest influence in her life, she replied, revealing, 'I would say Mrs Thatcher, because she's the first woman to be Prime Minister – she's come across in a really male-dominated world'. Lesley is *not*, as she says herself, a feminist: her answer to male domination is an assertion of individual superiority, not a collective opposition; she is as much in competition with other women as she is with the men.

The competitive element came out very strongly in the interview. Lesley referred several times to her ambition, her determination to do as well as men in her field, as in this exchange:

LESLEY: I'm really determined . . . I think being in an environment of boys as well, where it's a male-dominated field, it gives you the incentive to work harder, to say, I'm going to show them . . .
KIM: That you're as good as them?
LESLEY: Yes, if not better.

(Lesley, 4th year, C)

For Lesley, men are the standard against whom women's achievement is to be measured. None of the men said that they felt they had to do as well as the women; yet many of the women felt that they were being tested, that they had to prove themselves. In the following extract, Natalie is discussing the sexist attitude of one of the lecturers:

He picks on the girls: he's really mean to them. He always makes rude comments when they walk in half a minute late. 'Well, you're here again, are you? So you've decided to come this week, have you?' . . . He's always rude about their work, but not about the boys' work, except during the maths test when the girls got about twice as many marks as the boys, so he couldn't say anything.

(Natalie, 1st year, A)

The point here is not just that some male lecturers are misogynist, but that for a few women there is a continual battle to prove themselves as equal through competition with the men. It is not just a question of individual competition, but that they as women have to prove themselves as equal to, or preferably better than, the men as men. The existence of this competitive aspect, this need to prove themselves, shows that women, entering university with A level grades as good as those of men, cannot take their status as scientists in the department for granted: they have to demonstrate their worth first. Women have to choose the extent to which they wish to engage in this struggle; their involvement (or lack of it) in the battle is part of the process by which femininity is constructed and reconstructed daily. The battle is made all the more difficult by lecturers, like the one mentioned above, who would prefer not to have women in the department at all.

Many women, then, found themselves manoeuvring within the departments, trying to find an identity which would be acceptable both to them and to others. Lesley was the exception, not the rule, in taking on masculine values, in deciding to become a 'serious' scientist. There were far more women who found it easier to compromise their position and make use of what they saw as the advantages of being a woman:

I'm more prepared to ask for help than the boys are, you certainly get more help . . . you know, just doing practical or something, I'll ask my neighbour if he's done the bit before me, 'Have you any ideas about how to do this?' or 'Did you get things like that?', whereas I don't think boys ask as much . . . maybe they feel, 'I can't let them know that I can't do it', but I don't feel that at all, I just want to do it as best as I can.

(Felicity, 1st year, A)

Marianne had perfected the art of using femininity to advantage:

Actually, it's good being a girl. It was the same when I was doing my A levels as well. They used to say, 'Oh, you go and ask him for some computer paper or tell him the terminal's broken', so I think you do get a bit of preferential treatment actually. You might not, I might be imagining it, but sometimes you'll do the same work as one of the lads, and you'll get a better mark.

(Marianne, 4th year, C)

Although Marianne had earlier said that the women were treated as equals by 'the lads', it is clear that women are treated differently by the staff. Leaving aside the issue of whether always having to be the one who tells teacher that the terminal's broken is really preferential treatment, there is a more intimate, chatty relationship between the female students and the staff, as both Debbie and Marianne explained:

> I find they're probably friendlier towards the girls if the girls are prepared to be friendly to them, rather than, if the boys chat to them, they're not quite as chatty as with the girls.
>
> (Debbie, 1st year, C)

> I think the girls are more – not bossy, bossy's the wrong word – but we might go and say to the lecturers what we think or 'Can you give us some tutorial sheets on this', whereas the lads just sit back and take it, and if it's a crap lecture they'll just accept it's a crap lecture, whereas we won't, you see, we'll actually go and say, 'That wasn't up to much', and we'll go and ask them questions and stuff like that.
>
> (Marianne, 4th year, C)

The strategy here is to manipulate lecturers' perceptions of women to advantage; women can challenge lecturers without being threatening. Marianne recognizes that this is due to women's inferior social position and that there is a sexual element to the staff's greater willingness to chat to the women. She finds it easier to accept and use this, however, than to challenge it:

> There's no way you can get absolute sexual equality. With some of the lecturers you feel that you're being a bit sexually harassed – not physically – but there's one who's always making comments . . . he says, you're in the clean room, and he says, 'Oh, it's a bit hot in here, why don't you take your clothes off'. I mean, he's only joking, he never takes it too far, but he's the only one who's actually made any comment, it's just his sense of humour, he's not really a pervert.
>
> (Marianne, 4th year, C)

As with many other of the female students, Marianne's complaint about discrimination is immediately followed by a denial of the validity of the complaint, in her case five consecutive statements which rationalize the lecturer's behaviour: 'he's only joking, he never takes it too far, but he's the only one who's actually made any comment, it's just his sense of humour, he's not really a pervert.' This rationalization is a way of coping with the experience; she turns the lecturer's unacceptable behaviour into something acceptable by, in a sense, denying what has happened, or putting into a different context. 'Jokes', after all, are harmless; if the lecturer is only joking, then she need not feel threatened by him.

Fay, in the same year as Marianne, confirmed Marianne's account of differential treatment:

> FAY: We do get treated differently by some of them. I mean, you can't deny that, they call you by your first name and all the blokes get called by their second name . . . some of them treat you just the same as all the others –

the odd one treats you *carefully* – I don't know how to describe it. It's annoying, because they think you're not quite capable of it and you might just do something silly because you're a girl. And then some of them go the opposite way – because they're frightened of being seen to treat you differently, they treat you worse, because they're scared of – you know what I mean?

KIM: Giving you preferential treatment?

FAY: Yeah, but on the whole, no discrimination really.

> (Fay, 4th year, C)

The staff seem to be as puzzled as the male students about how to treat the women. The women are perceived as an oddity, perhaps even a threat, and therefore they have to be treated 'carefully' in case they do something really strange. Addressing women by their first name makes them seem less threatening, and less serious. For Fay, this is not enough to constitute discrimination, but it does mean that she has to tread a careful path and negotiate her identity. The issue of masculinity and femininity came up again in an interview with Louise, a third-year student at B:

I'd really like there to be more women, especially coming from an all-girls' school. It's something you miss, female company. It tends to be that you get to know plenty of blokes and hardly any girls, so when you go out at night, you tend to be one of the lads all the time, and it would be so nice to get dressed up and taken out for a change.

> (Louise, 3rd year, B)

Louise is talking about a common experience: the need to blend in comfortably. She is 'just one of the lads' – no longer conspicuous, no longer different, but the same as everyone else. Like Lesley, she talks about feminine identity in terms of clothing: getting 'dressed up' to be taken out, rather than in terms of mixing with other women. She sees her identity as defined by men – whether they see her as 'one of the lads' or as a 'woman'. Her notion of femininity is therefore a stereotyped one – being taken out by a man – and the alternative to it is being 'one of the lads'. There is no middle course; gender identity is always rigidly defined as polarities. It was not possible simply to regard one's sex as unimportant or inconsequential; it was a question of manoeuvring, becoming more 'masculine' (or more 'scientific') or more 'feminine' as the situation demanded. Thus Louise, in the example quoted above, feels a need to assert her 'femininity' in the face of pressure to be 'masculine'. Traditional notions of masculinity and femininity assert themselves.

Women's attitudes towards physics were far less direct and precise than men's. Physics was, like a number of other things, something they did because they enjoyed it: not necessarily something which was an overriding part of their lives. Natalie, for example, who was one of the most talkative of the science students, talked about playing in a jazz band and studying physics with equal enthusiasm, and switched from one topic to the other with apparent effortlessness.

In the same way, the women's self-image was rarely as clear-cut as that of the men: they did not, on the whole, see themselves as ambitious or important. When they talked about the courses, for example, they were often unhappy about certain important elements. Most of the women disliked computing, which was compulsory; whereas many of the men had had previous computing experience (and hoped to use computers in their careers), most women didn't, and had difficulty with the self-taught nature of the computing course, one women confessing to me that 'I'm a bit of a Luddite really'. Women also often disliked the abstract nature of the physics studied:

> I find that there isn't enough description very often and just too many equations and numerical things and I find that if some people talked English more often, that would help.
>
> (Julie, 3rd year, A)

> There seems to be a certain jargon to it and if you know the jargon, you're OK, but they're used to talking to people on their level and you find it difficult to talk to people who don't really know.
>
> (Melanie, 3rd year, A)

It will be remembered from Chapter 4 that Jane said she saw physics as a 'chatty, qualitative subject'; many women simply didn't regard physics in an instrumental way at all; it was just something they were good at and enjoyed. Women's preferences within the course tended to be for 'relevant' options: medical physics, for example, at the 'soft' end of the physics hierarchy. Far from seeing physics as central, either to their own lives, or to society, they down-played its significance:

> I know a science degree tends to be looked upon in better light than an arts degree because people think if you've done a science degree you must be clever – it's not the case at all, it's just what you're interested in.
>
> (Mary, 1st year, B)

In other words, women lacked a strong identification with physics; they did not see themselves as 'physicists', first and foremost as the men did. Their hobbies were often more diverse and people-oriented: music, theatre, reading, while the men tended to be more interested in computing and mechanics and sport (usually rugby). Melanie, a third-year student at A, showed a sharp awareness of the social meaning of the word 'physicist' – and a clear rejection of its connotations. She had said that her school friends (she went to a single-sex school) had tried to dissuade her from doing physics and encouraged her instead to choose medicine or veterinary science. I asked her why medicine or veterinary science were considered more acceptable, and she said that she thought they were generally agreed to be more suitable subjects for women. She illustrated this by talking about a female friend on the physics course:

> One of my friends goes up to people and says, 'What do you think I do?' and if someone says, 'Oh, English', she's really pleased and she likes them, but if someone says 'physics', she tends to be a bit doubtful.

When asked why this was, she replied

> Physics people have a reputation for being really boring and square and working all the time with computers and things.
>
> (Melanie, 3rd year, A)

The interest of this remark lies in the idea that this woman's friend, although a physics student, didn't want other people to think of her as a physics student, because she didn't like the image associated with physicists. She makes a deliberate attempt, not to contradict people's impression, but to distance herself from that image of physics, thereby tacitly accepting it. It is an image of a particular kind of masculinity that she is rejecting: an image of someone who is introverted, uninterested in the outside world and who is involved only in his subject.

Women's lack of a strong identification with physics is related to a lack of confidence in their ability to perform well in it. In Chapter 4 the attitude of Paul, a third-year student at B, blithely joking about his propensity to break lab equipment, was contrasted with the anxieties of Jane and Marie, trying desperately to understand how to cope with the lab work. Marie, in particular, saw herself as 'not intelligent but prepared to get down and work'. There were other women, however, whom one might expect to be a paradigm of self-confidence, who felt very unsure of themselves. One first-year student at A, for example, who had attended a girls' public school and had gained three A grades at A level, as well as gaining a distinction in her physics S paper, said:

> It's challenging my faith in my ability to do things . . . I think there's a lot of readjustment. I think there's a lot of people here who are brighter than me, and it's hard to say, to have the confidence to say 'Never mind about them, concentrate on you.'
>
> (Felicity, 1st year, A)

When asked how she knew other people were brighter than she was, she said:

> I don't know; the way they act, I suppose. You take so much from someone else's self-confidence; if someone's really self-confident, you tend to assume that they're bright. They might not be, but you know, you've all got the grades to come here and . . . I don't know.
>
> (Felicity, 1st year, A)

Similarly Jane, as indicated in Chapter 4, had felt her confidence being destroyed by going to a school where the teachers didn't believe she had any ability. Self-confidence, to a large degree, is a matter of other people's perceptions, and a matter of the student's own perceptions of how she is perceived by others. Felicity's self-image was shaped by a belief that she was less able than the other students; she had already decided that she probably wouldn't pursue physics as a career, even though that had been her intention when coming to university. She felt that she had been thrown in at the deep end, and felt lost in the individualistic atmosphere of the department, saying,

You tend to feel that everyone else knows a bit more about what's going on than you do.

(Felicity, 1st year, A)

The four women in the first year at B all exhibited the same lack of self-confidence in themselves as 'physicists'. One of them, Marie, was discussed in Chapter 4; her sense of confidence in herself had diminished rapidly since coming to university:

> I don't mind working. I worked really hard to get my A levels, because I knew I had to because I wasn't intelligent but was prepared to sit down and work . . . but here you don't feel as if you're getting anywhere when you do work, it really depresses you.

(Marie, 1st year, B)

This rigid division Marie makes between the concept of 'intelligent' and the concept of 'working hard' results in a self-label of 'hard-working but stupid'. At university, she feels herself to be losing out on both counts, with nobody to turn to for help. The other three women, however, had all been placed in the same corridor in their hall of residence (increasing Marie's sense of isolation). These three students, like Marie, were experiencing difficulty with the course. However, they coped with their problems by evolving a co-operative strategy:

> They're quite good . . . if you can't do something you can ask one of those two, and if you all can't do it, then there's not something wrong with you, there's something wrong with the course.

(Susan, 1st year, B)

And

> With three of us doing physics on the same floor, it's quite nice, because you can come back and say, 'God, I didn't understand a word of that', and hopefully one of the other two will have done bits of it for A level, and begin to explain it to you.

(Susan, 1st year, B)

Thus they had begun to challenge the individualist ethos of the department, which tries to make students compete and succeed as individuals. They built their identity through a system of mutual support, gaining confidence from each other, not through competition or high achievement on the department's terms.

Women in physics are unable to construct a straightforward identity for themselves as physicists, because to be a physicist is to be male. A sense of identity is achieved through difference; in this case women emphasize their difference from men (at the same time distancing themselves from science), or their difference from women ('leaving the skirt behind'). Women suffer from lack of self-confidence because of their inability to match the ideal of physicist which is male, individualist and instrumental. We shall now see how this lack of identification with the male norm led women away from the traditional career paths of physics graduates.

Only two of the female physics final-year students wanted careers in industry, and one of those intended to be a medical physicist – traditionally regarded as a 'softer' (and certainly a less well-paid) option. Three, however, intended to train as teachers, while three wanted jobs not at all connected with physics (two in management, and one who wanted to be a librarian). Whereas ten of the men, therefore, intended to stay with science, only four women intended to do so. Wanting to go into teaching or management rather than research and development does not necessarily denote lack of ambition. However, the reasons many of the women gave for their decisions were negative:

> I know I don't want to do research, it would drive me round the bend, basically, and I don't want to do theoretical research and that applies for doing research in a company as well – I just don't want to. It was either go into management or something like that, and then I thought I might want to do teaching, because at least it's using your physics.
>
> (Melanie, 3rd year, A)

> I don't want to do things that a lot of people do, like production management and stuff like that.
>
> (Sioned, 3rd year, B)

The student planning a career in information science saw it as a broadening out; she didn't want to stay with her subject:

> I dislike getting too specialized and I think if you stay with physics, you're bound to do that in some way or another.
>
> (Pauline, 3rd year, B)

The woman who was thinking of taking a year out to do VSO, or doing a Master's degree in 'science and the environment', said:

> I can't face the thought at the moment of going into a job and having to stick it there for *n* years.
>
> (Linda, 4th year, C)

These women all find the idea of a typical scientific career in industry uninspiring. Perhaps Linda's attitude was influenced by her experience in the industrial year out:

> It wasn't the bosses [who were sexist]; it was the fellows who used to work in the factory and the workshop. I used to go into the workshop and ask them to make lots of equipment and things, and they'd say, 'You shouldn't be doing things like this' – and I'd be covered in tar and grime, you know, my coat was filthy – and they'd say, 'You should be up in the office typing'.
>
> (Linda, 4th year, C)

While a sandwich science course teaches students to handle scientific concepts and enables them to gain experience of working in industry, it does not teach them how to handle this kind of hostility in the work-place. It is possible that in some cases, industrial experience has the opposite effect of that intended.

Although some of the women were enthusiastic about working – Louise, for example, who intended to enter medical physics, was very dedicated – some were very anxious about the difficulties of following a job and having a family. Exactly half of the final-year women, when asked what they saw themselves doing in ten years' time, mentioned the possibility that they would be married with children. This possibility was far from unproblematic, however, as the following quote nicely illustrates:

> I should think if I'm 32 I'll still be in my career, but I don't know because if I have children I don't want them till I'm about 28 . . . so at 32 they'd be about 4 years old, so I might be at home, because I don't really believe in going straight back to work; on the other hand, you can't necessarily afford to look after children for five years before they go to school, so I might be at home, or on the other hand I might be in my career.

> (Marianne, 4th year, C)

Or as another woman put it:

> I think I'd like to be married with a couple of kids, but then again I'll probably be working in a library somewhere, but hopefully I'll like it that much to stick at it.

> (Pauline, 3rd year, B)

Or another:

> I'd like to have a family but I'd like to have a job as well. I wouldn't want just to have children.

> (Melanie, 3rd year, A)

The conflict between family and career, particularly as outlined by Marianne, is one which throws once more into sharp relief the contrast between the wider social pressures to be feminine, womanly and so on (i.e. have a family and stay at home to look after it) and the more immediate social pressure to be a successful scientist following a career. Part of being a successful physicist is having a linear career: doing well, getting promoted, making money. Staying at home to look after children is not easily accommodated in this scheme.

The fact that women were worried about combining careers with parenthood and that the men weren't, need not surprise us; parenthood has, after all, always been regarded as a female vocation. Although one might expect that women who had made a conscious decision to take an obviously male-dominated subject as physics would be more likely to reject 'conventional' female 'roles', than arts students, this was not the case with the female science students in the sample; many were keen to have families although they were aware that this conflicted with their other plans. More surprisingly, perhaps, the female scientists viewed their long-term plans differently from the male scientists, not just in terms of marriage and children, but in terms of the sort of qualities they looked for in jobs:

> Hopefully I'll be in a job which I enjoy which will be really interesting, which will pay relatively well. I mean, I don't want loads and loads of

money, not at the moment I don't, because I've never had any so it doesn't bother me. I just want satisfaction basically, something where I'm interested. I don't want to be stuck in a job where I'm interested. I don't want to be stuck in a job where I'm bored, so I probably won't be working! I might even have kids or something, I don't know, I haven't really thought about that yet.

(Linda, 4th year, C)

It depends if this medical physics lives up to its expectations. If it does, hopefully I'll have been promoted – getting a decent living wage and stuff – I don't want anything spectacular, I just want a house and a car and a television, to be able to eat the kind of things I like to eat, holiday once a year, usual stuff.

(Louise, 3rd year, B)

The ambitions of the female science students were, on the whole, more mundane than those of the male science students. It's not that the male students envisaged themselves as doing anything particularly exciting (as one of them ironically said to me, 'I don't know what sort of ambitions you see scientists as having in life – designing a really lethal planet-splitting bomb or something?'), but they did see themselves as making their way up a career structure, which would bring financial rewards. The women, on the other hand, even though they mentioned money, were often quite negative about it, saying, like the student quoted above, that they just wanted a 'decent living wage'. In addition, the female students were much vaguer about what they actually expected to be doing. It would be something which entailed 'job satisfaction' but it was usually unconnected with physics. While many of the men appeared to have their careers mapped out already, the women lacked a clear image of themselves, whether as managers, scientists or parents.

The attitude of the first-year female science students was somewhat different from that of the final-year students. Some expressed similar desires for jobs which involved working with people – Rachel, for example, wanted to become a medical physicist for that reason, while some were still concerned with the problems of combining career with family:

I'd like to have something where I could get married and have children and still go back to it, have a part time job or something, but still in the same line.

(Suzanne, 1st year, A)

However, many of them were ambitious, some unrealistically so, Debbie even saying that what she *really* wanted was to be an astronaut. Even allowing for the fantasy element, the first-year students were more resolute in their ambitions. Like the final-year students, six mentioned marriage and children, but of these six, three talked in terms of *not* wanting those things. As one put it:

not being a housewife with children. That's a waste of a degree, really. I think you should be able to put something back into your country after all the opportunity, all the money you can get, you've got an obligation in a way.

(Debbie, 1st year, C)

That she sees the future as a choice between those two options is in itself interesting: either a scientist or a mother, but not both. She defines herself through distancing herself from traditional ideas about women's occupation. Kate Millett's (1983) point about the antagonism created between 'career woman and housewife' is valid; those women, like Debbie, who wanted careers were often hostile to those who wanted families; those who wanted families were sometimes disparaging about those who wanted careers. Other women were very materialistic, if not specific about what they wanted:

I'd like to have a job and a house of my own and a car. I don't know what I'll be doing – can't imagine it . . . I'd like to be independent, very independent.

(Rachel, 1st year, A)

I'd like to have some really high-powered job, executive style, kind of thing, I like the image. I really want an office as well, ever since I was little I've always wanted an office. That's my personal ambition – to have an office of my own and a secretary.

(Natalie, 1st year, A)

The response of the female first-year physics students was much closer to that of the male physics students (as in that last quote, for example, which seems deliberately to mimic male ambition) than it was to that of the female arts students who were, as we shall see later, distinctly unmaterialistic.

The attitude of the third-year female science students was epitomized by Jane, a woman discussed in Chapter 4, and whose values were diametrically opposed to those of Richard, discussed earlier. The opinions she expressed in the interview were representative of those physics students who had decided that they did not want to continue with physics, the majority of whom were women. The most significant fact about this group of students is that not only did they not envisage for themselves high-flying careers in physics, but also they did not, on the whole, envisage high-flying careers in *anything*. They were almost wholly without ambition – 'ambition' in the conventional sense of earning a lot of money, gaining respect, and achieving status. Jane, it will be remembered, was a third-year student who had some feelings of regret about taking physics and thought she might have been better off doing something else. She said

I didn't choose physics with a view to doing physics afterwards, you know. There's no way I could see myself working in laboratories or anything for my life, but I just wanted to make sure I was doing something I enjoy.

This looks suspiciously like rationalization; she may well have wanted a career in physics at one point. However, she had no intention of applying for scientific jobs, but was applying for jobs in retail management:

I've applied for retail because I like meeting people and that sort of environment.

> (Jane, 3rd year, B)

That comment indicates that she had no real commitment to retail herself; like many of the other female physics students she vaguely wanted something connected with 'meeting people'. She was aware, she said, that she was expected to have a strong commitment to the company she was applying for, a commitment she felt she didn't possess. Her attitude to the degree was similar; she was involved in a variety of different projects and activities outside her course – in fact when I interviewed her, she had just taken up two more, despite being the term before Finals – and although she thought she could get an upper second degree if she worked really hard, she explained that she was 'not that sort of person'.

When she was asked how she saw herself in ten years' time, her answer was clear:

> I'll probably hopefully be married and have about two children and I will have left my job if it's financially possible. I'm willing to make financial sacrifices for family. I think my Mum and Dad did a wonderful job: they've had a lot of financial hardships bringing us up and I really want to be able to give the same sort of time to my children. I don't want to be a flighty career woman . . . I would like to have a satisfying career for about five years but I could quite happily see myself married when I'm about 26, 27 and hopefully with children before I'm 30. I really don't want to leave having children until late 30s or even early 30s. I certainly want to have my first one or two before I'm 30. As long as I was able to have a roof over my head and food in my stomach and clothes for the children I wouldn't mind making financial sacrifices to be at home. I could quite happily sacrifice videos and things like that: they're not important.
>
> (Jane, 3rd year, B)

The contrast with the reply from Richard hardly needs pointing out. First and foremost, it is an obviously male/female contrast. Giving up their jobs to bring up children is what women have always done. But it is not just a male/female difference; some of the women (though not many) were ambitious and did want good careers. Jane's answer is, in fact, an explicit rejection of the values that are so important to Richard. She doesn't want material possessions, or financial reward or power of any kind. Her use of the derogatory phrase 'flighty career woman' (there's no such thing as a 'flighty career man') indicates that she feels those sorts of aims to be trivial. She sees her future as being centred around human relationships, not individual success. It would be easy to dismiss her attitude as the resutlt of conditioning, but to do that would be to ignore the fact that she is an intelligent woman, and that the conclusions she has reached are the result of considerable thought. Jane had already made a 'non-traditional' choice in taking physics. She has now decided, just as consciously as Richard made his decision, that she will not make the pursuit of a career her main aim in life. She doesn't simply say that she wants to have a family; she gives reasons which are based on the values that are important to her. The point is that she feels that a scientific career, or any successful career for that matter, would not be able to accommodate those values. Her position is similar to that of Mark, discussed in the last chapter, who wanted to become a nurse because he rejected the anticipated career paths of his fellow students. In other words, the rejection of physics as a subject is closely related to the rejection of the typical graduate career; it can be seen as a rejection of impersonality and instrumentalism in favour of human relationships and expressivity.

Women in science, then, are faced with a particular set of problems. The chief problem is that of the dual identity; trying to be a scientist on the one hand – which means proving that one is 'as good as a man' – and being a woman on the other – which, in its social definition, entails being uncompetitive. Further, while men were able to build their identity through a commitment to the coursework, to studying and pursuing a career in science, and through a self-definition as 'physicist' or 'physical scientist', women often saw science as being only one part of their lives; they had other interests which were as important to them as physics. Science was simply something they enjoyed and were good at, not an all-consuming interest, and in looking for jobs, many were keen to broaden their lives as much as possible. The conflict of identity was strengthened when women thought about their long-term futures; whereas men saw themselves as climbing the ladder of success, women were only too aware of having to make a choice between following a career and raising a family: being a physicist or being a woman.

We have already seen that physics lecturers, while showing an awareness of the 'problem' of the lack of women in physics, do not display an understanding of the difficulties and dilemmas faced by female physics students. We might reasonably expect that in English, a subject traditionally studied by women, the situation would be different. In the next chapter, therefore, we shall examine the way in which gender is constructed by both lecturers and students in English.

7

Gender Identity and Humanities Students

Introduction

In English, women are not in a minority, at least amongst the students. We have no reason, therefore, to think in terms of the 'problem' of women in English or communications, although we might find the position of the male students an interesting one. Is their position parallel to that of women in science? Do they face particular difficulties?

Given that there is no problem in recruiting students, either male or female to the liberal humanities, we might also ask whether the gender imbalance in these subjects is seen as a matter of concern to staff, or whether it is regarded as an irrelevance – nothing to do with the business of studying literature and the media. It is this issue which we shall examine first.

The issue of gender in English and communications

Let us begin by comparing two quotations, both from an interview with Dr M from Department B. Lest this seem an unfair juxtaposition it should be pointed out that in the interview itself they were separated only by my question 'Why do so many women do English?':

> I think that literature is actually the most intimate and complex and comprehensive account we have of the lives of men and women who have lived on this planet because it combines a philosophy in an essential sense, it combines social science in an essential sense, social studies, a study of culture, and it combines the modes of artistry that music and painting have, but it's verbal. . . . My perception of it is that people come because they think there is a rich store of past experience in literature, and I think that's what they intuitively go for.
>
> (Dr M, Department B)

This is a very large, very Leavisite claim for literature: to say that English is about the study of the 'most intimate and complex and comprehensive account we have of the lives of men and women', that it is about 'profound emotional structures' is to put it, as Leavis did, at the centre of the academic disciplines. Logically, perhaps, we might expect Dr M's answer to the next question would be concerned with explicating women's greater intuitive understanding, their ability to grasp complex and intimate accounts of life, or to get to grips with 'profound emotional structures'. However, he replied as follows:

> Well, I think there are well-known factors in the culture at large; whether they are, you know, ultimately cultural or biological or natural none of us really know, everyone has their private view on that subject. It is the obverse of the question, isn't it, of why more women don't do physics, and you know that I don't know that I've got any special wisdom to add to what's already been said on that topic, because you're partly dealing with whether people go to the *subject*, and whether people go to a *perceived* subject, whether it will be thought of in some ways as a slightly effeminate thing to do, and that might affect the choices, but it might be that people aren't affected by that, that they actually go for the nature of the thing itself. There may also be differences in career expectations; males may feel that they have to go into something which has a clear sort of career purpose, and it may be that there is still a very strong traditional sense that a career in that sense is somehow a lower priority for the female school-leaver; certainly I think it's probably the case that our students are still not so career-minded as some of the students that go into other subjects, that they come because they want to do that subject; maybe there's a kind of luxury element in that that perhaps young male school-leavers don't feel that they can afford.
>
> (Dr M, Department B)

The answer is a series of negatives; a career is not a priority for a woman, women don't do physics; maybe it's cultural or biological or natural. Considering the importance, to English, of the fact that it is studied by vast armies of women, Dr M has given the subject remarkably little thought; and his answer is entirely unrelated to his earlier eulogy of English as a discipline. Consider, too, Dr P's answer to my question, 'Why do women do English?':

> It may well be that this element of the aesthetic, the emotive, the playful, etc. is something women take to more readily than men, I don't know. One hesitates to make gender-based generalizations now because you're liable to be attacked for it, but yes, I think there is something in it actually; there may even be something physiologically; there have been thoughts passed around about different sides of the brain and so on, with some slight but possibly significant difference between the male and the female brain in this regard, but that is very theoretical. But I suppose I tend to say, it's not just cultural . . . I think there is something else, deeper.
>
> (Dr P, Department B)

Quite simply, then, women are biologically more disposed to studying English than men; if that is the case, then it is only reasonable to assume that women would be more successful at the subject than men. However, as we have already seen, women are notably *less* successful in English than men. Three of the four English lecturers believe that markers can be 'unbiased' and that there is a 'strong degree of consensus' about how to mark an essay. If that is the case, then the issue of the different degree classifications attained by men and women is not a problem; as it cannot be grounded in marking systems or the preconceptions of the marker, then it must be grounded in the students themselves. Both Dr P and Dr M regarded the issue of differential degree classes as unproblematic:

> I would think that that is true [that more men get firsts in B University]. It would make sense, wouldn't it? In a way, if the drift of the culture is to perceive this as a female subject, then the males that go in for it are males who have very positively chosen it or even quite a large number of such, so there will be a strong element of some selection of them wanting to do that, whereas if it's a female-perceived subject, then many girls may just go into it as part of the drift, just on that ladder.
>
> (Dr M, Department B)

This is reasonable, up to a point; it does not of course account for why the reverse does not happen in male-dominated subjects such as physics. Dr P's comment on the greater proportion of men obtaining firsts was:

> More men tend to be academic high-flyers, yes, vastly more. Basically, this is true. I think it's a subject that a lot of women drift into it, let's just say that. Able but weakish students who quite like English. Perhaps for these people the affective emotional thing is probably a bit too strong, they could do with a bit more intellectual stiffening, the rather weaker students. Men are often not encouraged to do English at school. If they do English, it's because they want to, because they've got some real commitment, some interest, it's slightly against the grain for them. But then once they get into it, if men are that much more competitive than women, which I'm inclined to think, then they start pushing ahead and advancing and so on. With firsts, I suppose there are more men, we don't get many anyway, two or three a year, I don't know. I think there probably is a preponderance of males, but not a vast preponderance. I always get the impression that the women high achievers are increasing in number, and have been somewhat over the years. You do notice it higher up in academic life, where certainly the majority of people in senior positions are male, but then the majority of people who apply to senior positions are male.
>
> (Dr P, Department B)

Dr P has already suggested that women are genetically more predisposed to study English than men. To go on to argue, then, that many women who do English only do so because they 'drift into it', and not because they are any good at it, is a double-think of some magnitude. It is, simply, an evasion of the problem; it is convenient to believe that women are biologically more suited to

English, and it is also convenient to believe that women do worse at it because they are not really as good as men. Either way, the end result is nothing to do with the practices of the department. Dr P makes use of dominant assumptions about men and women to explain differences in achievement: for women, the 'affective emotional thing' is 'too strong' while men are more 'competitive'. Thus are assertion and aggression (positive masculine emotion) rewarded, while affective response (negative feminine emotion) is penalized.

It seems that the issue of the proportions of men and women doing English, and their relative performance in English is, in fact, a non-issue. By setting the department up as objective and impartial, it is impossible to abdicate responsibility for inequalities of achievement amongst the students. It is possible to blame schools, society, biology, women themselves: but English departments themselves remain beyond doubt. The dissenting voice in all this came from Dr S in Department A. Talking about the discussion of marginal cases at examination meetings, she said

> Some male tutors' reports on female students say absolutely classic things, you know, about 'She is a rather sweet but unassuming person, who only reports ideas that she's found in books' and even when they're saying complimentary things, it's all about how sweet somebody is, or how unaggressive they are. Obviously what they're seeing and what they're looking for and even what they're praising, are in fact very non-competitive things, whereas some of the lads who make a good impression are clearly doing something else: they're talking a lot, being aggressive in argument and all the rest of it, and therefore very in quotes 'impressive', and I think a lot of them are into the whole competition anyway and can do that, and there are very few young men students, so they're special to start with, they're noticeable. So if you've got four girls called Sarah in your group and they're all quite shy and diffident about talking, then it's quite difficult to remember which Sarah is which, and if you've got one lad there, who's got a good sense of humour and a loud voice, then he does stand out and you think, 'This is a really good student who's contributing a good deal'; so I think when it comes to discussing students, the young men do stand out in that way.
>
> (Dr S, Department A)

Again, in Dr S's account, aggression and competitiveness are being rewarded – at least in men; and men, by virtue of their conspicuousness, are necessarily more interesting. It would seem, from this version of events, that women are in a double-bind, caught between trying to be unassuming and feminine or competitive and masculine.

The issue of gender, of why more women (and fewer men) do communications, as of why more women do English, is one which clearly impinges on a discipline which is concerned both with the social construction of people's identities, and with the practices of the media. I asked Mr E why so many women came on to the communications course:

That might have something to do with, this seeming to have career opportunities that other humanities or social science degrees don't have, and that then becomes attractive to women . . . I think that it means that a lot of your examples are drawn in terms of our sexual identities so that you're trying to say that apart from evident biological differences there are also cultural differences and you can use that as it were, the raw material for seminar discussions and papers and the like, and a lot of them do. And there are again sometimes arguments and debates about that, and again to some extent you're having to throw up things and let them make of it what they will. Some courses, I think, will say, 'This isn't a sexist course, this is a feminist course'; I wouldn't make those claims about this course. But it is a course, none the less, where feminism and sexism as cultural phenomena can be discussed and analysed and criticized.

> (Mr E, Department C)

The course, then, is explicitly aware of feminism and sexism as *issues*, issues which can be brought into the course and discussed and made open. In addition, Mr E is conscious of the need to make *men* aware of their position:

That means you have to address it as an issue and do it and not just in a kind of limp-wristed way which is 'I've got it sussed, I'm laid back, I know that women ought to be treated in a certain kind of way'; it also means getting the blokes to think about themselves as 'cultured' men, and how they arrived at that position, and how there might be problems about having arrived at that.

> (Mr E, Department C)

Once more, this contrasts with the English departments: A has a 'women and literature' course, not a 'gender and literature' course: understanding the construction of masculinity is not part of this English curriculum. Mr C believed that there were differences between the approach of men and women to communications, however:

There seems to be a group of women each year who, as it gets nearer to the exams, are constantly saying to you, 'If I do such and such, if I write that and do this, do you think that would help?' and you very rarely get blokes doing that. And I think that's got something to do with . . . that accumulation of attitudes and the like men have, as to how they tackle the problem. I think by and large, actually, the ones who turn out not only to be the most enthusiastic but the most diligent are the women. At the same time, they can both be among the weakest of students, also, more often than not, they're amongst the strongest of students, in the sense that they're prepared to live with those uncertainties we were talking about earlier, and go for it. You find that the ones who stand out tend to be the women, and that's quite nice, and maybe that's got something to do again with the fact that they're in a broadly supportive environment.

> (Mr E, Department C)

Mr E clearly sees the differences as being the result of social processes. Men are less openly anxious about examinations because of their cultural environment, while women might often do better because of their being on a course where women predominate. These differences are seen, not as inevitable, but as cultural and social, and therefore varied and changeable. Interestingly, too, he says that women are both the 'strongest' and the 'weakest' of students: a complete reversal of the orthodoxy on the subject (e.g. Rudd 1984; Heim 1971) which says that men tend to be found at the extremes and the women in the middle. Nothing could show more clearly the relationship between an understanding of texts and an understanding of the social world: where the lecturer in Department B, for example, saw certain qualities of literature as being immutable and inevitable (not socially produced), he also saw differences between men and women as being immutable and inevitable. To some extent, the immutability and inevitability of male–female differences will be reflected in those texts which are universally 'good'. The communications lecturer, however, sees both text and individuals as inextricable from a social world – which is not to say that texts and people are totally conditioned by society, but that there is a relationship which cannot be broken. The belief of the communications course that 'there are no certainties' can be carried over – *is* carried over – into the belief that there are no certainties about the attitudes, abilities or behaviour of men and women. Once that is recognized, it is possible to question social differences, and to change them.

The male humanities students

The interviews with the male arts students were the most informal and relaxed of the interviews conducted. Students talked very freely about their ideas and beliefs and their criticisms of the course. One student who was particularly forthcoming was Martin, a first-year student on the communications course. His account of his feelings about the course highlights clearly the contrast between the experience of higher education of the female physics students and that of the male arts students. Martin, who was mentioned briefly in Chapter 5 (p. 91), had attended a boys' grammar school until the age of 16, when he left to start a job in production engineering at a car-manufacturing plant where his father worked. He said, however, that

> I realized from the first day I went into engineering that it wasn't what I wanted to do.

> (Martin, 1st year, C)

He spent a year trying to get out of it, and eventually took a printing apprenticeship which he also disliked, and stayed for only nine days. He then went back to his school with the aim of taking some scientific A levels, but stuck that out for only six days. After that, he went back to the car plant and took an engineering apprenticeship, where he stayed for five years, taking an HND in the process: he came top in the course. He began work in manpower production for the company which he also hated:

I decided to leave the day I was offered the job.

Because of his interest in films, he decided to apply to study communications, a move in which he was encouraged by his mother, although his father was 'totally against what I've done'. It was a move, however, which he had not regretted: he was full of enthusiasm for the communications course, and contrasted it several times with the tedium of the HND he'd taken. He also contrasted the experience of being educated in an all-male environment with a mixed one; and he was remarkably candid about the transition:

It has broadened my outlook in ways I never dreamt it would, especially as far as women go, because throughout my life, going to an all-boys' grammar school and going to an engineering institute, women just don't take part at all and now I'm having to compete on level terms with women who are more intelligent – well, I don't know yet, but possibly.

(Martin, 1st year, C)

Asked how he felt about having intelligent women in the group, he replied:

That is a real kick in the teeth, to be honest. It really is, having come from such a male chauvinist background. That has been the biggest eye-opener, it really has. And I've been pleasantly surprised by the contrast, because it can be a bit boring sometimes, competing against blokes.

(Martin, 1st year, C)

The interview continued as follows:

KIM: Does it bother you that there are more girls than boys in the group?

MARTIN: Yes, there are more girls. I'd been led by people who came to the college to believe that there'd be a lot more women, but I'm not too sure of the ratio, but it's not too bad – well, I say 'bad', but that's probably the wrong word, isn't it? And when they first told me this, I thought, 'What sort of course is it going to be? It's going to be full of women. What sort of job is it going to lead to? Do I really want to do it? And I thought, 'Yeah, why not? I'm going to go into it with an open mind,' and I'm glad I did – as I say, it certainly broadens your outlook.

KIM: Do you feel any difficulty about being in a minority?

MARTIN: No, not really, no. It's good fun – I think I'd rather have it this way. You find as well that if you want to have a blokes' conversation or whatever with any of my friends on the course, you can divide up into little groups anyway. That's a natural thing to happen. If you want to talk about football or something like that, the girls will soon clear off and leave you to get on with it, the same if they want to talk about whatever they want to, hairdressing or whatever, the latest pop groups; you soon get a natural division. Also, the sort of course it is, there isn't a heavy demand on your time for lectures, so you tend to divide up and bump into each other in the library and if you want to discuss anything, if they've got questions they want to ask you, you just naturally do it. You don't think, 'God, she's a girl, I'm not going to help her, I'm only going to help the blokes'. That's what surprised me, I thought there would have been more of a division between the sexes.

(Martin, 1st year, C)

The implicit assumptions behind Martin's comments are particularly interest-ing, both in themselves, and as a contrast with Lesley's comments, quoted in Chapter 6. The most obvious feature is his view of gender differences, which appear to be very sharply defined in his account. He is surprised – he finds it a 'kick in the teeth' – that there are women who might, *possibly*, be more intelligent than he is. He thinks that a course composed mainly of women must be less demanding, less useful than one dominated by men. He enjoys being on a mixed course, especially as he is also able, when he wants, to have a 'blokes' conversation' – apparently about football – while the 'girls' talk about 'hair-dressing' and 'pop groups': quite trivial concerns. It also quite genuinely doesn't occur to him that he might ever need to ask a woman for help, even though most of the women on the course came from arts and social science rather than engineering backgrounds. In addition, he is very aware of 'compe-tition', in a way that most of the other arts students weren't. In fact, none of the other male arts students talked in terms of 'competing' against women, and none of the women mentioned it either. Like his attitudes towards women, it seems to be a product of the engineering background: competition with fellow students was considered to be an important part of the education.

If we compare this with Lesley's account in Chapter 6, we find some interesting similarities and differences. The similarity between them is that they both regard femininity with a certain degree of contempt: Martin does not aim to be 'as good as a woman', for example, or to prove himself in a female-dominated – a phrase that rests uneasily on the page – world. The differences are in their attitude towards being in a minority; whereas Lesley assumes that her course must be more difficult because of the number of men, that she has to work to be 'as good as' the male students, Martin assumes that his course is inferior because of the number of women and is worried that it might not lead to a good job. Most importantly Martin does not experience the sense of *being in a minority* in the way that Lesley feels it; he feels neither conspicuous nor ill at ease because of his belonging to a numerical minority.

Martin's sense of the superiority of masculinity was part both of his experi-ence as an engineer and of his experience as a communications student. As an engineer, he could believe that men were 'better' because no women did engineering. (And, mutually reinforcing, engineering was better because no woman did it.) As a communications student, he was better because he was in the privileged position of being in a minority: automatically superior as a man, and as an engineer, he could help the women with their work. The logic is circular, but it is there: as an engineer and as a communications student, Martin's identity as male is positively reinforced through rating women negatively.

Like Martin, most men regarded the fact that they were in a numerical minority as unproblematic; as this first-year student said:

> I just consider myself an individual having an understanding with my own tutors, so I don't feel myself in competition with girls. I'm aware of there being a lot of girls, but I don't know what the actual numbers are – ten to one I should think [sic].
>
> (Kevin, 1st year, B)

It is important that Kevin says that he considers himself 'an individual'. This is in contrast to some of the female science students who clearly felt part of a group, with a definite group identity, and who lacked a powerful sense of individual identity. He went on:

> I suppose there's a little bit of people regard arts degrees as 'feminine', so to speak; it doesn't really bother me, but you tend to think of arty people as being a little bit effeminate, I suppose; that's the impression you get from other people, probably more people at home, outside the system.
>
> (Kevin, 1st year, B)

There was some awareness, then, of arts degrees being considered 'effeminate'. However, within higher education itself, this was not the case; it was simply the view of outsiders.

Some male students mentioned feeling conspicuous:

> In my seminar I'm the only bloke. There are only two blokes doing English and French, and you get a lot of attention, people take more notice of what you say.
>
> (Gary, 1st year, B)

In this context, being in a minority sex is an advantage, not a disadvantage; men, by virtue of their conspicuousness, are more worthy of attention than women. This confirms Dr S's comment, quoted earlier, that because men stand out they are paid more attention.

Like some of the female physics students, some of the male English students had come from single-sex schools. This did not, however, appear to be a problem. Andy, for example, had been to a boys' grammar school:

> You didn't realize that English was a girls' subject, it was just the same as any other subject, and you didn't realize that certain subjects are orientated towards women or men; we had thirty blokes in each class, sixty in the whole year. It was unusual, yeah, unusual – and they're all so quiet, shocking . . . they just sit there during whole tutorials, heads down, not looking at anyone, and not saying anything.
>
> (Andy, 3rd year, B)

To Andy, English was not a gendered subject, and neither was science; the effect of finding out that English *was* gendered, however, a 'feminine' rather than a 'masculine' subject, did nothing to disturb his sense of ease or confidence in himself – and he was a supremely confident person. On the contrary, women appear as an unidentifiable mass, sitting quietly, not saying anything. It is the exact opposite of the situation of the female science students: coming from a single-sex environment to a mainly male one they felt uneasy. Men coming from a single-sex environment to a mainly female one felt more assured and more confident than before.

However, one man said that he felt isolated during seminars:

> For the American seminar I'm the only bloke in there with another six women, and I feel intimidated because they're all very loud and they're carping on about the lack of feminine fiction, feminist fiction on the course, and I feel if I say anything I'm going to be jumped on and it's going to destroy the tone and also I never feel inspired by the tutor in that one, he seems to cloud a lot of the issues.
>
> (Michael, 3rd year, B)

I asked whether the tutor agreed with the women:

> Yes, I think he tends to cop out sometimes, we did some Sylvia Plath and he said that he ought to feel embarrassed by it, but it was probably because he was a bloke, because of how personal it was, and all these women said how incredibly relevant it was, and I kept my mouth shut because I thought it was vaguely self-indulgent.
>
> (Michael, 3rd year, B)

Asked whether he thought women's writing in general was worth studying, he said:

> Show me a woman writer who's worth reading, then that's fair enough. I suppose the problem lies in the tutor's not giving you enough experience of who is good and who isn't. Virginia Woolf's the only woman writer we've done this term apart from Sylvia Plath. I just like to distance myself from the feminist cause a little because I think it's a bit hysterical sometimes.
>
> (Michael, 3rd year, B)

This student obviously does feel left out of this group, and isolated, in much the same way that some of the female students did. But there are differences, the main one being that he does feel more able to challenge the authority of the tutor, if not in person, then mentally. He does disagree with what is said in the tutorials, and feels fairly sure of his own opinions. His perception of Sylvia Plath's poetry as 'self-indulgent' is a conventional masculine charge against women's writing, and one which is illustrative of the differences in perceptions about literature between female students and male students; here emotional response is characterized as 'hysterical'. It is also interesting that Michael perceives the tutor as rather weak for tending to 'cop out' – that is not asserting his authority, and not telling the group what they ought to think about literature, or what they ought to be reading. This is not to deny Michael's sense of unease at being in the group; his response highlights the tensions inevitable in a mixed-sex discussion of an author who is concerned, at the core, with female identity and female sexuality.

Michael's description of feminism as 'hysterical' was not unique; feminism aroused hostility amongst other of the male students, for example:

> The only thing that can come of it [being in a minority] is if you get involved in a feminist argument, but I wouldn't say every single girl on the course was a raving feminist. And so, however many girls there are on the course, a fairly high percentage, maybe half of them, are feminists in their point of view, but a lot aren't.
>
> (Simon, 1st year, A)

Given that there was some attempt, in University A, to raise feminist issues in the course, one might speculate whether this had any influence, other than a negative one, on the men. One male student who discussed feminist ideas with me, said that 'I've never done a tutorial with another lad, always with other women'. When asked what this was like, he said:

> Sometimes it's bad, especially when you get these amateur feminists in, they kind of expect you to say things, I don't know. I'm a bit naughty, I used to say things which would annoy people but of course you get nowhere doing that, you just get people's backs up really, but especially in the first year I'm sure I was a bit chauvinist anyway. That's something as well, I've changed my ideas as well since being at university, I've probably become a lot more sympathetic towards the feminist stance . . . that's a thing about our department, anyway, a large number of women are, if not feminists, that's definitely where their sympathies lie.
>
> (Terry, 3rd year, A)

And he added:

> A career is for a bloke to write literature or to teach it and a pastime is for women to read it, to accept it and to get this indoctrination through literature.
>
> (Terry, 3rd year, A)

This combination of feminist awareness, on the one hand, and mockery ('these amateur feminists') on the other, is an example of the men's ability to maintain a sense of confidence and self-assurance despite being challenged; Terry is able to accept feminist ideas while deriding those women who hold them. Despite being in a minority of one, he was quite able to stand out against the opinion of others in the seminar group – accepting feminism but refusing to be threatened by it.

This self-assertion was characteristic of the male English students. For them, part of the point of English was to argue a case through, to get one's opinion across. The following two excerpts, for example, are from students talking about seminar discussions:

> I like picking out themes and discussing various subjects like psychology, history, politics . . . I don't like saying things are nice and beautiful and 'Isn't this a lovely image', I think that's a waste of time. I mean, English students are there to destroy and build up arguments.
>
> (Andy, 3rd year, B)

On an actual course level, the things I enjoy most are seminars – sitting down and putting across your arguments to someone else who puts theirs across and you just batter it around the table; I thoroughly enjoy that, I really quite revel in it.

(Ben, 3rd year, A)

This attitude towards seminar discussion is not confined to English students. Russell was a final-year communications student, highly articulate, very able and self-confident almost to the point of arrogance. When asked whether he got on with other students on the course, he said

Yeah, some of them, yeah, but I've personally got a bit of a name for kind of, I don't know why, but shooting people down a lot in seminars and stuff, I tend to take over a little and dominate, but I think some people are a bit worried about talking to me about work because they think that I do loads of it and I do loads of reading, you know, and therefore that I know it all; it's not true but I think that that's a kind of popular image that I've got. But I just spend most of my time talking to lecturers, seeing them outside and stuff, you know – they're more in my terms of reference than other people.

(Russell, 3rd year, C)

This characteristic of intellectual aggression is highlighted when seen in relation to female academics. In the male lecturer–female student or male lecturer –male student relationship, the hierarchy is easily defined; in the case of female lecturer–male student or even female lecturer–female student, the hierarchical relationship is not so straightforward. Female academics are not invested with the same authority as male academics, and therefore the tensions between femininity and academic success are once more highlighted, as they were for the female science students. The following is an excerpt from an interview with a male English student:

With my current tutor, I tend to be rather argumentative because she's a talker, she would talk if you let her – so I cut across her sometimes, which might mean she thinks I'm aggressive, but she might not have a bad impression of my academic ability, she probably respects me in that respect.

(George, 3rd year, A)

One only has to imagine a female student making the same remark about a male tutor to feel the force of this inversion of authority. George clearly sees his tutor as a *woman* and therefore does not accord her the same respect as he would a male tutor. He, like the other students, equates aggression with academic ability, but he does not allow his tutor the right to be aggressive or, for that matter, to talk at any length – 'She would talk if you let her'. George, therefore, defines himself through his difference from his tutor, by rating her negatively.

George's attitude to his female tutor, like the attitude of Russell to the other students in his seminar group, is, more than anything, an assertion of individuality. It was argued in the previous chapter that, for the English and communications students, the freedom to express an individual opinion was an integral part of the appeal of those academic disciplines. Individuality became an important part of the arts students' identity. Unlike the female science students, who struggled to 'fit in' with the department, who wanted to be accepted and who, on occasion, developed a collective identity, the male arts students wanted nothing more than to be different. Doing English (or communications) for them meant *not* being like every one else. One student, when asked what appealed to him about English, said:

> I like arguing. I like being pig-headed and putting forward my own opinions and discussing large numbers of subjects which are totally irrelevant to the appropriate topic. I don't like working logically and coming out with a precise answer.
>
> (Andy, 3rd year, B)

Doing English enables students not to be uniform, and at the same time to be successful; in physics women constantly felt that they had to keep up with other people, to attain the standard set by the department. In English, however, it is possible to assert oneself through rejecting those pre-set standards:

> It's good in that you don't have to say 'This is this' and 'This is this', all these facts are set out for you; there's a degree of personal appreciation of something. If you like something, you can tell someone why you like it, and they say 'Yes I like it because of this, or I don't like it because of that', but with economics or sociology or any of those subjects, it's all there and you just listen to it and you take it in.
>
> (Gary, 1st year, B)

As seen in Chapter 5, some students felt that the department was unable to accommodate their individuality and self-expression, that English at university was too rigid. The expression of individuality for these students takes the form of rebellion against the departmental norms and values:

> Our tutor was asking us last week what we were doing for the exam, and I thought, 'Well, there are so many thoughts going on in my mind the whole day, the whole week, that I just couldn't care less what the exam's like, I've got to go through it in the end, but to think that every thought you think has got to be related to your course and everything, is terribly closeted and quite grotesque, quite ugly because it doesn't give you any chance to be an individual'.
>
> (Robert, 3rd year, B)

There is still space, however, for Robert's form of rebellion within the department. His individuality was, in one way, an asset; he was able to express himself through a creative writing course which allowed him to explore, among other things, his interest in Freudian dream theory; he came out with an upper second degree. Unlike the female physics students he was able to do well without having to struggle constantly to accommodate himself.

The self-confidence of male students in asserting themselves and arguing their case in seminars can also be seen in the way some of them talked about the set texts. The following quote, for example, is from a man discussing the characteristics of black and feminist fiction, and how to recognize passages from various authors in examination papers:

> Black authors are going to be writing about things like identity and the fact of their existence and the need for recognition and the need to escape. . . . What you're taught I think on an English literary course is to apply a few basic rules to literature, so you'll apply a few basic rules for black fiction to this piece of black writing. When you know before you go in the kind of thing you're supposed to be looking for, it's just a matter of being able to pick it out.
>
> (Daniel, 3rd year, B)

Daniel is able to see English as the application of a 'few basic rules' because he distances himself from the experiences in the texts; he does not engage with them in the same way that a woman or black person would *have* to engage with them. Further, although men were willing to discuss their favourite authors – D. H. Lawrence, Kurt Vonnegut, Thomas Pynchon, Nabokov, Graham Greene, among others – they rarely talked of them in a personal or emotional way: unlike women, whose response to literature was more involved.

The desire for individuality, for freedom from social constraints, also emerged when the male arts students talked about their future lives and careers. English was certainly not perceived as a route to a career in the way that physics was. However, the English students were clear about the *kind* of future they wanted for themselves, and talked about their future lives in the same language that they used to talk about their subject: a language which expressed a concern with people, individuality and variety. In addition, many appeared to feel a moral repugnance towards many of the traditional graduate careers, such as management and accountancy.

Several students had considered teaching, journalism or VSO although few had done anything positive about embarking on these careers. Amongst the final-year English men, there were only two who were certain about what they wanted to do: one who intended to enter advertising ('It's about the one vocational course an English student's got, I think') and another who wanted to be an educational psychologist. Of the others, one had considered journalism, advertising or marketing (none of which he was very enthusiastic about); one wanted to be unemployed while working on his writing and photography; one wanted ultimately to do something 'socially useful' but had considered teaching abroad for a year initially; one expected (reluctantly) that he would become a teacher; one had vaguely considered the civil service; one wanted to write. Most of the students however, were more explicit about what they didn't want than what they did want:

> I know I'd much rather be involved with people than money. I wouldn't want to spend all my time putting money and business before people.
>
> (George, 3rd year, A)

I'm just not career-minded at all . . . I've always had this hopelessly vague notion of social responsibility in terms of doing a job. Just being tread-milled into accountancy or something is something I don't want to do.

(Michael, 3rd year, B)

This attitude of wanting to 'be involved with people rather than money' was very common. Whereas money usually featured highly in physics students' visions of the future, many of the English students, male and female, said that they neither wanted to work in business nor earn a great deal of money. Their values, then, what they looked for in life, were quite different.

Some of the students were embarrassed about their vagueness and their lack of commitment; at least one, however, regarded it as a positive decision:

What I want in life is not to know where I'm going – which is very different from the way I'm brought up to think.

(Terry, 3rd year, A)

The extremity of Terry's position is startling. It is, however, closely related to his view of English and university. In the same way that English is regarded as a valuable subject to study because of its scope and individuality, so many students wanted that freedom and potential in their future lives; they didn't want to be tied down by convention. For some, this meant conflict between their own wishes and familial or social ones; Terry, for example, knew that his family would expect him to try and get a respectable job. This was also true of Daniel, a final-year student at B. Like Richard, the physics student discussed earlier, he came from a working-class background where higher education was considered unusual, rather than normal. Although his parents had always encouraged him, without putting pressure on him in any particular direction, friends of his family regarded him as rather strange because he hadn't decided to enter a high-flying job. His eventual ambition was to become a child psychotherapist; he wanted to do voluntary work for a year, followed by a PGCE in primary school teaching; he then intended to teach for a few years before moving on to child psycho-therapy. In about ten years' time he thought he would either still be in teach-ing or have moved on to psychotherapy or educational psychology; he would, at any rate, be in some kind of youth work or work with children. As he says, 'I always see myself in a relatively low-paid but what I think is perhaps a more rewarding job'. He contrasts this attitude both with that of the other students and that of his acquaintance at home:

I see people rushing off, and the milk round is coming round and everybody is being chartered accountants and retail managers and things, and even that would sound better at home, if I said I was going to be an accountant. People are getting these jobs and I say, 'Well done' but I couldn't think of anything worse than being a retail manager so I don't know why every-body's desperate to get these jobs. It's partly because there's a lot more pressure, talking to students who are in their 30s now, there's an awful lot more pressure now to know exactly where you're going and know what you're going to be doing in so many years time that I don't think there was ten or twenty years ago. I don't particularly want to settle down in two years' time with my job and this job is going to last me till I retire . . . I'm not interested.

(David, 3rd year, B)

For Daniel, and for many others, variety, fulfilment, working with people and job satisfaction were all seen as more important than earning high wages or gaining social respectability. There was no difference in this between the female students and the male students; only a small number of either sex wanted to enter traditional management or executive-type jobs.

The traditional occupation of English graduates is teaching, and certainly some of the students saw their futures as teachers. Few of them expressed a great deal of enthusiasm for conventional secondary/primary school teaching, however, and other alternatives, TEFL in particular, were popular. TEFL was never regarded, however, as a permanent career, but just as something that might be done for a couple of years after graduating until something better turned up. The eventual decision on what to do with one's life was to be postponed because English, was not, after all, that sort of subject.

Similarly students' long-term plans tended to be vague, and occasionally unrealistic. Unlike the male science students, who generally saw their long-term futures in relation to the kind of job they would be doing, male arts students often talked in terms of friends or relationships:

I'd like to think that I would at least have had something published . . . I'd like to think I could make a living out of it, but the only way to make a living out of something like that is to compromise yourself, just to be read and heard . . . I'd like to think I would be living comfortably, with a comfortable association of friends. I'd like to think I'd be more politically active, and generally a lot more optimistic than I have been in the past.

(Robert, 3rd year, B)

Robert's vision of the future is untouched by materialism; he sees his needs as primarily emotional and intellectual. The same is true of John, who says

I can only look in vague terms at wanting to feel I'm doing something worthwhile, and that's interesting to me, I won't feel as if I've wasted opportunities or something. I've got no financial ambitions at all, I'm quite happy living on bare means, just as long as I can afford to get some books, get some records. I'm a very unambitious person, I always was, I think, at school; it's just that I want to be perpetually interested, keep myself alive up here, feel it's all worthwhile.

(John, 3rd year, A)

Some male students imagined themselves with families, but not in the same way as the women discussed in Chapter 6, who talked in terms of the conflict between career and family. Michael's own hope for the future, as he recognizes himself, is completely idealistic:

Sometimes I'd like to be married, have a big family, live in a cottage in the highlands or something, which is hopelessly unrealistic. I don't know, I can't see myself going into big business or getting a job in the city like a lot of people do, going into middle management, becoming an executive, I can't see that really. I do have ideas of trying it, to see if I could do it, then I'd pack it in, but I don't think I'll ever try it. I'll probably end up teaching, if I was very, very realistic. I think I'll end up in a school just like me dad.

(Michael, 3rd year, B)

Andy said sardonically:

Hopefully middle-class suburbia, working in an office, 2.4 children, wife, go on holidays every six months, vote Conservative – but I'm not totally scared by such boring constraints of conformity, it's hard to tell, I've got nothing against those things; if you haven't got enough confidence to do something different yourself, just lead an interesting life, it's the way you make it.

(Andy, 3rd year, B)

Most of the male English students were quite aware that what they wanted to do was completely at odds with the practical realities. While doing English at university gave them a degree of freedom to do and think as they pleased, they recognized that this was not possible in the outside world. Most of them, however, lacked any idea of what they would like to do after graduating.

The communications students were somewhat different. Unlike the English students, all the final-year students knew what they wanted to do after graduating. Of the four men, one wanted to go into television production, one wanted to be a cameraman, one wanted to be a newspaper journalist and the fourth, a particularly able student, wanted to do postgraduate work. The first-year students were more vague about what they wanted to do, although they were all interested in the media; the possible careers cited were working in video, playing in a band, being a television producer and setting up a pirate radio station! Most of the students were enthusiastic and self-confident; one final-year student said:

I'd really like ultimately to get into film production. I aim to produce a film, but that's an ideal. Once you get a steady job in television production, that's OK for a while, but then after that I'll perhaps go independent. Cinema is the ultimate thing to do in the end.

(Ken, 3rd year, C)

It is highly unlikely that they all achieved their ambitions, as journalism and television are very competitive fields. (The same applies, of course, to those English students who wanted to be journalists; it is not a very realistic ambition.) However, the students did not regard the course as solely vocational. Most of them had found the course stimulating and interesting in its own right; one student said that 'If I could have done any course in the entire country, I'd have done this one'. In addition, hardly any of them saw their futures in terms of financial and material success. They all stressed satisfaction in their work as the most important feature of the job they wanted to do. They were, on the whole, less materialist and less instrumental in their attitude towards work than the physics students, but more so than the English students.

Not surprisingly, the male communications students also saw their long-term futures in terms of the job they would be doing, although they generally appeared more interested in the job itself than in the material benefits it might bring:

> Hopefully I'll be working with cameras. That's what I'd like to do, and obviously I don't know what it's like to be in that situation for any length of time, because I've never really been in that situation apart from working in projects, but I would like really to be working in cameras of some description, either cinema or video or television.
>
> (Charles, 3rd year, C)

Like the male physics students, the communications students found it easy to define themselves in terms of their future careers. They generally saw themselves as independent, creative people, who would be successful in their field (there was surprisingly little doubt amongst students that they *would* be successful); they didn't reject all the trappings of conventionality like some of the English students; rather, they thought that careers in film, video and so on, gave them freedom to express that independence.

The male humanities students, then, were generally confident of their opinions and ideas and found little difficulty in settling into a largely female environment. Let us now compare their experience with that of the female humanities students.

The female humanities students

It would appear, initially, that the female English students are in an advantageous position. English is a 'woman's subject'; the women are in a majority and hence have strength in numbers. They do not face the isolation of the female science students. Similarly both English and communications are more 'mixed' subjects than physics and physical sciences; the sexes did not separate themselves during lectures but mixed and talked freely.

Despite their lack of isolation, however, many of the female students appeared to face other difficulties to do with their self-image, and many had doubts about their own abilities. We noted earlier that men saw in English a chance to assert their individuality; that they particularly enjoyed the cut-and-thrust of debate in seminars, for example. This assertion was not present amongst the women; indeed, many felt very reticent about participating in debate. In Chapter 5 Carole, a first-year student at B, was quoted as saying that she found seminars 'intimidating' and that there were 'an awful lot of clever people in our seminar'. When asked how she knew that they were more clever than she was, she said

> I think more confidence – probably I'm as intelligent as them really – or I tell myself, anyway – they just seemed to be very confident, and I felt really intimidated.
>
> (Carole, 1st year, B)

The contrast with the student who complained about feminist intimidation is marked; this student's doubts are much more to do with her own personal ability, or lack of it, than complaints about the behaviour of other students. Many of the female students were very self-conscious; one who was painfully self-deprecating throughout the interview managed to say something positive about herself, with several qualifications, when asked what she'd gained from the course:

> I think it teaches you to – you wouldn't guess it from this interview – I think it teaches you to express yourself a lot better. Like I told you, I'm not very active in participating in seminars, but it's brought me out a lot and also, in actually writing essays I think my style's improved a lot and I think that's bound to come if you're reading a lot of literature a lot of the time.
>
> (Diane, 3rd year, B)

The quietness of the female students was even commented on by a male student:

> It's amazing how quiet a lot of people are, especially girls; it's normally one or two people [who talk]; some people can sit in a seminar for one and a half hours and say absolutely nothing. I normally say more than most people . . . I always find it's better to say something or you get asked questions.
>
> (Andy, 3rd year, B)

Lack of confidence or assertion in seminars and tutorials can have an important influence on a department's impression of a student. In physics, students make their mark by performing well in the constant 'competitions'; the lab work, the problem sheets, the tests, the termly examinations. A student's achievement is usually very visible in physics: achievement is more easily measured and graded. In English, however, students are much less likely to know how other students are doing. The main form of assessment during term-time, the essay, is much more private, a matter between tutor and student. In addition, essay marks are not likely to vary greatly between students in the way that physics marks might vary. The main way in which a student can make an impression in English, then, both on staff and students, is by being talkative and (preferably) provocative or controversial in seminars: the reticence of some women in seminars is compounded by their invisibility – by being less conspicuous than the men, they can seem less interesting and less intelligent.

On the communications course, there was much less need for students to work to make an impression; as the course was substantially smaller than the two English courses, staff tended to know most of the students individually. Even so, some of the female students lacked confidence in their own ability. There was one final-year student, for example, who was very negative about her abilities. Despite wanting to have a career in television production, she perceived herself as both unambitious and not terribly competent. Vera has already been quoted on the topic of her single-sex education; her headmistress had wanted the pupils to be 'career women and be successful and dynamic and not get married'; 'it just didn't agree with me at all'.

Deciding to go to polytechnic rather than university involved a degree of willpower and rebellion as the pressure was firmly the other way (she had A level grades of BBD, so would have had no problem in getting into university); it was curious then that Vera had such little faith in her own ability:

> I feel I'm a bit of a waste. The staff would like to have more inspiring and intelligent people on the course. I want the course to be really good, and want it to get better, for them to spend more money on it, and I want them to be able to say, 'Look, we've got all these wonderful people who've got so much going for them, wouldn't you like to spend some money on them'; but I know that I'm not worth it, but other people who want to do the course *are*, and that's what I'd like, I just feel a bit of a disappointment, really.
>
> (Vera, 3rd year, B)

She also said

> I really wonder if I've learnt enough to be justified in getting a BA degree . . . it's something, you talk about people with a degree, you think they must be so clever, yet I don't feel clever at all.

These interview extracts may simply give the impression that the women in the sample were either lacking in ability or, at best, painfully shy. Yet in conversation, they were generally relaxed enough, easy and interesting to talk to, often lively. The anxieties they voiced were genuine feelings of inadequacy resulting from a social situation (finding themselves with a group of people who were superficially intellectual and articulate) in which they feel at a disadvantage. Women's sense of inferiority is heightened and re-created through a seminar system which rates articulacy and even aggression more than thoughtfulness. Despite the arguments of S. Bowles and Gintis (1976) about schools, the university seminar is not a situation in which passivity and docility are rewarded.

In an earlier section, we noted an hostility towards feminism amongst some of the male students. There was an ambivalence amongst some of the female students, however, towards feminist ideas, and this is partly the result of an awareness of others' perception of feminism. For example, Diana, a first-year student at A, mentioned a recent lecture on feminist criticism (by Dr S), of which she said,

> All the boys got annoyed about it but I think it was really good, it was really thought-provoking, and there was a subdued silence for the whole lecture.
>
> (Diana, 1st year, A)

She said that when the lecturer had asked the female students how many of them were feminists, only a handful of students had put their hands up. She continued:

I was thinking, if this was say eight or ten years ago, I'm sure all the girls would have put their hands up and it just seemed to me that it was a real shame that a lot of the girls aren't feminists now, I don't know why that is . . . I think I am feminist in a way, I think women should have equal rights in career terms, but I'm not really interested in it enough to really do anything about it.

(Diana, 1st year, A)

This perception contradicts that of Simon, who thought that half of the women were feminists; Diana hadn't been one of the students who put her hand up. While being aware of sex inequality and injustice, she is also aware of the image men have of feminists. What she is prepared to say publicly, the image of herself she puts across, is limited by that awareness. This was true, too, of a final-year woman at A, who enthused about the 'women and literature' course run by Dr S. However, she went on:

I'm not a feminist, I'm not aggressively feminist but I do believe in equal opportunity and equal pay and I do believe women should have the chance to do things because I think very much that people think you should have to choose between home and career, and I don't think you should have to choose.

(Gillian, 3rd year, A)

It has already been argued that students define themselves by comparing themselves with others, by trying to measure up to a pre-set standard. Carole, for example, thought that the students in her seminar group were more intelligent than she was because they were more confident and articulate. Female physics students tried to be 'as good as men'. This contradiction between femininity and academic ability also emerged in an interview with a female student at B. She had been talking about the numbers of women doing English:

I think it's ironic, though, that it's still, in these days of equal opportunity, the department is mainly female-orientated, female students and the sciences mainly male . . . it's probably a lot to do with primary school level, you know, you'd give a girl a book but you'd give a boy a car engine or something, it could be that, or it could be just a genetical make up of male and female minds, we don't know enough about it, it's very interesting. I don't know how many people there are in our year, about 100, and we know who the men are, and the boys, men and boys, we know who all the mature male students are, you know their names, and you know them by sight if you don't know them by name, but there are so many girls, I'm still meeting people today who I didn't realize had been doing my course with me for three years, and it's a very female-orientated subject.

(Susan, 3rd year, A)

This confirms that the men are, by virtue of being male, more conspicuous in the department; but then I pointed out to Susan that although most of the students were female, most of the staff were male:

> That's very ironic as well. It just goes to show that if males infiltrate into a supposedly female world of studying literature – *they're* the ones who wrote it. I mean, you look at before this century there were hardly any women writers and when there were, like the Brontë sisters, they all wrote under male pseudonyms, and it just goes to show that the males teach it as well. Because I don't think women tutors are taken seriously . . . there's a few of the female tutors that I do respect but there's a couple that I do think, Yes, you are useless, and you do rely on your femininity. They sit there and say, 'Well, what do you think of this?' instead of being forthright about it like a male tutor would be; they sit there and they giggle and rely on their femininity and 'Oh dear, I'm not sure what this means, ha, ha, ha' and it just makes you sick and I always hope that I'm not like that, but then I look around other female students and the female students are exactly the same in their attitude towards male tutors: 'Oh, I'm so sorry I haven't done my assessed essay, can I have an extension, please', smile, bat the eyelids, and obviously you can't help it but the sexual politics do come into contact with how you get on in the department.

> (Susan, 3rd year, A)

This diatribe is interesting for a variety of reasons. The general thrust of it is a complaint about female tutors and female students. It is worth noting that she equates the male appropriation of the female occupation – writing – with the greater numbers of men teaching English. (Despite what Susan says, there *were* a lot of women writers before the twentieth century, many writing under their own names; it is a measure of the success of literary critics in so rigidly defining the literary 'canon' that, not only is the work of these female writers now not studied, but also it is not generally known that they even existed.) Apart from attacking the 'feminine' strategy of some of the female students, she also attacks the female tutors for not being as 'forthright' as the male tutors; she accepts the equation of assertion and aggression with ability. That is, she sees the situation from a male viewpoint. The female academic has the problem of coping with male students' aggression and of defining her own identity in a way that is acceptable to students and to male colleagues. Whereas a male academic's role is clearly and precisely defined, the role of a female academic – and hence her relationship with students – is much more shadowy and vague.

Like the male students, the female students regarded their individuality, the right to assert their own opinions as an important part of their identity as English students. Whereas men's enjoyment of English, however, was often expressed aggressively – as a desire to engage in, and win, an argument – women's enjoyment centred much more round the quality of their own personal responses. In Chapter 5 for example, a female student was quoted as saying that English was about 'studying the soul of people': an emotive, but not untypical response. This kind of response can also be seen in the following extract from a third-year English student, who is talking about an option she did which she sees as opposing the dominant literary beliefs of the department:

> The best course I ever did was last year: an option called 'The Poet's Voice' and it's about modern poetry and stuff, but it's seeing videos of the poets reading their own poetry instead of getting it on a page, which is quite a cold process and just hearing what they say and how they speak, and also it was really interesting, it went into reggae and oral poetry and jazz; because I suppose that was a lot freer course in a way, because the essays you had to write on it were things that were quite personal really, your own poetry and stuff, so there was a big space for personal creativity which there is to an extent on the other course, but not a big extent really, because it's still quite orthodox, with quite established critical opinion; you can't really write 'I feel' much or anything.
>
> (Alice, 3rd year, B)

Men, too, often objected to having established opinion pushed on them, but their criticisms were more often to do with their right to express their own ideas rather than to show their feelings. Alice's criticisms, however, went much further to include the lack of female writers on the course. She talks, for example, about the American Literature part of the degree; it had begun with Poe and Melville until

> Now, at the end of a two-year course we're squeezing in black writers and women writers – I mean, it is bad actually, given the overall view of the course, because, up till now, I haven't done one woman writer or one black writer, it's been, like, all these big figures and stuff, so that's interesting, but it does seem a bit of a 'Oh well, we'd better put a couple of women writers on because there's a feminist movement going on', so it's going right up to books like Marge Piercey, 'Woman on the Edge of Time'.
>
> (Alice, 3rd year, B)

She also pointed out that there had not been one female author on the core English Poetry course. It is significant that issues of gender are raised only when *female* authors are studied, issues of race only when *black* writers are studied. Writers who happen to be women thus become 'women writers'; writers who happen to be black become 'black writers'; yet we never talk about 'men writers' or 'white writers'. The ideas of 'male as norm' and 'white as norm' are reinforced by a process which determines that female and black writers are studied first in terms of their identity as women or blacks, not in terms of their identity as writers. The way in which male writers construct their identity as men, or white writers their identity as whites, is not considered to be worthy of study.

Alice's feelings about theorizing and critical opinion are summed up by her response to my question about whether she read much literary criticism:

> Basically I think your own opinion is just as valid, and also it tends to get a bit tainted if you read too much.
>
> (Alice, 3rd year, B)

This view, which would be considered alarming in any discipline other than English, was one that seemed quite normal to Alice, and is, to a large degree, part of most English students' construction of English. In the following extract, for example, a student explains that what is important to her is the quality of her immediate, intuitive response:

> That's a problem I find in poetry, that I can appreciate it for what it is and what it's saying and what it's *doing to me*, but actually going into it in depth and looking at the way it's all been put together and language and everything, last year I found that a problem in seminars.
>
> (Jean, 3rd year, B, my emphasis)

A female mature student emphasized the importance of experience in enabling her to relate to and understand literature:

> Doing English I think it is an advantage, being a bit older, because I think you can sympathize with some of the things that the authors of these texts are saying better because perhaps you've experienced them.
>
> (Joan, 1st year, A)

This stress on an affective, emotional response to literature resulted, amongst some women, in a disdain for theory. Jennifer, for example, took psychology as her subsidiary subject and I asked her if she saw any links between psychology and English:

> When I said I wanted to do psychology, I invented some vague link between the two; I don't think there really is – apart from the fact that you can conclude that a lot of novelists are loonies, but they are anyway. . . . You can apply Freud to a lot of things, but it doesn't really get you very far, they completely ruined *Alice in Wonderland* doing Freud on it, because you just apply that to it and it becomes the most pornographic novel ever written, so it's just a waste of time.
>
> (Jennifer, 3rd year, A)

This reflected her more general attitude to theory:

> To me it doesn't add anything to a novel, in fact it takes an awful lot away, it just ruins it for me – it's probably because I'm not very technical.
>
> (Jennifer, 3rd year, A)

At most levels, the responses of the male and female students to literature are not very different; the majority of students came to English through a voracious love of reading, and felt that literature gave them an insight into the lives and ideas of others. There is, however, a profound contradiction for students in the responses they are supposed to feel towards literature. Earlier in this chapter, the head of department at B was quoted as saying that the study of literature was about 'affective, emotional response'; he then went on to say that some of the female students were *too* emotional in their response to literature. Because the curricula of English departments are dominated by the 'canon' of what is deemed worthy, one of the prerequisites of success for any English student is an acceptance of these definitions of worth. As Bowen has said of Leavis's writing, 'It is an attempt to produce readings of texts but, equally importantly, to *prevent, limit* and *restrict* them' (1985: 371). What both Leavis and Richards did – and what liberal humanist critics continue to do – is to refuse a set of absolute standards for judging literature, while at the same time denying the subjective or emotional basis of their own judgements; Leavis's judgements were right *because he said they were right*. The consequence is a spurious objectivity: a 'claim to be able to assess by a norm, yet the refusal to specify what that norm is' (Bowen 1985: 311). Similarly Richards's injunction to students of literature was – in Bowen's words again – 'emotionality and detachment, expression and mimesis, individuality and objectivity' (1985: 311). English students are caught between these injunctions to emotionality and detachment; this is particularly the case for women, of whom it may be said, if they are not cautious enough, 'the emotional, affective thing is too strong'. Whereas the male students, as we have already seen, used self-assertion and argument to establish their views, women, although not in reality more emotional, appeared so because they emphasized their spontaneous response to a text. As Gillian said:

> It's like, women being more emotional than men, they get more out of reading a work of literature than a man does. A man tends to, because of the way he is, want to get something concrete out of art, and I think that's why they don't accept it. They want an answer, they want something to show for what they've done, whereas a woman will do it for the joy of it.
>
> (Gillian, 3rd year, A)

The same, she said, applied to staff:

> I think they're very rational, I think they adapt to the academic way of doing English – rational, not for enjoyment – there have got to be answers, there have got to be right ways of doing it, there has got to be a meaning, they bring it down to a science, or try to.
>
> (Gillian, 3rd year, A)

The most striking difference between the female students and the male students of English – and the most difficult to communicate on paper – was the women's lack of a sense of self-importance. Whereas the men often talked at length about their hobbies – such as photography, rugby or politics – and their ideas about literature, science and their own futures, many of the women appeared to think that what they did or believed could be of little interest, and in some cases spoke quite negatively about their own abilities and interests. It wasn't that they *were* uninteresting to talk to: simply that some of them felt that what they said could not possibly be of value. The same was true of the female communications students who, although relatively ambitious, were sometimes quite diffident about their own talents.

The attitude of the female English students towards their careers was, in the short term at any rate, very similar to that of the male students. Few wanted conventional graduate jobs; most felt a positive distaste for anything conventional. Amongst the final-year women, two had decided to enter retail management; three were interested in teaching abroad; one intended to take a Master's degree; one had considered journalism (but definitely did not want to go into business); one was completely undecided.

> I wouldn't want to be working for the civil service or anything like that, I wouldn't like to be working for Sainsbury's, because a lot of people are doing retail management and that just bores me rigid. I don't know what I would like to be doing – it would be something that involved me writing, not a nine to five job; I know everybody says that, but something slightly more – I suppose, working with people. I know that's a bit naïve, but definitely outside business anyway, probably as far outside business as you can get.
>
> (Jennifer, 3rd year, A)

> I can't really envisage it [the future], but I hope that I'll have done something constructive, which is good, because I don't really want to have it so mapped out that I can tell.
>
> (Alice, 3rd year, B)

Often students who didn't know what they hoped to do were critical of those making conventional career choices. Alice summed up the feeling of many when she said:

> I'm here because I love English, not because I want a good degree or anything, but I think a lot of people are here because their daddies have said to them, you know, if you get a good degree, you can get a good job in this and that, advertising and everything.
>
> (Alice, 3rd year, B)

She went on:

> There's nothing I could do with it really, that I want to do with it.

Alice's own plans were vague: maybe TEFL, maybe busking abroad (she sang in a band), certainly not journalism. She wrote a lot in her spare time, and hoped to have some success with that, 'something creative', but as yet unspecified.

Another final-year student at B, Judith, who was a Christian, had already been accepted on to a PGCE course and wanted eventually to teach in a Third World country in some missionary capacity. Diane, in the same year, had applied for store management, but she seemed not to feel any great enthusiasm for it. When asked what she hoped to be doing in ten years' time, she said:

> God, no idea. Like I said, I've been applying for these jobs, I've only done eight application forms, which is not many. This lad who I was telling you about earlier . . . he did twenty-four application forms and I think he's terribly job-orientated, money-orientated, 'I am going to have a career, going to have two-point-two children' and all this sort of stuff, which doesn't appeal to me at all. I mean, it would be nice to get a bit of money and have a career and stuff but I think you can always keep applying for that sort of thing. It's nice to get letters saying 'You've got an interview with

us', but I don't think I'd be devastated if I didn't get a job because there's so many, particularly when you're so young, so many things you can still do. I quite fancy now, trying a bit of hospital radio, trying a computer course, things like that, seeing a bit of life, and I think particularly during the summer there are seasonal jobs to be had, and provided you can manage on the money, then I think it's quite a nice opportunity to get about and have a little experience of life.

(Diane, 3rd year, B)

The other student who wanted to enter retail management was also keen to assure me of her lack of ambition:

I'm not really career-minded, I don't feel the need to get to the top of anything. My only thoughts at the moment are to be happy and successful in whatever I'm doing. I'm not really thinking that far ahead.

(Lee, 3rd year, A)

Only one final-year English student said that her reason for doing a degree was because she wanted a career, and she was also the only student who said that she wanted to be 'successful' in conventional terms:

I don't want to be someone who's just another cog in the wheel, who's just working in an office, I want to do something that will make a change in either the field of art or in the field of communications or television, wherever I'll be working. I want to do something that is moving forward, that isn't stagnating and is challenging, and so I wouldn't sacrifice, because I mean, because women and men obviously do get married and nine out of ten women will have kids so I guess I'll have kids but I don't want them for ages yet because I think you should look after Number One first, so in ten years' time, I'd like to hope that I'd have a very strong career, loads of money behind me, not wealthy, I don't want to be *wealthy* wealthy, just well off and use the money I earn to supplement my own interest in fields of work I'd be working in, whatever it's going to be, and successful basically.

(Susan, 3rd year, B)

Susan was by far the most ambitious of the final-year English students but even so, she is aware of the difficulties facing any woman who has to choose between career and children – a point we shall return to shortly. Part of her desire to be successful is related to her not wanting to be the conventional housewife and mother; her ambition therefore has a sharper, feminist edge. Her next comment may seem ironic, in view of Jane's earlier remarks about starting a family:

There's no way after coming to a place like this, where you get a taste of freedom, you would sit down and accept being a housewife, and I imagine every girl at the university has the same thing. I mean, if you take a female science student, I bet she's going to forge a career for herself and not sit around.

(Susan, 3rd year, B)

Susan was an exception. Most of the English students did not talk about their futures in terms of wealth or success, and often they explicitly rejected those criteria. The physics students – at least, most of the male physics students, and a few of the female ones – saw wealth and success as important to them and their self-identity. This meant that they viewed their subject in different ways; for physics and physical science students, their degree was important in helping them to get a good job; for English students, the degree was often an end in itself.

Amongst the first-year students, there was a similar pattern of prioritizing people over money. A high number of students, both male and female – seven out of the sixteen – had considered teaching in one form or another, abroad or at home. Even the idea of teaching abroad, however, posed a moral dilemma for one student:

> I was thinking of teaching in this country . . . and then going abroad and teaching but I have qualms about that because you find that with something like VSO, you're teaching, you're imposing the English culture on another country and I don't think that's right so morally I don't know whether I could do it.
>
> (Geraldine, 1st year, B)

Another student posed the choice between journalism and social work in these terms:

> With journalism, you're not particularly serving a great purpose. Whereas with social work, you're actually doing something, helping people.
>
> (Carole, 1st year, B)

Obviously not all students experienced such angst over their careers; quite a few first years wanted to become journalists; one wanted to run her own interior design business. None the less, few saw their futures in terms of status or money.

Some of the female English students clearly felt that they *ought* to be ambitious, while at the same time lacking any strong inclination towards a particular career. For many of them, a social conscience seemed to preclude doing any of the normal graduate jobs such as management, while at the same time they wanted to do something rather more unconventional than teach. In fact, it is likely that for many of them – the men as well as the women – individuality was more important than their social consciences: they really didn't want to do the same as everyone else. The fact that *most* of them didn't want to do what everyone else was doing did make deciding what to do rather difficult.

The female communications students were more decided on their futures. Amongst the final-year students, one wanted to be a television researcher, one a newspaper journalist, one a television producer, and one wanted to work in radio. The first-year students, understandably, were less clear: one wanted to work in public relations, while the other three liked the idea of working in television. As with the English students, the emphasis tended to be on enjoyment rather than money:

I haven't really planned anything, but it would be nice to think I could get a proper career, something that I would really enjoy doing. Something that involved writing probably. I think the idea of writing for television is rather interesting.

(Sandra, 1st year, C)

Although the short-term ambitions of the female students were not very different from those of the men, it is in talking about the long term that major differences emerged. Women's feelings about their future were more ambivalent than those of the men; many were highly conscious of the difficulties of combining a career with raising a family. Susan, for example, although the most overtly ambitious of the female students, was also the only female final-year English student to mention the possibility of children:

A lot of my schoolfriends are married now and have a totally different mentality, but once you're here, all the girls I know here have a sense of freedom and a certain drive not to be tied down and to be career women in whatever fields and to make something out of their lives although they would like to get married at some stage, but we've got a standard joke that everyone gets married at about 28 and has kids at 30; I mean, that's the way it's going to be, we're going to have careers for eight years, then we're going to do this and we're going to work part-time after we have kids, it's just like a stereotyped thing.

(Susan, 3rd year, B)

Susan's own immediate ambitions were to teach English as a Foreign Language in Japan, and then to enter publishing or television. To her, being a 'career woman' is incompatible with being married and having children, although she knows she wants to do both. Having 'freedom' and 'drive' is seen to be in direct opposition to having a family, which she regards as confining.

The first-year female English students were more concerned about career/family conflict than the final-year students. In all, six of the eight women mentioned marriage or family. They had not, however, gone very far along the road of solving the conflict:

I'd like to have a job that I'm happy in and that was what I'd been aiming towards for years. I'd like to have got to where I'd aimed at. What that is, I don't know. By 29, I'd hope to have had a family, I suppose, but then again, there would be a conflict between career and family, it's frightening to think about it and I can't really say I have thought about it. Just have a job that I'm happy in, that's related to what I'm doing now.

(Diana, 1st year, A)

It's hard really because I would like to have children and I want to travel as well . . . I'd quite like to see myself set up abroad somewhere, with a job.

(Geraldine, 1st year, B)

I want to teach and I don't know whether I'll start teaching – I'm doing TT after I've finished here but whether I'll start teaching then or get another job I just don't know. I don't want to get married or settle down with kids. I want to work for a long time because that's what it's all about, that's what I've come here for, to learn, to be able to get a job, to be able to work; I don't know what I see myself doing; I suppose teaching, maybe get married later.

(Kate, 1st year, A)

I don't know. I haven't got a clue. I don't want to get married. And I certainly don't want children for quite a while, till I'm older. I suppose 'being a career woman'. I really don't know . . . I want to do VSO, but that lasts for two years usually . . . I think it would be a good experience. You feel as if you've done something to help humanity.

(Carole, 1st year, B)

In this respect, the female English students were no different from the female physics students: they experienced exactly the same conflicts about combining career with family. However, apart from its slight ambivalence about children, Carole's quote is interesting because of the contradiction between her apparent desire to be a 'career woman' and her desire to be useful and to 'help humanity'. The vagueness of many of the English students' replies when asked about future careers is perhaps because there are so few jobs in society open to graduates that are to do with 'helping humanity'; even fewer for *ambitious* graduates who want to help humanity.

Gillian, a final-year student, was a mature student who already had children. This, however, did not resolve the problem. Her age disadvantaged her; she was, for example, too old to enter the civil service, even though

Girls of 24 or 25 are going in and they might only stay for four or five years, whereas now I've got twenty-odd years to give.

(Gillian, 3rd year, A)

Even the experience of working for some years, both as a mother and as a clerk in the advertising department of a newspaper, before taking her degree, was not useful in terms of getting a job; she would be considered too old to receive training. None the less, she was not bitter; she intended to take a Master's degree and felt that doing English had been worthwhile. In reply to a question about what she saw herself doing in ten years' time, she said

I can't say what I'll be doing in ten years' time because I can't see myself not wanting to learn, so probably when I've done this, I'll do something else, and I might even do the OU as an associate member, just because I enjoy learning about different things . . . I think once you get into this kind of field of wanting to study, it's difficult, if you enjoy it, to give it up.

(Gillian, 3rd year, A)

Although they had far more idea of what they wanted to do than the English students, the female communications students shared the same anxieties about combining marriage and family as the female English and the female physics students. In all, six of the eight brought up the issue of whether they wanted children. The most determined woman, the one who had made a real effort to enter journalism, had thought at some length about it:

> Hopefully I will have got on in journalism – ten years' time – I'll probably have children by then. No, I can't see myself not having a family, I would like to have a family when I'm older, but I think I'm the sort of person that I can't see myself giving up my career, I'd like to work for at least that long. I'd really like to have a family but it conflicts so much. I think that's the trouble if you're having children, you have to have them young, and I think with journalism you have to really get into it, you know, ten years seems a long time but when you're training for two years it's not really long on a paper. I'd like to establish myself and be respected for my work. I'm so sure that I'm not going to do very well, I'd have to prove everyone wrong and myself wrong.
>
> (Helen, 3rd year, C)

One first-year woman said she wanted a family; she, like many of the other female arts students, was explicitly unambitious:

> I'm not dreadfully ambitious. I don't really see myself as a really successful career woman. I'd like a job that I enjoyed. I think that's my main hope, but I do also want to get married and have a family eventually.
>
> (Sandra, 1st year, C)

There was also a student who defined her future in terms of *not* being married:

> I won't be married [in ten years' time], that's for sure. How old will I be? Twenty-eight. Well, I might just be married, but I don't want to get married till I'm quite old. I'd like to think I'd got on quite well in the career I'd chosen; I'm not interested in money, I'd like enough to be happy, so I don't have to worry about it, but just job satisfaction, a job I can enjoy.
>
> (Rebecca, 1st year, C)

The interest of the comments about marriage lie not in whether or not women see themselves as getting married in the future, or not, but the fact that they define themselves as 'married' or 'not married': whereas men tend to construct their identity in terms of the sort of job they'll be doing, women tend to construct theirs in terms, not only of their job, but also in terms of whether they'll be married or single. It is very important to the women, when they think about what they'll be doing, and the sort of career they'll be pursuing, whether they will be married or not; and some of them are in the process of making quite complicated calculations as to when is the best time to get married and have a family. It is a *calculating* process for women in a way that it is not for men. Although, therefore, male and female arts students do not on the surface have very different ambitions, women's anticipation of successful, or at least happy, careers is often in direct opposition to their awareness, if they have children, of the need to do 'women's work' – bringing up a family. Women had very definite images of themselves as 'career women' or as 'mothers'; having a career was not simply about having a career, but being a particular kind of person: a 'career woman'. Being a 'career woman' clearly meant, for most of the women who used the term, being ambitious, single-minded and *selfish*; some were at pains to dissociate themselves from that image. Choosing to be a mother, on the other hand, meant being a warm, caring, *unselfish* person. For another group of women, 'being a career woman' meant being someone who was independent, who could look after herself; being a mother meant being boring, unambitious and trapped by convention. These images were the same for the female arts students as for the female science students; their ideas about what female graduates could and should do with their lives were shaped by a dominant discourse which divides women who behave like women (i.e. who become full-time mothers) and those women who behave like men ('career women').

Summary

At the end of Chapter 6, we noted that male physics students defined themselves rigidly as 'physicists', while female physics students felt a tension between their sense of themselves as women and their sense of themselves as physicists. In English, the boundaries were more fluid, but despite the predominance of women, men were still advantaged. Because men were in a minority, they were regarded as 'special'; their views were considered more interesting and more valuable than those of women. Men were not treated as a 'minority group'; on the contrary, they were able to compare themselves favourably with the mass of anonymous women around them. Male arts students in both English and communications were more self-confident than female arts students; being an arts student for them meant being an individual and having the freedom to form one's own opinions and ideas. Thus being an individual – in the sense of being opinionated, even aggressive – is an advantage in those subjects because individuality is highly valued. Women, too, in English and communications, enjoyed the freedom allowed them by those subjects to voice their own ideas and values; but they were both disadvantaged by being part of a mass, rather than a minority, and hampered by their lack of self-confidence in expressing opinions.

In many ways, the similarities of attitude that existed between the male and female science students, and between the male and female humanities students, were greater than those between men or women in either area. For example the science students, *on the whole*, tended to think that education should be useful, whereas humanities students saw education as valuable in its own right. However, there were differences of attitude between male and female science students, and these were greater than the differences between male and female arts students. Women in science were less materialist and less instrumental in their attitudes than the male scientists; both male and female arts students tended not to be materialist or instrumental. Women in science tended to stick together, and rarely sat with the men in lecture theatres; men and women in English and communications mixed much more easily together. The one major difference between male and female students in both areas was in their visions of their long-term futures. Men in physics saw themselves as having successfully climbed a career ladder, in management or science, and men in English saw themselves as successful individuals – not usually in a company, but as writers, or as making a living in some way that was essentially *different*; the women in all the disciplines, however, were concerned with the issue of whether they would choose family or career, or how they would combine both. Having a family rarely crossed the minds of the men; if it did, it was something they took for granted, not as something that would be a problem. Women saw the two things in opposition to each other, and never as complementary.

It was through this vision of their future lives that students' sense of themselves was most keenly expressed. Male scientists perceived themselves as ambitious and successful people, with money and responsibility. Female scientists, on the whole, were less clear about their futures; some, who saw themselves as 'caring' people rejected a career in physics altogether and stressed job satisfaction and mixing with other people over money and status. Male English students essentially saw themselves as 'different' – not taking part in the rat-race, but making their mark through other means: a rather romantic image. Female English students, like some of the male English students, stressed social responsibility as a prerequisite of their jobs; some, however, were clearly uneasy because they thought they *ought* to be ambitious, while at the same time not wanting to be in a job which was exploitative. Both the male and female communications students wanted to achieve success – both status and job satisfaction – through working in the media.

The numerical strength of female undergraduates in English and communications, then, is not equivalent to a female dominance of the subjects. Men in those subjects distanced themselves from its feminine image and exploited the advantage of being male; the fact that they *were* male in a predominantly female subject marked them out as special. Whereas in physics, women had to be seen to do as well as the men, there was no such pressure for men in English to do as well as the women.

English and physics, communications and physical science are not, then, parallel or symmetrical; they are asymmetrical. The dominance of men in physics and physical science is not mirrored by a dominance of women in English and communications. More importantly the environment of both the arts and the science disciplines ultimately favoured men, not women. The next chapter will look at how these findings relate to the hypotheses formed from the literature, and at what can be done to effect change.

8

Conclusion

Introduction

This chapter will review the findings and ideas of the previous chapters and discuss their implications. The preceding chapters have discussed the relationship between subject and gender; between academic constructions of arts and science and students' own sense of masculinity and femininity. It has been suggested that ideas about subjects, and ideas about gender, are, to a large degree, mutually reinforcing. Let us examine further the meaning and implications of that statement.

The subjects and the organization of learning

Physics and physical science

It was found that most physics and physical science students held a view of science as 'objective' and 'value-free': physics in particular was seen as a 'fundamental' subject, able to reveal universal and immutable truths about the nature of the physical world. Most physics students regarded academic disciplines as forming a hierarchy: the 'harder', the more 'certain' and the more 'useful' a discipline, then the more important it was. Only a few saw it as an uncertain subject, requiring intuition and speculative exploration. Physical science students tended to view their subject in almost entirely instrumental terms, regarding it as a concrete body of knowledge with useful application. The attempt to broaden the subject and blur boundaries between subjects had not been spectacularly successful: students still saw the course as being about physics *and* chemistry, rather than as a new discipline of 'physical science'.

This rigidity in the view of their subjects was mirrored by a rigidity in teaching methods. Each of the three departments was organized hierarchically, and this was related to the status of staff as imparters of knowledge; the 'educand', as Bernstein has it, has 'little status and few rights' (1971: 51). Students were dependent on staff for developing an understanding of the subject; full attendance at lectures, seminars and labs was very important. They were not, generally, required to discover for themselves; the point of experiments, for example, was to illustrate a received 'truth' rather than to allow students to make findings. Dissatisfaction with this method of teaching came largely from the very high achievers and the very low achievers; it is possible that both failure and success are related to non-conformism in physics – a disillusionment with the practice on the one hand, and an ability to see through and manipulate the practice on the other.

English and communications

Unlike physics, English was constructed by staff and students alike as 'uncertain' and 'subjective'; it was also seen by some as allowing access to artistic and universal truths about human behaviour. There was a strong emphasis on 'breadth': English's capacity to encompass a variety of related disciplines (such as history, sociology, philosophy). Women in particular attached great importance to the possibility of emotional response in English. English was constructed as a liberal humanist discipline which demanded personal and thoughtful response to the 'great' writers of English literature, with their range of moral perspectives and ideas.

The most important characteristic of English, in the view of students and staff, is its individualism: the possibility of holding different views from other people. Individualism is all to English departments; the aim of the seminar, for example, is not that students can reach collective agreement about a piece of writing or an idea, but that students put forward their competing perspectives in the cut and thrust of debate. It differs greatly, therefore, from physics and physical science, which demand consensus before learning can take place: English demands only consensus about the discourse, the way of talking about books. Whereas success in physics and physical science is related to the ability to understand, accept, and then (perhaps) manipulate, success in English is related to the ability to be assertive and original, to make an impression on the department. Students were much less dependent on staff (or other students) for their understanding of the discipline; they worked on their own, and to a large extent used lectures and seminars as aids to learning – they attended them if they thought they might be helpful; if not, they didn't bother.

Communications – perhaps surprisingly, given the different nature of the discipline – was discussed by its students and staff in very similar terms to those used by English students and staff. They talked of the wide variety of subjects encompassed by the discipline, of the potential for individual response and of the many approaches of tackling problems. They did differ, however, in that students did not talk about emotional response, as the English students did; further, they regarded communications as a more *relevant* subject, one which tackled current social issues and was not preoccupied with traditional intellectual and academic niceties. Students' relations with staff were very informal and, as in English, there was little sense of students' being dependent on staff.

Like the physical science students, communications students saw their course as at least partly vocational; it wasn't simply a course studied for its own sake.

In Chapter 1 I posed the question of whether physical science and communications provided fresh and valuable alternatives to the well-established disciplines of physics and English. The research suggested that, while physical science is dominated by traditional ideas about science – and its control over learning is more rigid even than that of physics – communications does provide a genuinely exciting and inter-disciplinary alternative to such disciplines as English, history or sociology. Although the course certainly has its problems (the first year in particular is very fragmented), it does allow students access to a wide range of ideas and theories, and provides students with means of making sense of the modern world, through the study of film and media. It is particularly refreshing that the studies encompass both intellectual aspects (such as the meaning of 'ideology') and the practical aspects of the techniques used by programme- and film-makers, and that these studies are firmly located in an understanding of how media institutions operate in society.

The chief difference, then, between the science and arts departments, was that students in the arts departments had a greater control over their own learning, and there was less emphasis in those departments on the formalities of marking, grading and assessing. This finding does support the arguments of T. S. Kuhn (1963) and Bernstein (1971); indeed, it is striking that the course (communications) which had the weakest boundaries between relevant and irrelevant knowledge, also had the most informal and least hierarchical staff –student relationships.

Gender

The most important point we can make about gender is that it is not simply concerned with the differences (biological or social) between men and women but that as a concept it has resonances which are used in all areas of society, including education. 'Masculinity' and 'femininity' are terms which embody certain values (although not the same values at all times). In particular, ideas of masculinity and femininity are often used in conjunction with ideas of conformity and rebellion.

An obvious example of this is Willis's (1977) study of working-class boys. Masculinity was an important part of the 'lads'' culture; yet it is their pride in their masculinity, and their devaluation of academic achievement as 'cissy', which leads to their ending up in poorly paid jobs and restricts their freedom to improve the quality of their lives. Masculinity was, therefore, a significant aspect of a culture of rebellion which eventually necessitated a fairly high degree of social conformity.

Another example of the use of gender in producing conformity is given by Lynne Segal in her book *Is the Future Female?* (1987). In a discussion of the army, she notes how new recruits are 'toughened up' by accusations of womanliness;

the whole ethos of the army depends on a contempt for women and a distaste for femininity. In this way, is the image of 'military manhood' maintained; argues Segal

> The image helps sustain the morale and self-esteem of the men already in uniform, most of whom, much of the time, will lead lives of relentless subservience, obedience and passive dependence – characteristics more typically attributed to 'women'.
>
> (Segal 1987: 187)

In both these examples, the inducement to conformity is powerful – no man wishes to be accused of effeminacy. Each example contains a paradox: in the first, it is that teenage rebelliousness leads directly to adult conformity; in the second it is that fear of the label 'effeminate' leads to conventionally 'feminine' behaviour. In both instances the men fail to realize their own subservient position in a social system because they have something to feel superior to: women.

The idea that 'masculinity' and 'femininity' can be used to induce conformity (or rebellion) is significant for this study. For most men, the fear of being thought 'unmasculine' is enough to make them conform to conventional masculine behaviour. For women, however (and, particularly, I shall argue, women in higher education), social pressure is much less clear. A woman can choose to behave in a conventionally 'feminine' way: for example, following an appropriate career such as nursing, which she might give up when she marries and has children. Yet while choosing this route might meet with social approval, it does not necessarily make her feel like a 'successful woman', because nursing and motherhood are not highly respected jobs. The woman who chooses, however, to become (say) an engineer would probably be met with a mixture of disapproval (for being unfeminine) and admiration (for making it a man's world): she might even receive the ultimate accolade of being considered 'as good as a man'. But which, in these two examples, is the conformist woman? We are conditioned to answer 'the former'. Arnot, however, has argued powerfully that, for many women, choosing the traditional feminine role is an act of *rebellion*. She argues that the 'inversion of the mental–manual division'

> allows working-class women to celebrate their femininity through a rejection of male culture which stresses the value of hierarchies, objective versus subjective knowledge and individual competition above cooperation. Paradoxically, then, femininity, the supposed essence of docility and conformity can become the vehicle for resisting forms of class reproduction.
>
> (Arnot 1982: 78)

The woman, therefore, who chooses to enter a typically masculine job, may be behaving in a conformist way because she has to obey – even more closely than the men – traditional hierarchies and values. This is not to make a value judgement, or to say that women shouldn't enter male-dominated professions: it *is* to say that, whichever choice a woman makes, the traditional divisions will be reinforced.

In Chapter 2 I suggested that women's experience of higher education might be 'confusing and contradictory'. This, indeed, proved to be the case; and it was also the case that, for most of the women, as for many of the men, the issue of choice (choice of subject and choice of career) was framed by questions of conformity and rebellion. These questions, however, were posed differently for the four groups in the study: male science students, female science students, male humanities students, and female humanities students.

For the male science students, the choice seemed clear-cut. Their version of 'masculinity' was a middle-class one, rather than a working-class one; instead of being concerned with physical toughness and class solidarity, it was much more bound up with the ideas of following a successful career: being competitive, pushy and earning a lot of money. These students had a self-image of 'successful physicist' which could equally mean 'successful man': they saw themselves as clever, ambitious, financially secure. The successful physicist is also one who uses his degree, who becomes a working physicist – either as an academic or as a research scientist in industry. For men, much of the appeal for physics is its high status; it is regarded as an important subject (this is also the appeal for some women who study it, of course). Studying physics affirms one's masculinity, and hence one's importance; it is a mutually reassuring circle. In the same way, physics's emphasis on certainty and on progress also provides reassurance: a sense of rightness and orderliness. The very certainty of physics gives the student a sense of confidence, of being in control. The physics students looked down upon the arts because they represented an alternative, less attractive set of values. The arts were strongly associated with pleasure, laxity, laziness, subjectivity – all 'feminine' qualities, as Hudson (1972) points out. One of the most common criticisms of the arts, it will be remembered, is that arts degrees didn't lead to a career. The contempt many of the science students felt for the arts was related to a high degree of subject loyalty and conformity to a fairly narrow view of what should be considered valuable: material success. The one student who clearly stood out in not conforming to the ideal of the successful physicist had chosen to enter the very traditional female career of nursing.

For the female science students, 'masculinity' was obviously far more problematic. A woman who chooses to study physics or physical science is engaging in an act of non-conformity, because these are subjects not traditionally studied by women. It is not necessarily an act of rebellion: for many of the women in the sample it was a relatively easy decision to make because they were encouraged by single-sex schools or scientist parents. Because physics is so bound up with notions of masculine success, many women felt that they had to prove that they were 'as good as men', as if men were innately better scientists. Some – particularly the first-year students – were driven too by the desire for material success. Most, however, felt a strong degree of tension – of being pulled in different directions. This is partly because women never can be 'as good as men'; men, being men, have a head start in that area. Women, however brilliant they may be academically, cannot be 'good physicists' if 'good physicist' equates with 'successful man'. The certainty of physics, so important to men, inspires less confidence in women because it depends on a negation of femininity, of those qualities which are socially acceptable but not intellectually acceptable.

Many women kept up their outside interests (music, reading, for example), and some intended to combine a career with raising a family. For these women, it was difficult to be a 'good physicist' *and* an ordinary woman; either one had to be sacrificed to the other, or, in some cases, there was an uneasy compromise. A subject like physics which has such strong boundaries that it regards even chemistry as quite inferior, demands a certain single-mindedness which the female students could not possess without a good deal of sacrifice. Indeed, it will be remembered that some of the female physics students were actively subverting their department's competitive ethos through mutual support and help.

Most of the male English and communications students saw themselves as non-conformists, rebellious. Partly they saw themselves as rebellious because they weren't doing (as they saw it) a conventional, boring, vocational subject. They were individuals, they had their own ideas, they were opting out of the rat race. But partly – and this is crucial – they saw themselves as rebellious individuals because their departments allowed them to do so. As well as defining themselves in opposition to students in other subjects (particularly science), they could define themselves in opposition to the women in their own subject: that quiet, anonymous mass. Outsiders might see English as slightly 'effeminate': the male English student knows better, however, because there is nothing easier than for a man to be 'masculine' in a subject where women predominate and where individualism, originality and assertiveness are highly valued. The women in physics had to try hard to be like the men; but the men in English (and to a lesser extent in communications) had only to show that they were different from the women – a much easier task. In English, therefore, nonconformism was closely allied to masculinity.

It was the female English and communications students who, surprisingly, were caught in the most difficult double bind. English's appeal for women lies both in its stress on the personal and the emotional, the lack of a need for conformity to predefined norms. For women, choosing English may actually be an act of rebellion (however mild); it is a way of making a space for women's concerns, an area where hierarchy and competition are apparently less important than breadth and sensitivity. English appears to allow women an escape route from an education system in which those qualities are not valued; it is one of the few disciplines to turn those vices into virtues: to prioritize the traditional concerns of women, to provide a space where conformity to dominant social norms is not particularly highly valued. English, similarly, may allow women to 'celebrate their femininity': women who do English (as, of course, a number of other arts subjects) need not feel that there is something wrong with being a woman, or with being feminine; they don't have to become 'as good as a man' to feel successful. Yet, as we have seen, this view of English that women have on entering higher education proves in many ways to be illusory. For one thing, women soon find that university English is less about the emotions and more about individualism. For another, it is hard for a woman to be noticed as an individual when there may be eighty women and twenty men in a department. Who can a woman show herself to be different *from*?

Perhaps the most important difference between physics and English is that physics, at least, has some sort of consistency: students accept the rules, or they don't. English seems to find it more difficult to decide what the rules are – although most of the staff would actively deny this. Do they want students to be subjective or objective, emotional or detached? Dr P, quoted in Chapter 7, who argued that English demanded an affective, emotional response, and who then went on to say that some women were *too* affective, *too* emotional, nicely summed up the double bind in which the female arts student is caught. It seems that English departments expect students to respond to texts in a subjective way; but their subjectivity has to conform to the objective and detached preferences of the department. When the students trying to respond in a subjective, individual and yet 'correct' way to texts are female, and the teachers, academics and critics who have determined what that 'correct' response is, are male, the result is a necessity to conform to male standards: what Bowen describes as the 'regulation of women's "response" by older men' (1985: 370).

Arguably communications as much as English values assertiveness; a significant difference from English, however, was that the issue of gender was part of the curriculum; *masculinity* as a social construct was discussed as much as femininity. Students, therefore, were encouraged to see communications in relative terms, as a social product rather than as an embodiment of absolute standards and values. This concentration on the social character of writing allows a greater awareness of the social character of gender.

Another paradox for female English students lies in their choice of career: male English graduates may express non-conformism by opting out of the 'rat race'; yet if the female graduates opt out of the rat race, aren't they simply doing what women have always done? The woman who decides not to enter industry as a trainee manager, but to do some casual TEFL work, and then maybe start a family before going into part-time teaching, is always open to the accusation that she is a 'typical woman': unambitious, conventional. Almost all the women in the sample, whichever subject they studied, felt this contradictory pull; almost none felt that they had resolved it satisfactorily.

There may be good reasons why physics and physical science demand a high degree of conformity, and English and communications a much lesser one. As we saw in Chapter 3, science is increasingly subject to the demands of industry in a capitalist society. The physics graduate who chooses to follow a typical career path will, in all likelihood, end up in a job which is well paid but in which he can exercise little control over his work. He will have financial freedom, but little intellectual freedom. As Gorz has so succinctly put it:

intellectual workers are both the beneficiaries and the victims of the class nature of Western science and of the social division of labor that is built into it.

(Gorz 1980: 272)

The intellectual worker – in this case, the scientist – is rewarded for his conformism by financial security and high social status. The difference between the middle-class workers and Willis's lads was that the latter were powerless to subvert the system; if they had rebellious attitudes, it didn't really matter. From the point of view of capitalism, it is much more important that the intellectual worker conforms, because his abilities make him potentially more subversive.

Arguably the reason English demands less loyalty (in the sense of conformity to a predefined set of beliefs) is because its graduates will have a much less important part to play. Most of the English students in the sample had little idea of what career they wanted, and few wanted to go into industry. The irony is that because English is a broader subject, with 'weak frames' and 'weak classification', the job opportunities of many of its graduates are limited; Shaw (1983) has explained Bernstein's statement that 'behind weak classification is strong classification' by applying it to women's education, saying that weak classification and weak framing lead to

> strong classification (a very restricted set of job opportunities for women) and strong framing (much stricter and more extensive social control).
>
> (Shaw 1983: 97)

Perhaps, then, the apparently greater freedom allowed by English is – as far as women are concerned – linked to less choice in the job market. At the same time, greater choice for women in the job market would almost inevitably be tied to an acceptance by women of traditionally masculine values.

Higher education and gender inequality

Higher education does not actively discriminate against women; rather, through an acceptance of particular values and beliefs, it makes it difficult for women to succeed.

Women are, to some extent, 'outsiders' in society – in Hacker's (1977) words, a 'minority group'. They are constantly caught up between wanting to have highly valued social qualities and conforming to acceptable social behaviour. Women in higher education are engaged in a process of negotiation and manipulation; their choices are, perhaps, based upon a more complex aware-ness of reality than those of men's. Thus women have access both to their own perception of reality and men's perception of it; they are able to manipulate men's perception both of the world and of women. This is particularly true in an area such as physics, where women manipulated men by using 'femininity' and 'helplessness'; it also explains women's reluctance to have a single-minded dedication to physics, either as a discipline or as a career, wishing, as they did, to combine this 'masculine' concern with more traditional 'feminine' concerns: the arts, looking after a family, involvement with people. Women – particularly educated women – are confronted with contradiction and uncertainty: their position is far less secure or certain than that of men.

Women's position in relation to men resembles the position of English – and other arts subjects – in relation to science. We can suggest that all arts subjects, including English, exist in the shadow of science. In one sense, they act as a 'negative reference' for scientists: science is important and valuable because it is not like the arts. In another sense, they constantly measure themselves against science, wishing to come up to the standards science is perceived to have set – an ultimately fruitless aim, because science can be superior only if the arts subjects are perceived as inferior. In subjects such as English, therefore, there is a constant struggle between many modes of thoughts, but in particular, between masculinity and femininity: between an emphasis on those negatively valued qualities such as emotion, a concern with people, uncertainty, intuition, and those positively valued qualities such as objectivity, certainty, scientific truth.

A simple functionalist model, of higher education reproducing or eliminating inequality, will not do. There is a relationship between higher education and society, and society's different elements; families, industry, schools. This relationship is not a straightforward one, because society itself is not straight-forward: its organization is riddled with contradictions and anomalies. One such anomaly is that a woman can become prime minister, and remain prime minister for more than ten years, when politics is one of the most male-dominated social activities. Yet there are other areas of society where women are increasingly successful: publishing, for example, or teaching, or medicine. 'Masculinity' and 'femininity' are fluid concepts; their meaning varies in different areas of society. Perhaps part of Mrs Thatcher's success lies in her ability to manipulate these concepts; to seem simultaneously more masculine than her colleagues, more feminine than other female politicians.

Higher education might be regarded as one of our more liberal social institutions: an arena where women are allowed in in reasonable numbers, and where they may even succeed. Yet it is this ultimately illusory liberalism that allows gender divisions to be maintained and renewed. Academics can afford to be complacent because their institutions and departments appear to be so meritocratic and egalitarian. The physics lecturer can say, 'Of course the department would like more women to take physics, but the problem is with the schools: they put girls off'. Or the English lecturer can say, 'Well, we do have a lot of girls coming here to do English, but they're a bit weak, really, too emotional'. Inequality of achievement is seen as the fault of schools or of society in general or as the result of student inadequacy: never the inadequacy of individual departments or institutions.

Disciplines like English and communications are regarded by some of their practitioners as potentially, and even actually, subversive of conventional beliefs about women and men. Yet it is very rare that this subversion of the values of the outside world leads to a critical examination of the practices of the institution. The fact that the issue of the social position of women, for example, may sometimes arise during a discussion of Shakespeare's comedies or Charlotte Brontë's heroines, does not, apparently, lead academics to speculate on why a large majority of English undergraduates are women, and an even larger majority of English lecturers are men: far less to do anything about it.

Because of the variations between subjects and departments in higher education, it is not possible to see higher education as a unified entity with one function or purpose. The antagonism which exists between different subjects suggests that they often have quite different aims. Yet they are part of the same system, a system which examines and grades students and sends them out into society and the graduate labour market. It is important to stress, therefore, that higher education is *relatively* autonomous; departments and institutions can pursue independent inclinations (such as research projects or the design of undergraduate courses), while having to comply with certain predetermined requirements.

Higher education does not reproduce gender inequality by actively discriminating against women. What it does is to make use of culturally available ideas of masculinity and femininity in such a way that women are marginalized and, to some extent, alienated. This is not to say that women cannot succeed in higher education; of course they can, and do, though at a price. But it is important to realize that higher education represents a separate stage in the educational process; it is not simply 'more of the same'. The one lasting impression I carry from this research is of how much more self-confident the men were than the women. This was particularly striking amongst the female physics students, especially those who had been to single-sex schools: they were bright, intelligent and able, yet they felt unsure of themselves in the environment of a university physics department. These were women whose self-image was undergoing a change: in school, they were clever, confident students who would have successful careers as physicists. University challenged that identity.

By 'lack of confidence' I do not mean passivity. The problem of much early research on gender and education was the assumption that many girls passively allowed themselves to be slotted into traditional roles. In fact, much of what appears to be 'passivity' is resistance: women rejecting the values of the school or the university or the polytechnic. However, whether women accept the dominant values (that women are less able, and can succeed only by being as good as men) or reject them (through refusing to play the game of academic success), the result is the same. As Arnot has put it, in a slightly different context:

> In neither the dominant nor the dominated gender codes do women escape from their inferior and subordinate position.
>
> (Arnot 1982: 85)

By the dominant gender code, Arnot is referring to the code of the bourgeoisie; the dominated gender code refers to the code of the working-class and ethnic minorities. If we substitute 'physics' for 'bourgeoisie' and 'English' for 'working-class', the meaning still holds. The point I am making, therefore, is that higher education, by making use of widely available ideas of gender, undermines its own apparent egalitarianism. At the same time, those ideas appear as 'natural' and 'inevitable', and, consequently, unchallengeable.

The possibility of change

Despite the fact that higher education will continue to play a part in meeting the demands of industry, by providing suitably qualified workers equipped with the appropriate attitudes, we do not have to take an overly deterministic view of the situation. Higher education can change, and will change. The impetus for change is unlikely to come from the present government, but can come from academics and, I hope, from students.

I should like to think that academics and students reading this book are able to recognize aspects of their own experiences and are moved to want to do something about it. The worst vice of higher education is its complacency: its belief that because it has always operated in a certain way, it should always continue to operate in the same way. Sociologists are not exempt from this: sociologists of education in particular have shown how inequality is created in schools: how working-class children, black children, female children are disadvantaged in the state education system. Teachers themselves are implicated as agents of social control. Yet how many sociologists have looked at their own institutions and pointed to the ways in which minority groups of students are disadvantaged? Sociologists have often seen higher education as the end; they show how schools disadvantage working-class children, for example, by pointing to *how few enter higher education*. My point is that higher education is *not* the end; that any theory of the relationship between education and inequality must look at higher education. It may seem like heresy to suggest this, but in fact, universities and polytechnics are *worse* than schools in many respects. For example, a number of anti-racist initiatives have taken place in schools, and schools are expected to provide at least some form of multi-cultural education: but how much multi-cultural teaching takes place at degree level?

There are a number of ways in which change can be effected in higher education. One important area is assessment: 'blind' marking of examination papers is already carried out at A level and should become the norm at degree level. At the same time, universities in particular should look more carefully at their marking practices, and ask themselves whether a higher degree of standardization might be obtained. Degree marking currently appears to be a very haphazard process, with large variations between universities, different departments within an institution, and often in the same department between different years. These variations do not necessarily disadvantage women, but they *may* be indicative of discriminatory practices in certain areas.

Admissions policies could also be examined. I do not doubt that most departments do not discriminate against women in admissions; but few actively encourage women to apply, or attempt to make their courses attractive to women. One of the problems with departments such as physics and engineering is that they generally have so few female students that they are unlikely to see why they should change any of their practices. An important way of getting more women into science, without making women feel isolated and marginalized, is to provide more women-only conversion and access courses – with the important proviso that women receiving a grant for these courses should still be able to receive four years of grant for their degree courses. (Given the current government's plans to introduce a loans system, this seems less and less likely.) Single-sex conversion courses enable women to find out what they are capable of and allow them then to follow science degree courses with greater confidence, and in greater numbers, than is currently possible.

Admissions policies also cover postgraduate admissions. These days it is immensely difficult for anyone who hasn't got a first-class honours degree to get funding to take a postgraduate degree in the humanities. While it is up to the government to change this, both science and humanities departments could look at the system by which undergraduate students are picked out as likely candidates for Ph.D places, and the unconscious discriminatory process which may underlie this. Institutions of higher education might also wish to consider ways of recruiting, and keeping, female staff. Nursery provision might be a start; positively discriminating in favour of female candidates would also be a useful step.

The most necessary, and the most difficult, change that higher education has to make, is to break down the disciplinary barriers. Departments should welcome students with mixed science and arts A levels; higher education should become a broadening out, not a narrowing down. *All* students should have access to, and some understanding of, scientific, social scientific and artistic ways of looking at the world; they should be encouraged to see the connections, rather than the differences, between these world-views. This is particularly hard for academics because they have so much invested in subject divisions; but polytechnics are already making small steps in this direction, and universities may slowly follow. Once we realize that being a scientist is not synonymous with being illiterate, and that having an English or a history degree is not synonymous with being innumerate, then we also begin to break down the barrier of gender that so limits and distorts the higher education world view.

Finally, I wish to end this book with a conventional plea: for more research. There is an enormous gap in the study of higher education, and it can be filled by more work on, amongst other things, admissions policies, the employment of male and female graduates, the dynamics of staff–student interactions in lectures and seminars, the gendered curriculum and assessment and grading policies. The research reported on here has made only a small contribution to our knowledge of gender processes in higher education; it is to be hoped that future research will extend that knowledge much further.

References

Acker, S. (1977). 'Sex differences in graduate student ambition: do men publish while women perish?', *Sex Roles*, 3, 3: 285–99.
—— (1980). 'Women: the other academics', *British Journal of Sociology of Education*, 1, 1: 81–91.
—— (1981). 'No woman's land: British sociology of education 1960–79', *Sociological Review*, 29, 2: 77–104.
—— (1984a). 'Sociology, gender and education', in Acker *et al.* (eds) (1984), pp. 64–77.
—— (1984b). 'Women in higher education: what is the problem?' in Acker and Warren Piper (eds) (1984), pp. 25–48.
Acker, S. and Warren Piper, D. (eds) (1984). *Is Higher Education Fair to Women?*, Surrey, SRHE/NFER.
Acker, S., Megarry, J., Nisbet, S. and Hoyle, E. (eds) (1984). *World Yearbook of Education 1984: Women and Education*, London, Kogan Page.
Althusser, L. (1971). 'Ideology and ideological state apparatuses', in *Lenin and Philosophy*, London, New Left Books, pp. 121–73.
Apple, M. (ed.) (1982). *Cultural and Economic Reproduction in Education*, London, Routledge & Kegan Paul.
Arditti, R. (1980), 'Feminism and science', in Arditti *et al.* (eds) (1980), pp. 350–68.
Arditti, R., Brennan, P. and Cavrak, S. (eds) (1980), *Science and Liberation*, Boston, Mass, South End Press.
Arnold, M. (1960), *Culture and Anarchy*, Cambridge, Cambridge University Press.
Arnot, M. (1981). 'Culture and political economy: dual perspectives in the sociology of women's education', *Educational Analysis*, 3, 1: 97–116.
—— (1982). 'Male hegemony, social class and women's education', *Journal of Education*, 164, 1: 64–89.
Arnot, M. and Weiner, G. (eds) (1987). *Gender and the Politics of Schooling*, Milton Keynes, Open University Press.
Association of University Teachers (1983). *The Real Demand for Student Places*, London, AUT.
Baldick, C. (1984). *The Social Mission of English Criticism 1838–1932*, Oxford, Oxford University Press.
Barnes, B. (1977). *Interests and the Growth of Knowledge*, London, Routledge & Kegan Paul.
Barnett, S. A. *et al.* (1983). 'The theory of biology and the education of biologists: a case study', *Studies in Higher Education*, 8, 1: 23–32.

Barrett, M. (1984). *Women's Oppression Today: Problems in Marxist Feminist Analysis*, London, Verso.

Barton, L., Meighan, R. and Walker, S. (eds) (1980). *Schooling, Ideology and the Curriculum*, Sussex, Falmer Press.

Beauvoir, S. de (1981). *The Second Sex*, Harmondsworth, Penguin.

Becher, T. (1981). 'Towards a definition of disciplinary cultures', *Studies in Higher Education*, 6, 2, 109–22.

—— (1984). 'The cultural view', in B. R. Clark (ed.) (1984), pp. 165–98.

Becher, T. and Kogan, M. (1980). *Process and Structure in Higher Education*, London, Heinemann.

Becker, H. S., Geer, B., Hughes, E. C. and Strauss, A. L. (1961). *Boys in White: Student Culture in Medical School*, Chicago, Ill., University of Chicago Press.

Bee, M. and Dolton, P. (1985). 'Degree class and pass rates: an inter-university comparison', *Higher Education Review*, 17, 2: 45–54.

Bell, C. and Newby, H. (eds) (1977). *Doing Sociological Research*, London, Allen & Unwin.

Belsey, C. (1988). 'Marking by numbers', *AUT Woman*, Autumn.

Bernstein, B. (1971). 'On the classification and framing of educational knowledge', in Young (ed.), (1971a), pp. 47–69.

—— (1977). 'Education cannot compensate for society', in Cosin *et al.* (eds) (1977), pp. 61–6.

Blackstone, T. (1975). 'Women academics in Britain', in Fulton and Blackstone (eds), (1975), pp. 43–67.

—— (1976). 'The education of girls today', in Mitchell and Oakley (eds), (1976), pp. 199–216.

Blackstone, T. and Weinrich-Haste, H. (1980). 'Why are there so few women scientists and engineers?', *New Society*, 21 January, pp. 383–5.

Bowen, J. (1985). 'The subject of English: psychology and pedagogy from Bain to Richards', unpublished Ph.D thesis, University of Birmingham.

Bowles, G. and Duelli-Klein, R. (eds) (1983). *Theories of Women's Studies*, London, Routledge & Kegan Paul.

Bowles, S. and Gintis, H. (1976). *Schooling in Capitalist America*, London, Routledge & Kegan Paul.

Bradley, C. (1984). 'Sex bias in the evaluation of students', *British Journal of Social Psychology*, 23, 2, 147–53.

—— (1985). 'Sex bias in examining reconsidered: a rejoinder to Rudd', *Studies in Higher Education*, pp. 91–3.

Brighton Women and Science Group (eds) (1980). *Alice Through the Microscope*, London, Virago.

Brown, P. and Jordanova, L. (1982). 'Oppressive dichotomies: the nature/culture debate', in Whitelegg *et al.* (eds) (1982), pp. 389–99.

Burgess, Tyrrell (ed.) (1972). *The Shape of Higher Education*, London, Cornmarket Press.

Burstyn, J. (1980). *Victorian Education and the Ideal of Womanhood*, London, Croom Helm.

Byrne, E. (1978). *Women and Education*, London, Tavistock.

Capra, F. (1979). *The Tao of Physics*, London, Wildwood House.

—— (1983). *The Turning Point*, London, Flamingo.

Chisholm, L. and Woodward, D. (1980). 'The experience of women graduates in the labour market', in Deem (ed.), (1980), pp. 162–76.

Clark, B. R. (ed.) (1984). *Perspectives on Higher Education*, University of California Press.

Clarricoates, K. (1978). 'Dinosaurs in the classroom – a re-examination of some aspects of the "hidden" curriculum in primary schools', *Women's Studies International Quarterly*, 1, 4: 353–64.

Clay, R. W. (1982). 'The academic achievement of undergraduate women in physics', *Physics Education*, 17: 232–4.

Cockburn, C. (1983a). *Brothers: Male Dominance and Technological Change*, London, Pluto.

—— (1983b). 'Caught in the wheels', *Marxism Today*, November: 16–20.

Cooper, B. (1984). 'On explaining change in school subjects', in Goodson and Ball (eds), (1984), pp. 45–63.

Cosin, B. R., Dale, I. R., Esland, G. M., Mackinnon, D. and Swift, D. F. (eds) (1977). *School and Society: A Sociological Reader*, London, Routledge & Kegan Paul.

Couture-Cherki, M. (1976). 'Women in physics', in Rose and Rose (eds) (1976a), pp. 65–75.

Crompton, R. (1986). 'Credentials and careers: some implications of the increase in professional qualifications amongst women', *Sociology*, 20, 1: 25–42.

Curran, L. (1980). 'Did she fall or was she pushed?', in Brighton Women and Science Group (1980) pp. 22–41.

Dale, R. R. (1969). *Mixed or Single Sex Schools?*, London, Routledge & Kegan Paul.

Deem, R. (1978). *Women and Schooling*, London, Routledge & Kegan Paul.

—— (ed.) (1980). *Schooling for Women's Work*, London, Routledge & Kegan Paul.

—— (1981). 'State policy and ideology in the education of women: 1944–80', *British Journal of Sociology of Education*, 2, 2: 131–44.

—— (ed.) (1984). *Co-Education Reconsidered*, Milton Keynes, Open University Press.

Deem, R. and Finch, J. (1986). 'Claiming our space: women in a "Socialist Alternative" post-18 education', in Finch and Rustin (eds) (1986), pp. 128–43.

Delamont, S. (1980). *Sex Roles and the School*, London, Methuen.

Department of Education and Science (1978). *Higher Education into the 1990s: A Discussion Document*, London, HMSO.

—— (1980). *Girls and Science*, HMI series: Matters for Discussion no. 13, London, HMSO.

—— (1985). *Higher Education in the 1990s*, London, HMSO.

Dyhouse, C. (1981). *Girls Growing up in Late Victorian and Edwardian England*, London, Routledge & Kegan Paul.

—— (1984). 'Storming the citadel or storm in a tea-cup? The entry of women into higher education 1860–1920', in Acker and Warren Piper (eds) (1984), pp. 51–64.

Eagleton, T. (1976). *Marxism and Literary Criticism*, London, Methuen.

—— (1983). *Literary Theory: An Introduction*, Oxford, Basil Blackwell.

Edge, D. (1975). 'On the purity of science', in Niblett (ed.) (1975), pp. 42–64.

Eichler, M. (1980). *The Double Standard: A Feminist Critique of Feminist Social Science*, London, Croom Helm.

Equal Opportunities Commission (1982). *Science Education in Schools: Response of the EOC to the DES consultative document*, Manchester, EOC.

Erickson, G. L. and Erickson, L. J. (1984). 'Females and science achievement: evidence, explanations and implications', *Science Education*, 68, 2: 63–89.

Evans, M. and Ungerson, C. (eds), (1983). *Sexual Divisions: Patterns and Processes*, London, Tavistock.

Fee, E. (1983). 'Women's nature and scientific objectivity', in Hubbard and Lowe (eds) (1983), pp. 9–25.

Ferry, G. (1984). 'WISE campaign for women engineers', *New Scientist*, 12 January: 10–11.

Feyerabend, P. (1974). *Against Method*, London, Verso.

Finch, J. and Rustin, M. (eds) (1986). *A Degree of Choice*, Harmondsworth, Penguin.

Firestone, S. (1979). *The Dialectic of Sex*, London, Women's Press.

Flood Page, C. and Gibson, J. (1974). *Research into Higher Education: 1973 Papers Presented at the Ninth Annual Conference of the Society*, London, SRHE.
Fowler, A. (1985). 'A critical point for literature', *Times Higher Education Supplement*, 8 March, p. 15.
Friedan, B. (1983). *The Feminine Mystique*, Harmondsworth, Penguin.
Fulton, O. (ed.) (1981). *Access to Higher Education*, Guildford, Society for Research into Higher Education.
Fulton, O. and Blackstone, T. (eds) (1975). *Women in Higher Education*, London, Staff Development Unit.
Gibbs, G. Morgan, A. and Taylor, E. (1984). 'The world of the learner', in Martin *et al.* (eds) (1984), pp. 165–88.
Glazer-Malbin, N. and Waehrer, H. Y. (eds) (1977). *Woman in a Man-Made World*, Chicago, Ill., Rand-McNally.
Goldberg, P. (1968). 'Are women prejudiced against women?', *Transactions*, 5, 5: 28–30.
Goodlad, S. (1976). *Conflict and Consensus in Higher Education*, London, Hodder & Stoughton.
Goodson, I. (1983). *School Subjects and Curriculum Change*, London, Croom Helm.
Goodson, I. and Ball, S. (eds) (1984). *Defining the Curriculum*, London, Falmer Press.
Gorz, A. (1980). 'The scientist as worker', in Arditti *et al.* (eds) (1980), pp. 267–79.
Grafton, T., Miller, H., Smith, L., Vegoda, M. and Whitland, R. (1983). 'Gender and curriculum choice: a case study', in Hammersley and Hargreaves (eds) (1983), pp. 151–70.
Greer, G. (1979). *The Female Eunuch*, London, Paladin.
Hacker, H. M. (1977). 'Women as a minority group', in Glazer-Malbin and Waehrer (eds) (1977), pp. 137–47.
Halloun, I. and Hestenes, D. (1985a). 'The initial knowledge state of college physics students', *American Journal of Physics*, 53, 11, November: 1,043–55.
—— (1985b). 'Commonsense concepts about motion', *American Journal of Physics*, 53, 11: 1,056–65.
Hammersley, M. and Atkinson, P. (1983). *Ethnography: Principles in Practice*, London, Tavistock.
Hammersley, M. and Hargreaves, A. (eds) (1983). *Curriculum Practice: Some Sociological Case Studies*, London, Falmer Press.
Harding, J. (1979). 'Sex differences in examination performance at 16+', *Physics Education*, 14: 280–4.
—— (1981). 'Sex differences in science examinations', in Kelly (ed.) (1981), pp. 192–204.
—— (1983). *The Science Education of Girls*, London, Longman for the Schools Council.
—— (ed.) (1986). *Perspectives on Gender and Science*, London, Falmer Press.
Harding, S. and Hintikka, M. B. (eds) (1983). *Discovering Reality: Feminist Perspectives in Epistemology, Metaphysics, Methodology and Philosophy of Science*, Reidel, Dordrecht.
Harris, A. S. (1974). 'The second sex in academe', in Stacey *et al.* (eds) (1974), pp. 293–316.
Hartmann, H. (1981). 'The unhappy marriage of Marxism and feminism', in Sargent (ed.) (1981), pp. 1–41.
Head, J. (1980). 'A model to link personality characteristics to a preference for science', *European Journal of Science Education*, 2, 3: 295–300.
—— (1981). 'Personality and the learning of mathematics', *Educational Studies in Mathematics*, 12: 339–50.
Hearn, J. and Parkin, P. (1983). 'Gender and organisations: a selective review and a critique of a neglected area', *Organization Studies*, pp. 219–42.

Heim, A. (1971). *Intelligence and Personality: Their Assessment and Relationship*, Harmondsworth, Penguin.

Henriques, J., Hollway, W., Urwin, C., Venn, C. and Walkerdine, V. (1984). *Changing the Subject*, London, Methuen.

Hine, R. J. (1975). 'Political bias in school physics', *Hard Cheese*, nos 4 and 5, pp. 93–6.

Hollway, W. (1982). *Identity and Gender Difference in Adult Social Relations*, unpublished Ph.D. thesis, University of London.

—— (1984). 'Gender difference and the production of subjectivity' in Henriques *et al.* (1984), pp. 227–63.

Hubbard, R. (1981). 'The emperor doesn't wear any clothes: the impact of feminism on biology', in Spender (ed.) *Men's Studies Modified*, Oxford, Pergamon, pp. 213–316.

Hubbard, R. and Lowe, M. (eds) (1983). *Woman's Nature: Rationalizations of Inequality*, Oxford, Pergamon.

Hubbard, R., Henifin, S. and Fried, B. (eds) (1979). *Women Look at Biology Looking at Women*, Cambridge, Massachusetts, Schenckman.

Hudson, L. (1967). *Contrary Imaginations*, Harmondsworth, Penguin.

—— (1970). *Frames of Mind*, Harmondsworth, Penguin.

—— (1972). *The Cult of the Fact*, London, Cape.

Humm, M. (1983). 'Women in higher education: a case study of the school for independent study and the issues for feminism', *Women's Studies International Forum*, 6, 1: 97–105.

Johnson, S. and Murphy, P. (1986). *Girls and Physics*, London, Department of Education and Science.

Keddie, N. (1971). 'Classroom knowledge', in Young (ed.) (1971a), pp. 133–60.

Keller, E. F. (1983). 'Gender and science', in Harding and Hintikka (eds) (1983), pp. 187–206.

Kelly, A. (ed.) (1981a). *The Missing Half: Girls and Science Education*, Manchester, Manchester University Press.

—— (1981b). 'Science achievement as an aspect of sex roles', in Kelly (ed.) (1981a), pp. 73–84.

—— (1985). 'The construction of masculine science', *British Journal of Sociology of Education*, 6, 2: 133–54.

—— (1986). 'Gender differences in teacher–pupil interactions: a meta-analytic review', paper given at BERA annual conference, September, Bristol University.

—— (ed.) (1987). *Science for Girls*, Milton Keynes, Open University Press.

Kelsall, R. K., Poole, A. and Kuhn, A. (1970). *Six Years After*, Higher Education Research Unit, Department of Sociological Studies, Sheffield University.

—— (1972). *Graduates: the Sociology of an Elite*, London, Methuen.

Knights, L. C. (1975). 'Literature and the teaching of literature', in Niblett (ed.) (1975), pp. 127–38.

Kolodny, A. (1981). 'Dancing through the mine-field: some observations on the theory, practice and politics of a feminist literary criticism', in Spender (ed.) (1981c), pp. 23–42.

Komarovsky, M. (1946). 'Cultural contradictions and sex roles', *American Journal of Sociology*, 52: 184–9.

Kuhn, A. and Wolpe, A.-M. (eds) (1978). *Feminism and Materialism*, London, Routledge & Kegan Paul.

Kuhn, T. S. (1962). *The Structure of Scientific Revolutions*, Chicago, Ill., University of Chicago Press.

—— (1963). 'The essential tension: tradition and innovation in scientific research', in Taylor and Barron (eds) (1963), pp. 341–54.

Lakatos, I. and Musgrave, A. (eds) (1970). *Criticism and the Growth of Knowledge*, Cambridge, Cambridge University Press.

Lanser, S. S. and Torton Beck, E. (1979). '[Why] are there no great women critics?', in Sherman and Torton Beck (eds) (1979), pp. 79–91.

Leavis, F. R. (1972). *The Great Tradition*, Harmondsworth, Penguin.

Lees, S. (1987). 'The structure of sexual relations in school', in Arnot and Weiner (eds) (1987), pp. 175–86.

The Leverhulme Report (1983). *Excellence in Diversity: Towards a New Strategy for Higher Education*, Guildford, SRHE.

Lewis, I. (1983). 'Some issues arising from an examination of women's experience of physics', *European Journal of Science Education*, 5, 2: 185–93.

—— (1984a). 'Being a woman physics student', in I. Lewis (ed.) (1984b), pp. 109–27.

—— (ed.) (1984b). *The Student Experience of Higher Education*, Kent, Croom Helm.

Lewis, J. (1981). 'Women lost and found: the impact of feminism on history', in Spender (ed.) (1981c), pp. 55–72.

Maccoby, E. E. and Jacklin, C. N. (1974). *The Psychology of Sex Differences*, California, Stanford University Press.

Macdonald, M. (1980a). 'Schooling and the reproduction of class and gender relations', in Barton *et al.* (eds) (1980), pp. 29–49.

—— (1980b). 'Socio-cultural reproduction and women's education', in Deem (ed.) (1980), pp. 13–25.

Mahony, P. (1982), 'Silence is a woman's glory: the sexist content of education', *Women's Studies International Forum*, 5, 5: 463–73.

—— (1985). *Schools for the Boys: Co-Education Reassessed*, London, Hutchinson.

Manthorpe, C. (1985). 'Feminists look at science', *New Scientist*, 7 March: 29–31.

Marks, P. (1976). 'Femininity in the classroom: an account of changing attitudes', in Mitchell and Oakley (eds) (1976), pp. 176–98.

Martin, F., Hounsell, D. and Entwistle, N. (eds) (1984). *The Experience of Learning*, Edinburgh, Scottish Academic Press.

Measor, L. (1983). 'Gender and the sciences: pupils' gender-based conceptions of school subjects', in Hammersley and Hargreaves (eds) (1983), pp. 171–91.

—— (1984). 'Pupil perceptions of subject status', in Goodson and Ball (eds) (1984), pp. 201–17.

Merchant, C. (1982). *The Death of Nature*, London, Wildwood House.

Miall, D. S. (1989). 'Welcome the crisis! Rethinking learning methods in English studies', *Studies in Higher Education*, 14, 1: 69–81.

Middleton, S. (1987). 'The sociology of women's education as a field of academic study', in Arnot and Weiner (eds) (1987), pp. 76–91.

Millett, K. (1983). *Sexual Politics*, London, Virago.

Mitchell, J. (1973). *Woman's Estate*, Harmondsworth, Penguin.

—— (1979). *Psychoanalysis and Feminism*, Harmondsworth, Penguin.

Mitchell, J. and Oakley, A. (eds) (1976). *The Rights and Wrongs of Women*, Harmondsworth, Penguin.

Moers, E. (1977). *Literary Women: The Great Writers*, New York, Anchor/Doubleday.

Morgan, V. and Dunn, S. (1988). 'Chameleons in the classroom: visible and invisible children in nursery and infant classrooms', *Education Review*, 40, 1: 3–12.

Newbolt Report (1921). *The Teaching of English in England*, London, HMSO.

Niblett, R. (ed.) (1975). *The Sciences, the Humanities and the Technological Threat*, London, University of London Press.

Oakley, A. (1972). *Sex, Gender and Society*, London, Maurice Temple Smith.

—— (1982). *Subject Woman*, London, Fontana.

O'Donnell, C. (1984). 'The relationship between women's education and their allocation to the labour market', *Studies in Higher Education*, 9, 1: 59–72.

Ormerod, M., Bottomley, J. M., Keys, W. and Wood, C. (1979). 'Girls and physics education', *Physics Education*, 14: 270–6.

Overfield, K. (1981). 'Dirty fingers, grime and slag heaps: purity and the scientific ethic', in Spender (ed.) (1981c), pp. 237–48.

Parrinder, P. (1979), 'Sermons, pseudo-science and critical discourse: some reflections on the aims and methods of contemporary English', *Studies in Higher Education*, 1, 4: 3–13.

Physics Education Committee (1982). *Girls and Physics*, London, The Royal Society and the Institute of Physics.

Pidgeon, D. A. (1967). *Achievement in Mathematics*, London, NFER.

Plowden Report (1967). *Children and Their Primary Schools: A Report*, London, HMSO.

Ravetz, J. R. (1971). *Scientific Knowledge and its Social Problems*, Oxford, Clarendon.

Rendel, M. (1980). 'How many women academics 1912–76?', in Deem (ed.) (1980), pp. 142–61.

Rich, A. (1979a). 'Toward a woman-centred university', in *On Lies, Secrets, Silence*, London, Virago, pp. 125–56.

—— (1979b). 'Taking women students seriously', in *On Lies, Secrets, Silence*, London, Virago, pp. 237–46.

Richards, J. R. (1982). *The Sceptical Feminist*, Harmondsworth, Pelican.

Robbins Report (1963). *Report on Higher Education*, London, HMSO.

Roberts, H. (ed.) (1981). *Doing Feminist Research*, London, Routledge & Kegan Paul

Robinson, E. (1972). 'A comprehensive reform of higher education', in Burgess (ed.) (1972), pp. 47–66.

Rose, H. (1982). 'Making science feminist', in Whitelegg *et al.* (eds) (1982), pp. 352–72.

—— (1986). 'Nothing less than half the labs', in Finch and Rustin (eds) (1986), pp. 226–49.

Rose, H. and Hanmer, J. (1976). 'Women's liberation: reproduction and the technological fix', in Rose and Rose (eds) (1976b), pp. 142–60.

Rose, H. and Rose, S. (eds) (1976a). *The Radicalisation of Science*, London, Macmillan.

—— (eds) (1976b). *The Political Economy of Science*, London, Macmillan.

—— (1980). 'The myth of the neutrality of science', in Arditti *et al.* (eds) (1980), pp. 17–32.

Rose, S. (1987). 'Time to sing a song for science', *Guardian*, 4 May, p. 13.

Rowbotham, S. (1973). *Woman's Consciousness, Man's World*, Harmondsworth, Penguin.

Rudd, E. (1984). 'A comparison between the results achieved by women and men studying for first degrees in British universities', *Studies in Higher Education*, 9, 1: 47–57.

Saraga, E. and Griffiths, G. (1981). 'Biological inevitabilities or political choices? The future for girls in science', in Kelly (ed.) (1981a), pp. 85–99.

Sargent, L. (ed.) (1981). *The Unhappy Marriage of Marxism and Feminism: A Debate on Class and Patriarchy*, London, Pluto.

Scholes, R. (1974). *Structuralism in Literature*, New Haven, Conn., Yale University Press.

Schwarz, B. (1986). 'Cultural studies: the case for the humanities', in Finch and Rustin (1986), pp. 165–91.

Scott, M. (1980). 'Teach her a lesson: sexist curriculum in patriarchal education', in Spender and Sarah (eds) (1980), pp. 97–121.

Scott, P. (1984). *The Crisis of the University*, London, Croom Helm.

Segal, L. (1987). *Is the Future Female?*, London, Virago.

Sharpe, S. (1976). *Just Like a Girl*, London, Pelican.

Shaw, J. (1980). 'Education and the individual: schooling for girls, or mixed schooling – a mixed blessing?', in Deem (ed.) (1980), pp. 66–75.

—— (1983). 'Models of learning and their role in reproducing educational inequality', in Evans and Ungerson (eds) (1983), pp. 89–102.

—— (1984). 'The politics of single-sex schools', in Deem (ed.) (1984), pp. 21–36.

Sherman, J. A. and Torton Beck, E. (eds) (1979). *The Prism of Sex: Essays in the Sociology of Knowledge*, Madison, Wis., University of Wisconsin Press.

Showalter, E. (1978). *A Literature of their Own: British Women Novelists from Brontë to Lessing*, London, Virago.

Smith, J. (1983). 'Feminist analysis of gender: a mystique', in Hubbard and Lowe (eds) (1983), pp. 89–109.

Smith, S. (1984). 'Single-sex setting', in Deem (ed.) (1984), pp. 75–88.

Snow, C. P. (1959). *The Two Cultures and the Scientific Revolution*, Cambridge, Cambridge University Press.

Spear, M. (1984). 'The biasing influence of pupil sex in a science marking exercise', *Research in Science and Technological Education*, 2, 1: 55–60.

Spender, D. (1980a). *Man Made Language*, London, Routledge & Kegan Paul.

—— (1980b). 'Educational institutions: where co-operation is called cheating', in Spender and Sarah (eds) (1980), pp. 39–48.

—— (1981a). 'Sex bias', in Warren Piper (ed.) (1981), pp. 104–27.

—— (1981b). 'Education: the patriarchal paradigm and the response to feminism', in Spender (ed.) (1981c), pp. 155–72.

—— (ed.) (1981c). *Men's Studies Modified*, Oxford, Pergamon.

—— (1982). *Invisible Women: The Schooling Scandal*, London, Writers & Readers.

—— (1983). *Women of Ideas*, London, Routledge & Kegan Paul.

—— (1985). *For the Record: The Making and Meaning of Feminist Knowledge*, London, Women's Press.

Spender, D. and Sarah, E. (eds) (1980). *Learning to Lose: Sexism and Education*, London, Women's Press.

Stacey, J., Béreaud, S., and Daniels, J. (eds) (1974). *And Jill Came Tumbling After: Sexism in American Education*, New York, Dell Publishing.

Stanley, L. and Wise, S. (1983). *Breaking Out: Feminist Consciousness and Feminist Research*, London, Routledge & Kegan Paul.

Stanworth, M. (1981). *Gender and Schooling: A Study of Sexual Divisions in the Classroom*, London, WRRC.

Steedman, E. (1980). *Progress in Mathematics*, London, National Children's Bureau.

Stéhelin, L. (1976). 'Science, women and ideology', in Rose and Rose (eds) (1976a), pp. 76–89.

Steinem, G. (1985). 'Why young women are more conservative', in Steinem (1985) *Outrageous Acts and Everyday Rebellions*, London, Fontana, pp. 211–18.

St John Brooks, C. (1983). 'English: a curriculum for personal development?', in Hammersley and Hargreaves (eds) (1983), pp. 37–60.

Swann Report (1968). *The Flow into Employment of Scientists, Engineers and Technologists*, Report of a Working Group of the Committee on Manpower Resources for Science and Technology, London, HMSO.

Taylor, C. W. and Barron, F. (eds) (1963), *Scientific Creativity: Its Recognition and Development*, London, Wiley.

Thomas, K. (1988). 'Gender and the arts/science divide in higher education', *Studies in Higher Education*, 13, 2: 123–37.

Thompson, N. (1979). 'Sex differentials in physics education', *Physics Education*, 14: 285–8 and 317.

Thomson, J. (1984). *Learning Liberation: Women's Response to Men's Education*, London, Croom Helm.

UCCA (1986). *Twenty-Fourth Report, 1985–86*, Cheltenham, UCCA.

UGC (1988). *University Statistics 1987-8*, vol. 2, Cheltenham, Universities' Statistical Record.

Walden, R. and Walkerdine, V. (1982). *Girls and Mathematics: The Early Years*, Bedford Way papers 8, London Institute of Education.

Walker, B. (1981). 'Psychology and feminism – if you can't beat them, join them', in Spender (ed.) (1981c), pp. 111–24.

Walkerdine, V. (1987). 'Some issues in the historical construction of the scientific truth about girls', in Kelly (ed.) (1987), pp. 37–44.

Wallsgrove, R. (1980). 'The masculine face of science', in Brighton Women and Science Group (eds) (1980).

Warren Piper, D. (ed.) (1981). *Is Higher Education Fair?*, SRHE.

Watson, J. (1959). *The Double Helix*, Harmondsworth, Penguin.

Weiner, G. (1980). 'Sex differences in mathematical performance: a review of research and possible action', in Deem (ed.) (1980), pp. 76–86.

Weinrich-Haste, H. (1984). 'The values and aspirations of English women undergraduates', in Acker and Warren Piper (eds) pp. 116–31.

—— (1986). 'Brother Sun, Sister Moon: does rationality overcome a dualistic world view?', in Harding (ed.) (1986), pp. 113–31.

Weisstein, N. (1979). 'Adventures of a woman in science', in Hubbard *et al.* (eds) (1979).

Whitelegg, E., Arnot, M., Bartels, E., Beechey, V., Birke, L., Himmelweit, S., Leonard, D., Ruehl, S., and Speakman, M. A. (eds) (1982). *The Changing Experience of Women*, Oxford, Martin Robertson.

Whitty, G. (1977). *School Knowledge and Social Control*, Milton Keynes, Open University Press.

Whitty, G. and Young, M. (eds) (1976). *Explorations in the Politics of School Knowledge*, Driffield, Nafferton Books.

Whyte, J. (1986). *Girls Into Science and Technology*, London, Routledge & Kegan Paul.

Williams, R. (1975). *The Long Revolution*, Harmondsworth, Penguin.

—— (1981). *Culture*, London, Fontana.

Williamson, B. (1986a), 'Priority to the power of ideas: an evaluation of the Green Paper on higher education', *Journal of Educational Policy*, 1, 3: 271–80.

—— (1986b). 'Who has access?', in Finch and Rustin (eds) (1986), pp. 67–91.

Willis, P. (1977). *Learning to Labour*, London, Methuen.

Wolpe, A. M. (1977). *Some Processes in Sexist Education*, London, WRRC.

—— (1978). 'Education and the sexual division of labour', in A. Kuhn and Wolpe (eds) (1978), pp. 290–328.

Woodhall, M. (1975). 'The economic benefits of educating women', in Fulton and Blackstone (eds) (1975), pp. 27–30.

Young, M. F. D. (ed.) (1971a). *Knowledge and Control*, London, Collier-Macmillan.

—— (1971b). 'Curricula as socially organized knowledge', in Young (ed.) (1971a), pp. 19–46.

—— (1976). 'The schooling of science', in Whitty and Young (eds) (1976), pp. 47–61.

Young, M. and Whitty, G. (1977). *Society, State and Schooling*, Ringmer, Falmer Press.

Index

The Society for Research into Higher Education

The Society exists both to encourage and coordinate research and development into all aspects of higher education, including academic, organizational and policy issues; and also to provide a forum for debate – verbal and printed.

The Society's income derives from subscriptions, book sales, conference fees, and grants. It receives no subsidies and is wholly independent. Its corporate members are institutions of higher education, research institutions and professional, industrial, and governmental bodies. Its individual members include teachers and researchers, administrators and students. Members are found in all parts of the world and the Society regards its international work as amongst its most important activities.

The Society discusses and comments on policy, organizes conferences, and encourages research. Under the imprint SRHE & OPEN UNIVERSITY PRESS, it is a specialist publisher of research, having some 40 titles in print. It also publishes *Studies in Higher Education* (three times a year) which is mainly concerned with academic issues; *Higher Education Quarterly* (formerly *Universities Quarterly*) mainly concerned with policy issues; *Abstracts* (three times a year); an *International Newsletter* (twice a year) and *SRHE News* (four times a year).

The Society's committees, study groups and branches are run by members (with help from a small secretariat at Guildford), and aim to provide a forum for discussion. The groups at present include a Teacher Education Study Group, a Staff Development Group, and a Continuing Education Group, each of which may have their own organization, subscriptions, or publications (e.g. the *Staff Development Newsletter*). A further *Questions of Quality* Group has organized a series of Anglo-American seminars in the USA and the UK.

The Governing Council, elected by members, comments on current issues; and discusses policies with leading figures, notably at its evening forums. The Society organizes seminars on current research, and is in touch with bodies in the UK such as the NAB, CVCP, UGC, CNAA and with sister-bodies overseas. It co-operates with the British Council on courses run in conjunction with its conferences.

The Society's conferences are often held jointly; and have considered 'Standards and Criteria' (1986, with Bulmershe College); 'Restructuring' (1987, with the City of Birmingham Polytechnic); 'Academic Freedom' (1988, with the University of Surrey). In 1989, 'Access and Institutional Change' (with the Polytechnic of North London). In 1990, the topic will be 'Industry and Higher Education' (with the University of Surrey). In 1991, the topic will be 'Research in HE'. Other conferences have considered the DES 'Green Paper' (1985); 'HE After the Election' (1987) and 'After the Reform Act' (July

1988). An annual series on 'The First Year Experience' with the University of South Carolina and Teesside Polytechnic held two meetings in 1988 in Cambridge, and another in St Andrew's in July 1989. For some of the Society's conferences, special studies are commissioned in advance, as *Precedings*.

Members receive free of charge the Society's *Abstracts*, annual conference Proceedings (or *Precedings*), *SRHE News* and *International Newsletter*. They may buy SRHE & Open University Press books at discount, and *Higher Education Quarterly* on special terms. Corporate members also receive the Society's journal *Studies in Higher Education* free (individuals on special terms). Members may also obtain certain other journals at a discount, including the NFER *Register of Educational Research*. There is a substantial discount to members, and to staff of corporate members, on annual and some other conference fees.

Further Information: SRHE at the University, Guildford. GU2 5XH UK (0483) 39003